J.D.

Brock Beard

J.D.

.

Prologue

Dale Earnhardt took the white flag in third place. Ahead of him were his son, Dale Earnhardt, Jr., and race leader Michael Waltrip, both in cars Earnhardt owned. Behind him were an ever-increasing number of competitors, all of them vying for a win in the 2001 Daytona 500. In the sport's biggest race, Earnhardt was unquestionably its most prolific driver. His aggression made him "The Intimidator," a seven-time NASCAR champion with seventy-six wins. But on that day, Earnhardt drove defensively, blocking the three-wide pack threatening to overtake his black Chevrolet.

Then, in the final corner, it happened. Earnhardt's No. 3 wiggled left, cut right, and slammed nearly head-on into the outside wall. When the dust settled, Ken Schrader, his car collected by the impact, checked on Earnhardt. Later that day, we would all learn the reality of what he saw.

On February 18, 2001, Dale Earnhardt became the first driver to lose his life in a NASCAR Winston Cup Series race in nearly a decade, dating back to an unseasonably cool August day in 1991. That race wasn't the Daytona 500, the sport's biggest event, but a ninety-lapper at Watkins Glen International, one of only two road courses on the schedule. It happened to a driver who was running near the back of the pack and had for much of his career. The driver's name was John Delphus McDuffie, Jr., but no one ever called him that. To everyone, he was J.D.

Through four decades, J.D. McDuffie drove for his own team, maintained his cars out of a tiny shop down the street from his home, and personally hauled them to and from the track on the back of an old truck. He ran No. 70, the number he once raced to victory on the dirt bullrings of his youth. But that success never crossed over into NAS-CAR. He never won a race, never finished on the lead lap, and his hand-crafted machines set a record for last-place finishes. But racing was McDuffie's life, his way of providing for his wife and two children, and for 653 starts he lived it. No winless driver had ever stuck it out for so long. None have since.

On the surface, J.D. McDuffie's career seems like the exact opposite of Dale Earnhardt's. But in reality, they had much in common. In fact, they helped each other. In 1977, two years before Earnhardt's first win, McDuffie set up a late model sportsman car for "The Intimidator" to run at Charlotte. In 1986, Earnhardt's car owner Richard Childress sold McDuffie one of his old No. 3 Wrangler Jeans-sponsored race cars, a chassis which in time would become McDuffie's final No. 70. In 1991, when McDuffie lost an engine in Daytona 500 practice, both Earnhardt and Childress raised enough money for him to rent a new one.

Contrary to what some have written, the engine McDuffie leased didn't belong to fellow owner-driver Jimmy Means. "No, that's not true," said Means, "If J.D. needed a motor, he'd have gotten it for free." Such was the friendship between the two drivers. Means and McDuffie were often mentioned in the same breath as two Davids fighting an ever-increasing number of Goliaths. In a tragic twist, the last time it happened had fatal consequences.

The nature of sport doesn't leave much room for stories like this. Competition is about the winner, the champion, the one who defeats all challengers. Viewers and media alike don't spend much time thinking about the others who were there, the ones who made the victor work for his trophy. That is, unless the defeat is itself spectacular. The first baseman who missed a ground ball. The kicker who missed a field goal. The veteran racer who died without a win. In each case, a single moment can overshadow an entire career.

But there was much more to J.D. McDuffie than his final moment, and much more to that moment than is widely known. What follows, for the first time, is the full story, featuring the memories of those who knew him best. It's also about his family, his team, and his life, which for McDuffie were one and the same.

CHAPTER 1
Four Decades

> *"We're gonna run better, you know.*
> *You couldn't call me a quitter."*
>
> —*J.D. McDuffie, 1986*

South of Durham, at the heart of Lee County, the city of Sanford sleeps soundly in the North Carolina sandhills. For years, Sanford was known as "Brick Capital of the U.S.A.," its natural deposits of clay and shale the bread-and-butter for the Sanford Brick & Tile Company and Borden Brick & Tile. Bricks quite literally laid the foundation for Sanford; whose rectangular red buildings still dot the brushy landscape. The same earth also happened to be perfect for dirt track racing. Every weekend, clay would scatter into dust over a cluster of quarter-mile ovals: Asheboro, Danville, Rockingham, Dillon, and Sanford itself. Yes, bricks were Sanford's business, but racing was its pride.

First came Herb Thomas, the farmhand who legend has it learned to race by wheeling a dump truck down narrow roads. Thomas was NASCAR's first two-time champion, claiming the national title in 1951 and 1953. He racked-up forty-eight wins in 229 starts over ten seasons, half of those wins in '53 and '54 alone. Three times, Thomas won the longest and most grueling race on the calendar, the Southern 500 at the Darlington Raceway. His "Fabulous Hudson Hornet," a low-slung teal coupe with the No. 92 on each fender, became one of the most feared cars on bumpy dirt tracks across the south.

By the 1960s, Thomas retired from racing, his hand forced by a savage wreck during a race in Shelby, North Carolina. By then, Sanford had found his heir-apparent. He was handsome and mild-mannered, a literal "shade tree mechanic" who worked on his 1960 Ford Starliner under the pines surrounding his home. He'd made a few NASCAR races in 1963, even finished eighth twice, but Darlington proved harder than Herb Thomas made it look. The driver failed the rookie test and was prohibited from starting the race. At the end of the year, he went back home for a couple years to hone his skills on the local circuit. Teamed with another local driver, Delbert McLeod, the man picked up where he left off, dominating on the dirt.

In 1966, the driver gave NASCAR – and Darlington – another try. More struggles awaited. He passed his Darlington rookie test, only to crash so hard that it knocked him unconscious. He then blew his only motor trying to make the World 600 at Charlotte and lost out on a chance at a share of one of the season's biggest purses. By summer, he was in jeopardy of missing the big race at Daytona. An article in the *Sanford Herald* alerted the town to the driver's situation. So, Mayor E.W. Fields declared June 23rd to be "J.D. McDuffie Day."

"If it's possible that anyone in Sanford never heard of stock car racing," read *The Daily Independent*, "then they'll hear about it on June 23."

That day, crowds lined the streets of downtown Sanford and watched thirty-five cars rumble down the road. Among them was Herb Thomas' Hornet, loaned from a South Carolina museum, its driver back behind the wheel for the first time since his retirement. 1965 Daytona 500 winner Fred Lorenzen was there. So was defending NAS-CAR champion Ned Jarrett. Janice Harris, the newly crowned Miss North Carolina, presided over the parade that afternoon. All converged at the Lee County Fairgrounds for a question-and-answer session with fans. NASCAR tickets were auctioned off, as well as a Honda motorcycle, the proceeds going to Sanford's favorite son.

"He has a long way to go before he'll equal the success of Sanford's last Grand National Racer," the *Independent* said of McDuffie. "But Herb Thomas, the king of racing a decade ago, started out small also."

In the end, the festivities raised $2,500 for McDuffie, which allowed him to buy a blue 1964 Ford race car from the Holman-Moody shop. Huggins Tire Service provided him with a set of fresh dirt track tires. Two days later, those tires carried McDuffie to a sixth-place finish at the Greenville-Pickens Speedway. It was the second-best finish he'd have all year.

* * * *

In January 1973, Bobby Hudson was, by his own admission, "a little twenty-year-old snotty nosed kid." The youngest member of L.G. DeWitt Racing, Hudson was on his first coast-to-coast trip to Riverside. The team's No. 72 Chevrolet would run that weekend with Benny Parsons behind the wheel. One night, the team parked its cab-over hauler next to others at a motel. In their room, Parsons and crew chief Travis Carter set up a table and began shuffling cards. Soon, others walked in, including crew chief Harry Hyde and owner-driver Grover Cleveland "G.C." Spencer.

The group welcomed Hudson over, and they all played poker. "They just took me under their wing from the second night on," he said. "They always treated me like one of them, that made me feel special to be involved with them."

Hudson sat next to J.D. McDuffie – "Jay" as he was called – who he'd known since he was a teenager. In the late 1960s, Hudson's father raced against J.D. and his older brother Glen at the Rockingham dirt track. The two struck up a friendship. "He was kind of a – I'm not saying he was a loner – J.D. was bashful," said Hudson. "And I used to be like that a lot. But J.D. was very, very, bashful."

McDuffie never asked for help, but Hudson made sure he got it. At DeWitt, he was in charge of making sure the parts the team gave to McDuffie were usable. "J.D. was our number one customer...He only got A-1 pieces. We didn't sell any garbage to him, he got the cream of the crop. He probably got some parts before they were [worn] out." The brake pads, rotors, and tires coming off Parsons' No. 72 were much appreciated. One time at Riverside, McDuffie could only run a single qualifying lap because it was all the stock Chevrolet rods in his engine could take. "I can't afford the new stuff," said McDuffie in 1977. "But the used parts I buy from Benny Parsons usually are just as good as new. It's a matter of putting them together right."

But playing cards wasn't a time for business. It was a driver's favorite pastime. Long before today's many sponsor and media obligations, it was common for drivers and teams to be seen at the same hotels and bars as fans. When practice was over, or rain started to fall, everyone talked about where they were going to play cards. They set up in hotel rooms, in the back of the Wood Brothers' hauler, on the red-eye flight from Los Angeles to Charlotte, and even in the Motor Racing Network (MRN) radio booth, usually ten people at a time. The location changed frequently as NASCAR intervened, trying to shake off the last vestiges of its rough-and-tumble past.

As hard as he worked, McDuffie wasn't above having a good time. When his finances allowed it, he enjoyed throwing dice in Atlantic City on the way to Dover or stopping in Las Vegas on the way to Riverside to chat with racing enthusiast Mel Larson at his Circus Circus casino. McDuffie preferred blackjack, and he was good at it, too. In 1983, when he burned the clutch on his car hauler outside of Las Vegas, he went into the Sands, bet the team's tire money for the race in Riverside, and walked out with $1,300. One trip to the salvage yard later, he was back on the road.

In the garage area, poker reigned supreme. At the card table, as at the race track, Hudson made sure he had McDuffie's back. "We would both shove a knee under the table. If I had a lot of horsepower, that's what we called it when we're around the race track – if I had a lot of horsepower in my hand in my deck of cards, I'd poke his leg which meant 'we can still play, but I've got a lot of it.' And he would do the same thing to me. He'd bump my leg, and that was the only thing we ever did as far as looking out for each other, just hanging out with the guys and having a great time."

While no one member at the table had a clear advantage, McDuffie didn't win often, except for one night at Darlington. "[I]t seemed he could not lose," recalled writer Tom Higgins, "and almost every pot was a big one. When the game broke up around midnight, J.D. walked from the room with bills protruding from every pocket, including his shirt. With the stub of a cigar clinched in his teeth, J.D. couldn't have grinned any wider if he had just won the Daytona 500."

* * * *

Then as now, the 2.5-mile Pocono Raceway in eastern Pennsylvania remains one of the most unique tracks on the NASCAR circuit. Not only because of its three turns, each modeled after a different more conventional four-turn oval, but also how effortlessly the nearby resort community shifts from a quiet honeymoon destination to a haven for rowdy race fans.

In the mid-1980s, Jim Slezak worked in marketing and media coordination at the Pocono track. For each of the twice-yearly visits NASCAR made to the speedway, he would host a barbecue picnic the first evening to welcome drivers and crews. All the big names came – Dale Earnhardt, Neil Bonnett, Harry Gant, and Cale Yarborough – each mingling over barbecued hamburgers, hot dogs, and ribs. It was something Jim's young son David looked forward to every year. David had been coming to the track since he was nine. He watched Tim Richmond take the checkered flag in the Like Cola 500. His favorite driver was Terry Labonte, the 1984 series champion, but he was also intrigued by J.D. McDuffie, who was always the first to show up at the picnic.

The picnic was a welcome change of pace for McDuffie. His lunch often consisted of an opened loaf of bread and bologna scattered amongst his tools in the garage. "J.D. was always the guy who would show up at like quarter to five before we'd open officially," David recalled, "and he'd walk in with his cigar and he'd grab a couple things and we'd say, 'J.D., how you doing?' 'Good.' Never really very talkative, just kind of minding his own." One time, David walked up to the driver as he ate quietly at a far table. He pulled out the only slip of paper in his wallet, a card that read "J.D. McDuffie Fan Club." The club didn't offer many perks, but for a couple of dollars gave fans a chance to help keep McDuffie Racing in business.

"Hey," said David to J.D. "I'm part of your fan club, I'm a big fan." The driver smiled. "Good to hear." And that was it. "It was (just) one of those things – you'd ask him a question and you'd get one-word responses back. He wasn't a mean guy in any way shape or form. He just – I don't know – the gift of gab, I mean, just talking like you're a young fan, how many of them do I see like this, you know, tell me a little about you, he wasn't like that at all."

Some young fans had more success. Once, while waiting in line to qualify, McDuffie climbed from his car and walked over to some children standing by a fence on pit road. He signed autographs for several minutes. "I love to talk with the kids and tell them about the cars," he said in an interview. "I'd rather talk with them than just sit in the car waiting to qualify." Others, especially those who came by the garage, found him polite, but singularly focused on his work. When Doug Schneider's father brought him by the shop in 1990, McDuffie showed him around briefly, took a photo with him, and went right back to tuning up his car.

From that moment at the picnic, David was determined to learn more about the man in car No. 70. He tracked down a tent that sold J.D. McDuffie t-shirts. The shirts were as plain-spoken as the driver – his name in red lettering beneath a giant blue AC Spark Plug, the car number printed even smaller, almost apologetically, near the bottom. He tried to learn more from his father. "You ask me about any driver and I could give you all these stories, but you ask me about the one guy who I have almost no stories on." David listened intently. "Let me tell you, every single time, David, I walked up and down that garage area where I had to meet a driver, every single time I went, J.D. McDuffie was under the hood of his car or he was sitting on his car."

David waited. "Okay, tell me more." His father shrugged. "I wish I could. That's my point. I could tell you all these Elliott stories, I could tell you all these Harry Gant, Yarborough—but J.D. every single time he had the cigar in his mouth and was under the hood of his car." Jim's co-workers could add little more. They, too, described a man who worked alone, honking his car hauler's high-pitched horn as he drove away, last to leave the racetrack.

* * * *

Maurice Leggett knew the way to Sanford. He'd been driving there from Lumberton nearly every week since December 1990, when he wrote a piece on McDuffie for his local paper, *The Robesonian*. On Tuesday, August 6, 1991, he headed down Willett Road toward a small neighborhood. Suddenly, he was there once again. At the far end of a 1.36-acre lot sat a 100-by-50-foot two-bay garage.

The driver was there to greet him. Five-foot-ten with thick gray-and-black hair and a bushy mustache. The 52-year-old McDuffie had hardly changed since 1966. Neither

had his circumstances. His shop, built by friends two decades earlier, was still just three blocks down the road from
the home he shared with his wife and two children. In the
past, his family traveled with him to nearly every race, following in their car on road trips as far west as California
and as far north as Delaware. They'd watch him race, then
stand with him by the hauler after it was over, waiting for
the man from NASCAR to bring by his share of the purse.
But as time went by, even they couldn't keep up with the
grueling schedule.

The grind was getting to McDuffie as well. Throughout
his career, he'd averaged just $2,000 in earnings per race.
Without a corporate sponsor to supplement this income, he
could only scratch together a few extra dollars from a small
network of supporters. Once, after a fender-bender in his
street car, the insurance settlement went directly into his
race car. It was always just enough to keep the shop open
and make it to the track, but not enough for new cars or parts.
He had to run old equipment – even tires – discarded by larger teams. A practiced mechanic, McDuffie knew which parts
were still good, and if they weren't, would often be able to
figure out how to make them good again. So, for decades,
McDuffie Racing remained a fixture at each race.

For all the obstacles he faced, McDuffie outlasted
many big names. In May 1991, while some of his contemporaries, like Cale Yarborough and Richard Childress, participated in the "Winston Legends," an exhibition race for
retired drivers, McDuffie prepared his No. 70 for the weekend's main event. Under the hood of his Pontiac were parts
and pieces that years earlier carried super-teams like Hol-
man-Moody, DiGard, and Blue Max Racing to a combined

five championships. By 1991, all three teams closed, the contents of their shops sold at auction. McDuffie made sure to show up and place his bids. Days before Leggett arrived, the driver had just returned from another auction in Charlotte, bidding alongside fellow independent driver Philip Duffie. He hoped what he purchased would get his No. 70 through the final three months of the season.

Everything in the garage looked well-worn – dusty, grimy, dented – but every piece neatly organized and within arm's reach. On one side of the room were suspension springs – black, yellow, and white – arranged on a hand-crafted shelf. Pistons on another, lined up carefully next to some eight-track tapes. The seat, steering wheels, and dash-board gauges came from the metal rack on another wall. Robbie Benton, the rear tire changer for Petty Enterprises, built a row of cabinets that provided more storage space. Paneling, painted white in the indeterminate past, offered more shelf space above. Two bright red fuel cans on one side. Cardboard boxes of miscellaneous parts on the other, accessible by a hand-crafted stepladder.

Only a few signs decorated the flat white walls. A large decal from AC Spark Plugs. A pit board with the STP logo. A white banner that read "Welcome Race Fans: Detroit Gasket Racing." At the far end of the room, an old Pepsi machine stood next to a pair of steel rims, each perched atop the pedestal of a black oil drum. Next to that, the entrance to his office, where framed pictures on the wall documented races past. He didn't keep his trophies in there – those were always at his home.

The garage could hold five or six cars, but beneath the fluorescent lights, there was just one Pontiac Grand Prix stock car. Earlier that year, McDuffie rolled the car into the small paint shop at the back of the garage, giving it a coat of bright red. He tuned the engine in the engine shop next door, looking for any change in horsepower on the analog gauges of his old dynamometer. Then he pieced the car together with practiced care, using tools from a simple red toolbox that, on race day, doubled as the team's humble "war wagon." But for all that work, the red No. 70 car was now torn apart and sitting on jack stands, as it had been for two months since an on-track accident. McDuffie's other car – his *last* car – was chained to the back of his truck. He called the truck "Old Blue."

The words "Not For Hire" were painted in front of "Old Blue's" driver's door. It was no stretch of imagination for the 1970 Chevrolet ramp truck to be confused for a flatbed wrecker. Spare truck tires and equipment were tied down to an elevated platform above the cab. A set of Goodyear racing slicks fit in a purpose-built cradle that dangled over the nose of his race car. A dozen side lockers like those on a fire engine held his tools and pit equipment. Only after seeing all this would anyone notice the faded NASCAR Winston Cup Series decal from 1986, then the words hand-painted beneath:

J.D. McDuffie Racing
Sanford, N.C.
 # 70

The ramp truck was once the vehicle of choice for NASCAR drivers – Paul Goldsmith's team used a nearly identical model in 1965 – but by 1991, teams had already graduated to the eighteen-wheelers so common in the sport today. NASCAR didn't like it, either. At least one official told him the truck was "an eyesore" and urged him to up-grade his equipment. Another time, according to his wife, an official blocked his path. "Where do you think you're going?" the man asked. "I'm coming to race," said J.D. "Where are you going?" The man grabbed the truck's driver's side mirror. "You can't go in there. You gotta turn around and get outta here." The driver's response was swift. He flung him off the door and sped into the garage.

During this time, McDuffie threatened to use an even older "Old Blue," a 1960 GMC that had sat rusting in the grass outside his shop for more than a decade. The "ramp" of that model was little more than two iron girders welded to the back of a stripped-down bed, dangling his race cars precari-ously over the pavement. "I've got a good mind to get that thing out of the weeds and bring it to the next race," he said. But he decided against it. After at least one other incident, NASCAR officials stopped blocking "Old Blue's" path.

In truth, McDuffie had upgraded his car hauler one other time. Behind his shop sat a forty-foot trailer acquired from short track legend Dick Trickle's ASA team in 1988. The plywood-lined trailer could only fit one car, but with the help of a local grading company which provided a truck in exchange for sponsorship, he made it work. Unfortunate-ly, it had become impractical to use it. McDuffie could hardly read or write, having left school at a young age, and was not at all clear on how to keep the truck properly regis-tered. After he was ticketed multiple times for not paying the diesel tax and road tax, McDuffie parked the trailer in the weeds and brought "Old Blue" back into service.

Aside from the cost of renting a rig and registering his trailer, the 1970 "Old Blue" proved a cost-saving measure when it came to fuel. At the time, NASCAR teams didn't have a way to store excess racing gasoline after an event. Since "Old Blue's" 427 cubic inch Chevrolet motor ran on gasoline instead of diesel, McDuffie filled up the truck's dual 150-gallon saddle tanks with it after every race. For years, that was exactly how he got back to Sanford.

There was a time where McDuffie wouldn't let anyone else drive "Old Blue." After all, only he could figure out all the little quirks that kept the truck rolling. How the gearstick rattled once you drove over fifty-five miles per hour. How a broken fan belt could be replaced by a length of rope. Only after he broke his sternum at Daytona in 1975 did he hand over the wheel to someone else on the crew. Now, all these years later, there was no one else available to drive. So now, he did that, too, his uniform hung in the back of the empty crew cab.

Whichever of his friends could show up at the track would be his pit crew for the weekend. And if not enough were able to make it, he'd hand-pick volunteers at the race track. It must have been a lonely experience. That April, after he failed to qualify for the 400-lapper at North Wilkesboro, *Winston Cup Scene* reporter Deb Williams was dining at a local restaurant. McDuffie walked in alone, wearing the sports jacket he'd been awarded for his only pole position in 1978. "He sat down at a table by himself and even though it appeared as if he was expecting some-one, no one ever joined him," recalled Williams. "He ate quietly, speaking to no one, and then left."

Once, after failing to qualify for a race, McDuffie was

asked if he thought about retiring. "Yeah, I get to feelin' that way for a little while sometimes. Like today, for instance. It can sure get discouraging, but then I get back home and start working on the car again, and I figure, 'Well, maybe next time...'" And so he'd load up "Old Blue," drive back to Sanford on race fuel, and find a way to squeeze a little more power out of his engine.

In the tradition of "J.D. McDuffie Day," Leggett set up fund-raisers to help. On January 13, 1991, he published an article in *The Robesonian* declaring "How you can become an actual Winston Cup racing sponsor." To cover the costs of pre-season testing for the Daytona 500, Leggett solicited donations between five and fifty dollars. Each donor would get their name on No. 70 at either Rockingham or Darlington, plus autographed pictures of the driver and Leggett's bonus articles on McDuffie Racing. More funds came April 4 with Leggett's twenty dollar a plate buffet dinner at Lumberton's Ramada Inn. By the day of the Darlington race three days later, no less than fifty-seven names and businesses covered the panel above the blue car's right-rear tire, including Leggett, *The Robesonian*, and the Ramada, plus a large part of the population of Henderson, North Carolina. The slew of white lettering must have spelled the difference: in qualifying, McDuffie edged Mark Stahl for the fortieth and final starting spot. It was the first race he'd made all year.

As Leggett and McDuffie wrapped up work, the driver talked about his plans going forward. He would be on the road for the next two races in Watkins Glen, New York and Brooklyn, Michigan, then meet up again in Lumberton on Labor Day weekend for NASCAR's return to Darlington.

The upcoming "Budweiser at The Glen," set for Sunday, August 11, was at one of McDuffie's favorite venues, a rolling 2.428-mile road course. "I like running up there," McDuffie said to Leggett. "It's just like driving at home."

Neither knew it then, but this would be the last time the two ever spoke.

CHAPTER 2
They Know Who It Is

"I thought he had a lot of potential. Those who only re-member him from the last few years didn't see the young J.D. who was a hot-shot driver."

—H.A. *"Humpy" Wheeler, 1991*

It was love at first sight.

The year was 1958, and Ima Jean Wood was working at a condenser company in Sanford. During her shift, she met a young man who was working in the back of the shop. When asked what attracted her to J.D. McDuffie, she gasped. *"Everything.* Handsome. Good looking. He didn't talk a lot, but when he talked they listened. He only talked when he needed to, so I had to talk twice as much (laughs)." On July 19, 1959, the two married and made their home on Baker Street. Hours before the ceremony, J.D. was still hard at work on his race car, replacing a busted radiator.

Ima Jean knew of stock car racing from her father, who often listened to NASCAR on the radio. She also knew of its dangers. The first broadcast she remembered was when two-time champion Joe Weatherly lost his life in a crash on the road course in Riverside. But right away, she knew her husband was determined to race, and that racing would be-come a big part of her life as well. She first watched J.D. compete at the Jalopy Speedway. It was at this dirt track in Hillsborough, sixty miles north of Sanford, that McDuffie made his racing debut in 1956. After he took the checkered flag in second, J.D. met her in the stands, clothes covered in dust. He took her by the hand and led her to the exit. "Let's get outta here before they want the money back," he said. With that, his $300 share of the purse made it safely home.

To supplement their income, J.D. and Ima Jean worked several jobs. J.D. tried his hand as a lumberjack but was injured by a falling tree. He also considered becoming a boxer, but there weren't any gyms in Sanford. It hardly mattered – racing was always his passion. J.D. worked during the day, tuned on his car at night, and raced on the weekends. "He went off to the track down at Rockingham and got bruised up," recalled Ima Jean. "Somehow the radiator-motor support broke and ruined the radiator, so he stayed out all night in the grass and dew fixing that."

Even in those early days, J.D. McDuffie was known for bucking long odds just to compete. Hours before one particular race, he discovered his trailer had snapped an axle. Unable to fix it in time, J.D. decided to drive his race car to the track, ten miles away. Two miles ahead, Ima Jean led the way in their street car, watching for the police. The two made it to the track without incident, but the delay caused them to miss practice. Certain that J.D.'s tires weren't warm enough to race, his competitors jeered him. That is, until he won the race handily.

Moments like this endeared Ima Jean to her husband. "When he was on the short tracks, he was king of the road," she said. "He could sling some dirt."

* * * *

John Delphus McDuffie, Jr. was born December 5, 1938 in Lee County. It's unclear where exactly in Lee he was born. His parents, John Delphus, Sr. and Ruby Lee, were sharecroppers who worked on fields of cotton, corn, and tobacco all over the county. The family lived in at least seven different homes, many without electricity. J.D. never saw a light bulb until he was nine. "That one bulb was the brightest thing I'd ever seen," he later recalled. Adding to the grueling pace of farm life, the McDuffies never once used a tractor. All they could rely on were mules, horses, and their own brute strength. Lessons learned on the fields never left the youngest McDuffie.

It was a simple life, a slow life. From an early age it was clear J.D. wanted to go faster. One of the earliest pictures of the driver seemed symbolic of the career that awaited him. It shows J.D. no more than five years old sitting in a wagon. The wagon appears to be broken, the rear wheels missing, and the bed slanted downward onto the sand. The boy gives the camera a determined stare, hands clutched tightly to the wagon's sides as if still trying to get it to roll. By then, those same hands had steered John Sr.'s Ford Model A through the woods as he sat in his father's lap. It was the first car he ever drove.

McDuffie went to his first race when he was ten years old. He, his older brother Glen and Uncle Reuben, a used-car dealer from Greensboro, were spectators at Bowman Gray Stadium. Since its construction during the Great Depression, Bowman Gray had only hosted college football games, but in time hosted races on the standard quarter-mile oval track surrounding the field. Horses came first, then cars, and when the McDuffies took their seats on May 18, 1949, the track had just been paved. Bill France, Sr., who had just moved his family from Daytona Beach, ordered the paving, and the stars of his National Association for Stock Car Auto Racing, or NASCAR, were there to break in the new surface.

"It was sumpin' to see," McDuffie recalled. "Curtis Turner, Billy and Bob Myers and Glen Wood – all of them racing. It was a bunch of fast cars, noisy you know, which you really liked. Thought it was a big rack back then. I liked the smell of racing before I ever raced. Got close to the track, you could smell the rubber off the tires, the gas, the racetrack. It's something I thought I'd want to do." That night, Fonty Flock, age twenty-nine, took the checkered flag. But J.D. wasn't there to see it. Overcome by exhaust fumes, he left the track with Ruben. But by the next morning, the young boy knew what he wanted to do with his life.

From the start, McDuffie had to be resourceful. His parents had no background in racing, much less the funds to help him get started. To make ends meet, he found work at a local Ford dealership. The shop's mechanic found an eager student in McDuffie. There, he learned hands-on how to set up a car, and even built his first go-kart engine out of an old washing machine motor. He also became a mechanic at Keith Motors, Sanford's Buick dealership. Years later, McDuffie's boss N.V. "Vic" Keith would feature prominently in his NASCAR career.

In 1956, a seventeen-year-old McDuffie dropped out of school to pursue his racing career. He and Glen picked up a '36 flathead Ford and entered it at Hillsborough. He chose car No. 70, explaining it was easy to paint and hard to forget. "Somebody says 70," he said, "they been around racing a long time – they know who it is."

Before long, he was right. By 1962, when J.D. graduated

from sportsman to late model competition, he became a star of the new Independent Racing Association. The IRA was a throwback to pre-NASCAR stock car racing, a loose confederation of a handful of North Carolina dirt tracks. Bullrings up and down the Carolinas invited racers just like McDuffie to drive their hand-crafted machines every Friday, Saturday, and Sunday. The tracks were all close enough together to attract many of the same drivers, and some promoters paid the entire field "tow money" – between ten and fifteen dollars – to make sure they could get back home.

The drivers of the IRA had much in common with McDuffie. "Winding" Wayne Andrews got into the sport when his older brother lost interest in racing his '37 Ford. The teenage Andrews said he was twenty-one on the IRA's release, though admits he was much younger at the time. He drove No. 4. He picked the number because it was the easiest number to paint. "Anybody can paint a four," said Andrews. "So that's what we done. Out of the blue, we picked up number four, it was straight lines, and we stuck with it." The lessons learned in the IRA served Andrews well. In the years ahead, he'd make six starts in NASCAR's Winston Cup Series, run two seasons in Grand National East, and claimed the final championship for the NASCAR Grand American Division in 1972. Years later, he still looks back fondly at his days in the IRA. "We didn't make any money, but we had friendships that lasted forever, and that's what it was about."

One of the most aggressive drivers Andrews faced in the IRA was "Big" John Sears, who made his way into NASCAR in 1964. "Now, John would put the chrome horn to you," said Andrews. "You know that, no doubt about it. He'd put me in the wall several times at Rockingham. Sort of – well – you know when you're running and when you're running on the limit, you was right on the edge anyhow, especially on dirt, and it didn't take much to put you around, and John would do that. And he'd done it to everybody…anybody was running up front and winning, that was his target. John was alright, we got a long alright, but sometimes we would get a little riled up at each other because of some incident on the track, but next week was another race, so you'd forget about it."

McDuffie, however, always raced Andrews clean. "We basically respected each other," he said. "We might've rubbed fenders and stuff like that, but as far as intentional stuff, we never did do that. J.D. was very mild mannered, laid back, and you know if he was running, he'd run good, and if he had a night off or something wasn't right, you come up behind him, he'd let you by, but any other night if he was running good, he would run you just as hard as the next guy. We never, to my knowledge, had any problems with each other at all. When you run with somebody like that, or different people, you're gonna have some people who'll be a thorn in your side, but J.D. wasn't that way, not racing dealing with him, and I know in NASCAR, I don't think that ever occurred, to my knowledge."

McDuffie's favorite stop on the IRA calendar was the Rockingham Speedway, a tight three-eighths-mile clay oval off US-1 that hosted the series' Saturday races. The track didn't have an outside wall, only a ditch that caught cars racing too high in the corners. Tom Clegg had never seen anything like it. "It was the first time I'd ever been to a dirt track," Clegg said of his trip to Rockingham in 1961, "and it had a reputation back then of being a rough place, but it wasn't. There was kids everywhere and it was just a nice fun place." Clegg remembered delivering papers by the McDuffie house as a kid, but it wasn't until his first trip to Rockingham that he realized who his neighbor was. "He (J.D.) was one of the heroes. Everybody liked him."

Another person drawn to the action at Rockingham was one H.A. "Humpy" Wheeler, at the time a promoter for Robinwood Speedway in Gastonia, North Carolina. "I kept hearing about Rockingham and the drivers down there," said Wheeler. "I saw two super-duper race drivers that night – a guy from Ellerbe, named Big John Sears, and J.D. McDuffie. I believe J.D. won the race."

Wheeler was so impressed that he invited McDuffie, Sears, and their fellow competitors to Gastonia. McDuffie didn't disappoint. "It was a great race," said Wheeler. "With two laps to go, J.D. rooted John Sears out and won the race. At that point, I remember J.D. was as good a race driver as I'd ever seen, and I'd probably only seen 500 races by then." Wheeler, who would go on to have great success promoting events at the new Charlotte Motor Speedway, predicted big things for the man from Sanford. "He became one with the car. I thought that night he could probably be a big-time star driver if he could get out of his locale and run other races."

McDuffie was also a favorite of the local media for his spectacular victories. He racked up several thirty, thirty-five, and forty-lap features, including Chevrolet's first-ever win at the dirt oval in Dillon, South Carolina. He once raced from sixth to first on the opening lap and stormed to a decisive win. "J.D. McDuffie of Sanford is having himself the most successful racing season he has ever enjoyed," said the *Richmond County Journal*. "McDuffie was earlier this year commended by both track officials and drivers for his good sportsmanship over the past several years in competition." An article in the July 27, 1962 edition of the *Richmond County Journal* proclaimed, "McDuffie Is Driver To Beat At Speedway." At the end of 1962, McDuffie was crowned Rockingham's track champion.

At one point, McDuffie was the top-earning driver at Rockingham, where a win earned him $100, but that wasn't enough. Working on his own cars was expensive, and at other IRA tracks the only prize he won was a trophy and a case of Pepsi. Looking for a new challenge and a more stable source of income, J.D. looked to NASCAR and its national championship purse. "To him the competition was NASCAR," said daughter Linda. "That top race, you know, the Grand National drivers, that's what he wanted – that was the challenge he wanted every week to compete against teams that had millions of dollars of backing versus what he had."

On July 7, 1963, J.D. McDuffie made his first NASCAR start in Myrtle Beach, South Carolina. He entered a 1961 Ford previously driven by Curtis Turner, one of the men he'd saw race at Bowman Gray as a child. Paul Clayton's team ran No. 70 that season, so J.D. McDuffie's car carried a big "X" instead. Car "X" finished twelfth in a field of eighteen. The driver took home $120 for his efforts.

So began one of NASCAR's longest careers.

CHAPTER 3
Too Independent

> *"The 30-year-old, stocky, dark-haired, cigar-chewing*
> *mechanic from nearby Sanford is not likely to win the*
> *rich speed classic, except for some miracle performed*
> *from Up There. He doesn't even give it a second*
> *thought."*
>
> —*Bob Myers, The Charlotte News,*
> *March 7, 1969*

In 1969, J.D. McDuffie's No. 70 on the NASCAR Grand National tour was a Buick Grand Sport. He received the car two years earlier from Vic Keith, his old boss at Keith Motors. In exchange for the car, the company's name was painted on each rear fender, and it was often put on display in Keith's showroom. McDuffie still worked at the dealership during the week, and Keith would give him a day off to go racing.

As nice as the car looked in its bright gold paint, it was a handful to drive. It rode high off the ground and produced just 360 horsepower, less than three-quarters the power of a top NASCAR engine at the time. The car also blew engines regularly. On Lap 104 of the Daytona 500, the power plant let go in front of Cale Yarborough, causing the defending race winner to crash out of the race. Twelve of the seventeen races the Buick failed to finish that year were because of the engine. "Everybody knows General Motors doesn't participate in stock car racing," lamented McDuffie that season, "and it's near impossible to get high performance engine parts."

But, that same year, the Buick started forty-five of fifty-four races. Twelve times it finished inside the Top 10, including a stretch of three in a row at Beltsville, Bristol, and Nashville. His best finish of the year was sixth, which he first scored at Richmond, then backed-up at Greenville-Pickens. When the points were tallied, McDuffie sat fourteenth in the championship standings. Eighty-four points-earning drivers ended up in his rear-view mirror. "There's another consolation," McDuffie said with a smile, "I'm driving the fastest Buick in stock car racing."

That year, it was the *only* Buick in stock car racing.

* * * *

Such was the life of an "independent" – also known as an owner-driver – someone who owned and maintained the same cars he raced. It was – and remains – the hardest possible way for a racer to make a living. From the start of his career, J.D. McDuffie's No. 70 was much slower than a handful of "factory drivers," racers fully funded by Ford or Chrysler. Without their backing, it was McDuffie who had to bang out the dents if he crashed, McDuffie who swapped out engine parts if the motor let go, and McDuffie who raised money to do both. The odds were against him. Yet, somehow, he always made it work.

Much of McDuffie's endurance was thanks to the close group of friends who made up his crew. Much of his 1969 crew had been with him since he ran in the IRA: Cecil Wicker, Earl "Bud" Sloan, Curtis Ward, Bully Hutchins, Tommy McDonald, and Wilbur Thomas.

Thomas, nicknamed "Bad Eye" for being blind in one eye, had known McDuffie since grade school. He lived in Broadway, what he called "a wide spot in the road" outside Sanford, on his family's soybean and tobacco farm. At the edge of the farm, built on what was once a cow pasture, stood a thirty-by-thirty yellow building that became McDuffie's first garage in the 1960s. On race day, Thomas would back his farm truck into a ditch, so the bed was level with the field. McDuffie would then drive No. 70 across the field and onto the truck – his first race car transporter.

"I never got up with anyone who loved racing as much as J.D. did," Thomas recalled. "He stayed with it. He studied it all the time."

When his chores allowed it, Thomas traveled with McDuffie to the track. Even then, money was tight for independents. Tires were always an issue as the team could only afford half as many as bigger teams. "I know we went to run South Carolina one night," said Thomas, "J.D. had a new motor, he run good, he run the whole race, and it run good, and he came down and asked if I had a little money. He said 'Well, I need $300 – I'm not winning enough to make the tire money.' So, I loaned him money to pay the tire money. Back at the big tracks they gave you a set of tires, but at the short tracks you had to buy them, and they was dirt back then and the dirt would eat them up. So, he would buy three sets of tires and run that night and wore them out, he ran the whole race. He ran pretty well I think he finished inside the first ten, but he didn't make enough to pay the tire bill."

In time, Thomas became McDuffie's first crew chief – or technically his second. At least three times in the past,

J.D. Brock Beard

McDuffie served as his own crew chief, climbing from his car on every pit stop to refuel No. 70. But such a thing wouldn't be tolerated at Daytona. "The NASCAR official come by down pit road and introduced himself, he was gonna be the official looking after us at that race, and asked J.D. 'who's your crew chief?' And I was just standing there. J.D. says, 'Well I ain't got one.' He said, 'Well you've gotta have one,' so he said 'Hey, well 'Bad Eye' here, [he's the] crew chief,' so that's the way I got it."

Thomas was just as spontaneous as his friend. When the team wanted to bring water to the garage, Thomas decided to build a well. He went to a local hardware store and bought ten sticks of dynamite for a quarter a piece, stuck them in the ground, then ran the fuse through his barn. "We was in the shop when it went off. It blowed mud all over the shop, roots throwed across the road, mud all over the grass, all over the top, and the highway out here. Bad Eye came in and said, 'we've got running water!' From then on, we could wash our greasy hands."

That story was recalled by Jimmy Byrd, or "Byrdie," a good friend of both Thomas and McDuffie. Without a farm to tend, Byrd was in the Broadway garage more often than Thomas, making him McDuffie Racing's only full-time employee. For fourteen years over 400 NASCAR races from 1970 to 1984, Byrd shared crew chief duties with Thomas, and was also the technical wizard behind the scenes. Like many other mechanics of his day, Byrd tried to make the most of the gray area between the rules in the NASCAR rulebook. One rule in particular owes its existence to Byrd's efforts with No. 70.

"The rule book said you've gotta have a full-bladed

fan," he recalled. "But the rulebook didn't have no dimensions on how long the blades had to be. So, I picked us a six-cylinder fan, cut all the blades at a quarter-inch (laughs). Bill Gazaway, Jr., he said 'you can't run that.' I said 'yeah, I can, too.' I said, I got the rulebook out, I said 'the rulebook says full-bladed fan, it don't say how long the blades have got to be.' I said, 'I left a quarter-inch of the blade on there.' So, he didn't take it...The following week at Richmond, rule change: blades have gotta be four inches long (laughs)."

Byrd was also a talented car builder. He often built Chevrolets – the driver's favorite – from parts and pieces the team scrounged together: Monte Carlos for the super-speedways, Lagunas on the short tracks. Byrd learned much from McDuffie, particularly when it came to setting up the rear end. If the gear's teeth matched and the metal had a mirror shine, it was good enough to run again. He also specialized in springs and shocks, convincing McDuffie to move away from using the same right-front spring from one race to the next. What Byrd didn't know, he learned from other mechanics in the garage area and brought back to Broadway. Figuring out the steering geometry used by "factory teams," for example, required a bit of subterfuge.

"When I figured it out, J.D. had a Chevelle built in South Carolina and then Richard Petty had one built at the same place, and he got the car that J.D. was supposed to have gotten, and we went to get it, they let Richard have it, so we had the next one that came off the jeep. And I asked Richard, 'did your roll center come off a quarter-inch from floor level?' And he told me, he said 'it checked a quarter of an inch.' Well, I figured out right then I knew how to do it (laughs)."

* * * *

Back in the 1960s, McDuffie Racing's grassroots ef-fort wasn't unusual. In fact, independent drivers made up a sizeable portion of NASCAR's starting grid. Fighting to make ends meet, the group helped each other survive. It was common for McDuffie to select a spot on pit road next to Neil Castles, Wendell Scott, Roy Tyner, and his other con-temporaries, allowing them to share the few volunteers each brought to the track. When one of them pitted, the others would come and help, and when one fell out, the crew would stay with whoever was still running.

There was cooperation, but also heated competition. As the few "factory drivers" battled amongst themselves on the lead lap for victory, the independents would run a race among themselves for what amounted to "best in class," tak-ing care to stay out of the leader's way. "I feel like I'm a competitive driver," said McDuffie in an interview. "I just don't have the equipment to run up front. So, I race with (the) other guys like myself, on back in the field. People may not be aware of it, but there's some good racing going on back there."

For years, NASCAR supported the independents. Bill France, Sr., the sport's founder, wanted to build his sport around a group of returning drivers – not just the big names, but those who filled out the fields. To this end, France of-fered to pay the top twenty-five drivers in the point stand-ings over each off-season to make sure they could afford to come back the following year. With only a handful of big names back then, and the field open to just about anyone with a car, this provided an incentive for drivers across the country.

McDuffie was among the best at reaching France's pay threshold. He made up for poor finishes by running as many races as possible. He refused to test experimental setups for other owners for fear of losing his rank in points. He also did his best to stay on good terms with NASCAR officials, avoiding costly penalties or disqualifications. Thus, for six-teen straight years – from the time he became a full-time competitor in 1968 through 1982 – he made the top twenty-five every year, and in so doing ran all but fifty of those 531 combined races.

Back then, France was always at the track, and would loan his drivers money if they needed help. "If you got in a jam," recalled a crewman, "J.D. if he got tight, he'd go to the race track and see Bill and borrow some money to eat off of and sleep off of. He would take out $100 a race – back when they ran fifty or sixty races a year." After a good run, when McDuffie went to the pay window, the clerk would tell him "I'm gonna take off $100 of what you owe Bill" and hand him the rest in cash.

But NASCAR was changing. It evolved in ways that made life more difficult for the smaller teams. In 1963, when McDuffie made his NASCAR debut, the dirt tracks of his youth were already being taken off the schedule. Clay ovals made up just seventeen of the fifty-five races that year, then dropped three seasons later to fifteen of forty-nine. By 1972, when Bill France, Sr. handed the family business to his son Bill Jr., the dirt tracks were gone com-pletely. So were races under 250 miles in length. In this new "modern era" of NASCAR, dirt track stars like

McDuffie had to start from square one and learn how to race on the sport's new paved superspeedways.

That same decade saw corporate sponsorship replace "factory teams" as the new business model for NASCAR. Independent drivers running near the back of the field found themselves having to make sales pitches to skeptical executives, hoping to get their logos on their cars. A reporter told Ima Jean McDuffie her husband couldn't get a sponsor "because he had two children, but so did the Pettys, David Pearson, all of them." An anonymous sports marketing executive attributed it to something else. "J.D. was a very quiet guy whose fingernails were a little too greasy – and that's not a knock on him...He couldn't get up in front of a microphone and be brilliant. He couldn't walk into a room and charm a bunch of CEOs."

With expanding television coverage and the increasing presence of national brands, there were also more cars and drivers than the field could hold. Qualifying was no longer a certainty, and independent drivers now had to make sure they could put together a fast lap in time trials. Failing to make the field meant no share of the purse, and teams sent home were stuck with another financial burden. No one felt this burden more acutely than independents like McDuffie.

One time at Talladega, McDuffie's No. 70 lost a motor on its first practice lap. Without a backup, he swapped in an engine designed for much shorter tracks, which wasn't fast enough to make the cut. When asked if he was going to stay and watch the race, the driver shook his head. "Can't afford to hang around...We've already spent between $500-$600 just to get here. If we'd made the starting lineup, we'd have taken home at least $1,200, which would have at least covered expenses. As it is, we're going in the hole on this one...I don't care to hang around if I don't race. I ain't much of a spectator."

McDuffie worked nearly year-round, determined to keep pace with the sport's many changes. "I usually take it easy for a couple of weeks around Christmas," he said, "but the rest of the time we just work right on through." When ESPN's pit reporter, Dr. Jerry Punch, asked McDuffie why he did so much work, the driver answered, "Who else is gonna do it? Plus, who's in that car driving it? And if something fails, who do I blame? Me!"

Despite all his work, McDuffie was never quite able to close the gap. More often than not, race day was a matter of survival. He'd have to pull over to let the faster cars go by. McDuffie remained a gentleman about it – never interfering with his fellow competitors, nor summoning the dreaded "move over" flag from NASCAR officials.

McDuffie didn't have any enemies in the garage area, either. Those on the inside seemed to understand his plight. "It was just making a living for him," said Richard Petty. "He wasn't trying to be a hero or nothing, just as long as he could come to the race track, run his race car, finish the race, get that money to get on to the next race and he was as happy as a june bug." Others weren't so kind.

In 1976, McDuffie joined a group of eight other independents at the Darlington Raceway to discuss a way to keep small teams in the sport. "We're not looking for a welfare line," said James Hylton, the driver who'd been appointed the group's spokesperson. "Make the money available so we can win our share. Put it into the purse or whatever it takes so when the year ends I can see that I have made a little money from racing." When asked to meet with the group, Bill France, Jr. refused, wanting instead to meet each driver on an individual basis. He was also skeptical about where the talks would go. "We (NASCAR) are not going to do anything to discourage competition," said Bill Jr. "You can't give them (the drivers) a place in the sun."

But on April 24, 1976, France changed his mind. He spoke to the group at the Martinsville Speedway. After two hours, Hylton announced that he was pleased with the outcome. "As far as I'm concerned, it's over," he said. "Mr. France agreed that we needed help and promised a permanent solution to our problem by mid-June."

The solution was a two-tier payout structure designed to help independent drivers, called "Plan A" and "Plan B:"

Plan A	$2,000 bonus to highest-finishing owner-driver $1,900 to second-highest finishing owner-driver $100 less for third-highest on down the rankings
Plan B	$2,000 bonus to owner-driver with the highest earnings all season, including total "Plan A" bonuses.

McDuffie was a beneficiary of both bonuses, but soon discovered that NASCAR took twenty-one days to send a "Plan B" bonus.

Despite these new incentives, which were later replaced by contingency awards made available to the entire field, the challenges facing independents only grew more overwhelming. Unable to qualify for races, much less make the top twenty-five, owner-drivers began to leave the sport in greater numbers. And as more money brought more full-sponsored teams into the sport, the door wasn't just shut, but locked.

* * * *

The sport's rapid evolution also changed the media's perception of McDuffie. Once, writers cheered him on like any other driver. When previewing the Southeastern 500 at Bristol on April 8, 1977, the *Kingsport News* did a feature on the independent, optimistically titled "McDuffie Eyes 1st Win." The article made its case that "McDuffie is one of the more successful independent drivers on the NASCAR circuit," having finished twelfth in the standings the previous year, and that "[i]t is at the tracks of under a mile in length where McDuffie feels he stands the best chance against the well-financed drivers and their sponsored cars." McDuffie started a strong twelfth that Sunday, but with just two cautions slowing the three-hour race, fatigue made him pull off the track in the final laps.

"There's different ways to define 'competitive,'" McDuffie once said. "Now, if you mean do I expect to run up front and lead the race, naw, I probably won't be able to do that. I ain't got the equipment for it. But there's a lot of us on back in the field who have pretty much the same equipment and we can race each other. All the racing ain't done at the front of the pack. Look on back there in the field sometime and you'll see a bunch of us going at it."

But racing at the back of the pack didn't interest the media as much as raw statistics. Later articles focused on the number of starts McDuffie had made without a win.

Four articles from 1982 through 1990 commemorated his 503rd, 542nd, 614th, and 646th starts. Looking back, it seems unfair he was singled out. His 653 races may have been the most, but not by much. Neil "Soapy" Castles never won after 498 green flags. Buddy Arrington went winless through 563. Perhaps the reason the man from Sanford was viewed differently was simply that he refused to get out of the car. Castles stopped driving in 1976. Arrington followed in 1988. Both went on to become car owners, putting young drivers like Dale Earnhardt and Dale Jarrett in their cars. McDuffie, meanwhile, remained in his No. 70 so long that he eclipsed Arrington's 0-for-563 in 1984 – four years before Arrington retired. "I'm running as hard as I can," McDuffie said in an interview. "It might not look like it sometimes, but I'm going as fast as I can."

Another misleading statistic was that McDuffie never finished on the lead lap. While factually true, this didn't mean that McDuffie didn't have his share of strong finishes. In 1966, when independents outnumbered "factory drivers," it was possible to finish multiple laps behind the leaders and still finish fifth – more than enough to stay in the top twenty-five in points. Only in the latter part of his career, when many big teams were capable of finishing on the lead lap, did an identical run mean a poor finish. "Used to be there was a time when we run in the Top Ten regularly," said McDuffie, who earned 106 Top Tens in his career, "but there's so many beefed up teams now it's rough. And don't none start like I did: with nothing. The only way I've survived all these years is to do my own work. It gets tough sometimes when you don't have enough equipment to run with. We just try to run as high as possible without ruining the equipment 'cause we got to run the same car next week."

Still, writers of the day didn't know what to make of the man from Sanford. Some, like Jack Chevalier of *The News Journal*, kept it good-natured: "J.D. McDuffie rides on forever, at the end of the field. Happy to be there on a Sunday afternoon with a bunch of good ol' boys he has ridden with forever." Brian Schmitz of *The Orlando Sentinel* joked that J.D. could win if he had "a 20-car crackup involving the top cars, a Rolls Royce engine and a healthy head start – plus directions to victory lane." McDuffie had heard them all. "I've been called an underdog so much that I've started barking at the moon and runnin' rabbits," he said.

But others seemed insulted by his presence. One wrote that J.D. stood for "Junk Dealer." Another, Ralph Paulk of *The Akron Beacon Journal*, said that McDuffie's "passion for speed and unyielding desire to take the checkered flag – one more time – is a sad, pathetic obsession."

The most pervasive of these critics was Larry Woody of *The Tennessean*. Whatever his motivation, Woody spent most of the 1980s publishing one-liners at the driver's expense:

"J.D. makes a strong argument for reincarnation. In his first life, he must have been a snail. He may come back next time as a tortoise. He's not a born loser. It's an acquired skill."

"Can he end the losing streak today? No, of course not. He doesn't stand a chance. Not a prayer. McDuffie has about as much chance of beating the likes of Darrell

Waltrip, Bobby Allison, Richard Petty, Cale Yarborough and Buddy Baker in a Grand National race as Phyllis Diller has of beating Bo Derek in a wet T-shirt contest."

"McDuffie has the same luck with race cars that Woody Allen has with women. The day McDuffie wins a race is the day Mr. Ed wins the Derby. Or Richard Simmons starts a bar brawl."

"They'll be ice skating in Hades before it happens. Frogs will fly, fish will sing, and Alexis Carrington will say no. In other words, don't hold your breath waiting for J.D. McDuffie to win a race. J.D. hasn't won in 24 years so why start now? His won-lost record is 0-614. That ought to cheer up Vandy coach Watson Brown."

Publicly, McDuffie could care less what others thought of him. He didn't complain about what he didn't have – even when other independents did. He simply enjoyed the pleasure of being out there. The phrase "With 'GOD' You're Always A Winner," painted on McDuffie's car, seemed to indicate he was embracing his underdog status. In reality, the self-deprecating phrase was the slogan for The Chapel, Inc., Brother Bill Frazier's ministry, which began broadcasting Sunday morning services at race tracks by public address in 1972. "I'm not proud of losing 503 races," said McDuffie in 1982. "But I make a living and I enjoy what I'm doing, and that's more than a lot of people can say, right?"

But undoubtedly, his struggles affected him deeply. "I saw a lot of heartache," said daughter Linda. "I saw a lot of promises made to my dad. He really didn't go into a lot of in-depth conversations about stuff like that because he just, you know, got so disappointed in people, he just got tired of people letting him down all the time...seeing him like that all my life was hard because he was such a great man."

McDuffie hardly ever got angry, even when he had reason to be. But when he was mad, you knew it. He'd tense up, grind his teeth, and the muscles in his temples would twitch. Then, just that quickly, the storm would pass. Few interviewed for this book could remember more than one occasion of him lashing out, a moment which stood out in its rarity. The time he confronted officials after a scoring error put him one lap down. The time he threw a timing light across his garage after he spent two hours trying to get it to work.

By all accounts, only once did the media stir his temper, and it wasn't for any of the quotes listed above. It was in 1982, when Jesse Outlar of *The Atlanta Constitution* compared J.D. to Herman "Turtle" Beam, another winless independent. Beam was what older short trackers called a "strumbo," so notoriously over-cautions behind the wheel that he only failed to finish eleven times in 104 starts. In this sense, McDuffie was, in fact, quite different: he fell out of 294 of his 653 starts, and in 1980 set a career record for most Winston Cup Series last-place finishes which stood until 2014. That wasn't the only difference.

"Don't you compare me to Turtle Beam!" he boomed. "I don't drive like he did. When I'm out there, I drive to *win!*"

* * * *

Once, J.D. McDuffie was asked whether he resented the success of his more well-heeled competitors. "Naw, not at all," he said. But he couldn't help but crack a smile. "Well, maybe a little. It'd be nice to see how I could do if I ever got a top ride. But that's not going to happen, so there's no use worrying about it. I'll just keep doing the best I can with what I've got."

But there *were* offers. Opportunities for an easier life. Many times, McDuffie was lured by other teams to serve as their mechanic. They heard of how he could set up a nine-and-a-half-inch rear gear with his bare hands, feeling the sticking points in the shims until he had it just right to run 500 miles. How he could piece together an engine out of two discarded sets of pistons, finding the best eight that would get the job done. Or the time he took a torch to a bent axle he'd laid across two old tires, then painstakingly hammered and rolled it straight again.

One of McDuffie's strongest offers came from Junior Johnson, who had graduated from one of the sport's best drivers into one of its top car owners. Johnson offered to have McDuffie and his family move to North Wilkesboro, where everyone on the team lived within a short distance of Junior's shop. He told Junior no.

McDuffie was also given the chance to drive for other teams – big teams with sponsorship and new cars ready to be driven. In 1978, car owner M.C. Anderson offered him a full-time ride in the No. 27 Oldsmobile the following year, replacing the lead-footed Buddy Baker. By merely signing his name on the dotted line, McDuffie wouldn't have to get his hands dirty and just focus on each race. There was a guaranteed paycheck. Security. McDuffie turned him down just the same. His contemporaries shook their heads.

"He was too independent," said Glen McDuffie. "When you get a big sponsor, you kind of got to do some things like they want to do."

Simply put, McDuffie loved the life of an owner-driver. He had his shop, his cars, his friends and his family. And, at times, it was remarkable what that alone could accomplish.

CHAPTER 4
The Bailey Years

"I also have to say something about Bailey Excavating of Jackson, Michigan which has helped me a lot on the financial end."

—*J.D. McDuffie, 1978*

While a national brand never sponsored McDuffie's No. 70, many small businesses still did. Among them were Wilder's Nuts and Bolts, Signs By Fritz, D.L. Philips Company, and Insurance World. He was once featured in promotional materials for Carolina Bank, which closed with, "The Carolina Bank is proud to have J.D. as a customer, Sanford is proud to boast 'He is Ours' and the Carolines [are] proud to have the opportunity to salute – J.D. McDuffie, Jr. – NASCAR's future."

But for the majority of McDuffie's career, two family businesses featured prominently over all others: Bailey Excavating and Rumple Furniture.

* * * *

Based in Jackson, Michigan, Bailey Excavating went into business as contractors in 1973. From the start, founder William "Bill" Bailey was a race fan. When NASCAR rolled into the Michigan International Speedway, a fast, two-mile oval in Brooklyn thirty-five miles to the south-east, many drivers and teams would stay at the Holiday Inn in Jackson, and Bailey would rub elbows with them over coffee.

In 1975, Bailey met with an owner-driver named Henley Gray. Active on the NASCAR circuit since 1962, the Georgia-born Gray landed a regular sponsor with paving company Belden Asphalt. Conversations with Gray and company president Rex Belden made Bailey consider sponsoring a team of his own. Gray recommended the driver he relieved at Bristol earlier that season.

"Henley came up...and said here's somebody I'd like you to meet, his name's J.D. McDuffie," recalled Bill Bailey's son John. "He's like me, an independent, and he's struggling." With some reluctance, McDuffie elaborated. "Yeah, I'm struggling," he said. "I blew an engine I don't have enough money to get home." Right then, over hotel coffee, Bailey decided to help. He gave McDuffie enough money to get back to Sanford. When NASCAR returned to Michigan that August, Bailey paid for a set of tires. That Sunday, and for at least 130 races afterward, No. 70 carried Bailey Excavating's logos over the rear wheels.

Sponsored at last, McDuffie was able to afford to move into a new shop. When the Baileys met him, the driver was still working out of Wilbur Thomas' garage, which was no larger than an oil change shop. The decision was made to construct a brand-new building with room enough to assemble each No. 70. And so, some ways down Willett Road, the blue pre-fabricated metal walls of a Mesco building took shape. In front stood a sign from the Sanford Metal Building Corporation, beneath which read, "Future Home of NASCAR Racing J.D. McDuffie."

The Baileys also upgraded McDuffie's car hauler – his second "Old Blue." Though the driver didn't want to admit it, the miles had caught up with his old GMC. During a trip west to the Riverside, the harmonic balancer fell off in Arizona, stranding McDuffie and his crew chief in the desert. As they had on the track, the two came up with a creative solution, cutting off part of the truck bed, but by then it was nightfall. In the twenty-five-degree cold, the two men stayed warm by gathering tumbleweeds into a pile and setting them ablaze. Then, when they finally got going, the fan belt snapped. Fortunately, this had a much simpler solution: take the belt off the race car.

Bill Bailey bought one of two Chevrolet ramp trucks from Gordon Van Liew. Van Liew, the Texan owner of Vita-Fresh Orange Juice, sponsored open-wheel USAC drivers since 1962, most notably Bobby Unser and Larry Dickson. In 1972, Van Liew spent a brief time in NASCAR, fielding Vita-Fresh Chevrolets for Ronnie Chumley, then the following two seasons with Tony Bettenhausen, Jr. Bettenhausen's No. 9 was carried on the back of one of two matching bright-orange ramp trucks. Bailey bought one of them, and McDuffie put it right into service. The truck remained orange for a couple weeks until the driver got a chance to paint the body blue and roof gold. He hand-painted the words "Old Blue" on the front of the hood.

Mechanical gremlins still wouldn't leave McDuffie Racing alone. In 1977, during a trip to Talladega, the engine blew, and this time there was nothing the driver could do. Fortunately, he was approached by a man from a Chevrolet dealership who offered to help. The man towed "Old Blue" to his dealership and dropped in a new engine. McDuffie didn't have any money but asked what he owed. The man waved him off. "Put my name on the car and good luck," he said. It was done.

John Bailey, fifteen in 1975, spent a year working alongside the driver. He stayed in Sanford, sharing a bedroom with J.D.'s son Jeff. "He was like a dad to me," recalled John. "J.D. come in there in the morning, grab my foot, and say, 'Come on, boy, gotta go to work,' and left Jeff in bed. We'd work all day and come home and eat a lot of scrambled eggs because they didn't have a lot of money, eat some scrambled eggs, put some Texas Pete on them, watch M*A*S*H, and go back to work until eleven, twelve o'clock at night."

One of John Bailey's biggest projects was helping McDuffie prepare for an opportunity to drive for long-time friend Junior Johnson. Though McDuffie had declined Johnson's offer to become his mechanic, he had driven one of his cars before. In 1972, Johnson entered into an agreement to sell him the No. 12 Coca-Cola Chevrolet Monte Carlo his team would run at Charlotte. For $15,000, McDuffie could have the car – so long as his driver Bobby Allison didn't wreck it. Allison brought it back in one piece, and McDuffie picked it up at Johnson's shop in North Wilkesboro the following day.

There was just one catch: Bill Gazaway, then NASCAR's director of racing operations, had warned Johnson not to bring the car to the track again, but in Johnson's words, "he didn't say *you* couldn't!" The car's nose was pushed out two-and-a-half inches and was fitted with bigger front fenders, making it sleeker on the series' fastest tracks. When McDuffie inquired about the fenders, Johnson offered to give him the correct ones to get it through inspection. McDuffie then repainted the car from Coca-Cola red to his traditional blue and gold. Unfortunately, when McDuffie brought the car to Rockingham, Gazaway wasn't fooled. On top of the fender issue, the car's drip rails were filled with Bondo. McDuffie drove it in the race, but this time was also told never to bring it again. Allison, driving another Johnson No. 12, won the race.

The Johnson car Bailey worked on in 1982 didn't have such a checkered past – as far as anyone could tell. It was a Mountain Dew-sponsored Buick identical to the No. 11 driven by the popular Darrell Waltrip, a car he nicknamed "Elvira." Waltrip needed a good finish in the season finale at Riverside to secure his second-consecutive Winston Cup championship, but "Elvira," though a proven winner, wasn't his first choice. Knowing the car was available, McDuffie contacted Johnson's engine builder Brad Puryear, asking if he could drive it instead. While Johnson first said "no," Puryear leaned on his boss, who invited McDuffie to come down and have the driver's seat fitted. The Johnson crew went over the car from end to end, even replacing a fan whose blade had a minor nick in it. By his arrangement with Johnson, McDuffie would take home all the prize money he earned at Riverside, and all he needed to bring was his own crew. Both Jimmy Byrd and Wilbur Thomas joined McDuffie on the journey west.

While Waltrip earned the pole at Riverside, McDuffie secured fourteenth on the grid. He enjoyed a solid eighteenth-place finish in the race and led his only lap of the season. So, as Waltrip came home third and clinched the title, McDuffie and crew went home with $3,450 in prize money.

* * * *

John Bailey was about the same age as Jeff and Linda, J.D. and Ima Jean's two children. Despite their father's occupation, the two enjoyed a modest upbringing in a quiet town. But being the children of a race car driver did have some advantages. In 1976, J.D. won an $8,000 boat for gaining the most positions during the Dixie 500 at Atlanta, rallying from thirty-fifth to thirteenth. The boat was a mid-engine Ski-Tique water-skiing boat with a 302-small block Ford engine, a welcome distraction for family trips twenty miles north to Jordan Lake.

McDuffie's mechanical know-how also provided his children entertainment on land. "We did race go-karts once in a while, we rode motorcycles," said Linda. "[W]e had an old car that basically we would go tearing through the woods with, you know, just (laughs) I could probably drive before I could walk you know? So we would be tearing up, just going down the woods completely wide open, you know looking back on it I don't know how we lived."

"I can't tell you how many times the cops come over to the house," said Linda. "[W]e would ride our motorcycles, the problem is we'd outrun the cops and they would go over to the house because they knew who we were, you know, go to the door and mama was 'what do you want me to do?' it was stuff like that. It wasn't – we weren't trying to be buttholes, we were just being kids."

Most of Jeff and Linda's time with their father was spent down at the shop, or at the race track. Linda still remembers hopping in the car with J.D. at Rockingham and Talladega. "Let's go!" she'd yell, and out they went, driving on banking so high it felt like the car would tumble clear down to the bottom.

Linda never understood why her classmates didn't respect him the way she did. One day in the third grade, she came home from school in tears. The next day, J.D. walked into class and talked to her classmates about racing. "When a tire blows," he said, "you ain't got a choice." Linda never had any problems with them after that. "He was so cool," Linda said. "He was like an astronaut."

One of Linda's most cherished memories is of Charlotte, the cat her father always kept at the garage. "They were in Charlotte for the race, and they found a little kitten at the motel, and my dad ended up taking him back home and he named her Charlotte, because that's where they found her." When Charlotte was struck by a car in May 1991, her father was devastated. "He came home and told my mom with tears in his eyes that he had to bury his cat...People forget that, how kind he was. He had a big heart."

Jeff, three years older, was being positioned by her father to take over the team. Driving six-cylinder dirt cars, Jeff won seventeen races when he was fifteen years old, much to the chagrin of his older competitors. When he turned eighteen, he began working on J.D.'s pit crew, including crew chief and tire changer duties. That same year, he made the first of five Winston Cup starts alongside his father, competing locally at Rockingham and North Wilkesboro. Each time, Jeff drove a second car renumbered with some combination of "7" and "0." Each time, he finished ahead of his father, earning a career-best sixteenth at Wilkesboro in 1982.

Linda, meanwhile, continued to work behind the scenes. She started off cleaning her father's office and the bathroom, but soon learned how to work on the car. She even drove "Old Blue," though her father insisted on shifting because the transmission was temperamental. Her first car was a blue 1983 Chevrolet Monte Carlo SS, the first year they were built. She still has that car today. Around that time, Linda asked her father if she could compete in a "powder puff" race against other women…In time, she decided not to pursue it. "I should have been the boy," said Linda.

* * * *

In 1974, a friend got J.D. McDuffie in touch with two brothers from Pennsylvania named Ron and Darryl Butler. The brothers' company, Butlers Inc., worked in high-performance auto parts and engine building. Before long, Ron was providing the machine work for McDuffie Racing, using parts the driver provided. Darryl, meanwhile, saw an opportunity to promote the tire company the two of them founded in 1957: McCreary Tires.

While Goodyear had just replaced Firestone as NASCAR's exclusive tire manufacturer, the Butlers saw a chance to get McCreary the press needed to acquire more distributors. "We've got to prove that our tire works," said Darryl. "And, it has already been proven." Since McCrearys saved McDuffie twenty dollars a tire over the Goodyears, the driver agreed to put them on No. 70.

Carrying logos for Butlers Inc. and Glenn's Landscaping – one of the brothers' other businesses – McDuffie turned in several strong runs on McCrearys. He soon found the tires wore quickly, so quickly that they couldn't be run on superspeedways like Daytona. Part of this was because they weren't the right width for a full-sized stock car. But they were fast enough while they lasted, and in time, McDuffie began to figure them out. He finished sixth at Riverside in 1975, then a season-best fifth at Richmond that fall. McDuffie's most famous ride on McCrearys was still to come.

* * * *

The one-mile Dover International Raceway, formerly known as Dover Downs after the horse racing track in its infield, remains one of the most challenging on the NAS-CAR tour. Known as "The Monster Mile" for its proclivity for big accidents, the steeply banked track was also one of McDuffie's favorites. When there weren't enough cars to start the race, the Sanford driver was called by Dover's track promoters to come up and fill the field. As a result, he made forty-one of his forty-two attempts on the oval, second only to Rockingham for most starts at a single track.

McDuffie's persistence afforded him a number of passionate Dover fans – "the Yankees loved him," a crewman said. Some handed him cigars, putting them in his pocket as he passed. Others worked on his team, most notably the "Delaware Dogs," so named for doing the dirty work when the circuit came to the track. One of the "Dogs," Rick Tori, brought his young son Curt. "I was the only kid that was allowed to sit in his car," said Curt, who would go on to drive in the American Race Truck Series and in ARCA.

Heading into Dover in September 1978, McDuffie Racing brought one of the best cars in their stable. Jimmy Byrd had completely rebuilt the Monte Carlo the previous off-season. He first took it to his own garage, cleared away his woodworking tools, and stripped it down to the chassis. One of his first additions was a new roll cage purchased from Banjo Matthews, a former driver who had become one of the sport's top car builders. When Byrd brought the car to the Broadway shop for finishing touches, he added more engine parts from Benny Parsons. The car was then painted Bailey blue and gold with a glimmering acrylic sheen. With a set of fresh McCrearys, the car was ready to hit the track.

McDuffie was an unlikely, but not improbable, candidate for the pole. He entered the race 11th in points, having finished eighth the week before at the Richmond Fairgrounds. His best qualifying runs had come in three of his previous seven starts. He started fourth at Nashville, ninth at Michigan, and fifth at Bristol. He'd also cashed-in on those strong starts, leading his only laps of the season in two of those races – one lap at Nashville, then three at Michigan. But, for one reason or another, McDuffie never won a Winston Cup Series pole.

The 1978 season wasn't making the goal easier to reach. Through the first twenty-three races of the season, just eight drivers had won poles, and all of them drove for top teams. Leading the group was David Pearson, whose fleet Purolator Mercury from the Wood Brothers took six poles. Cale Yarborough's Junior Johnson-prepared Chevrolet picked up five. Neil Bonnett, driving for Rod Osterlund, scored three of the first six. Even unheralded Lennie Pond, who scored his only Winston Cup victory that season with Harry Rainier, picked up four. Joining the group were Benny Parsons with two, and Bobby Allison, Darrell Waltrip, and Buddy Baker, who each had just one.

But, this time, Byrd had something for them. He was particularly aggressive with the setup, including the camber. "They said they wanted it set at 105 degrees, and I told the man we're putting it in at ninety-five degrees, or top dead center, and that thing would fly." The team also acquired more engine parts from Benny Parsons, which required some experimenting with the gear ratio. "We started out with a 422 gear and ended up with a 391 gear. It turned so many R.P.M.s, we had to keep gearing it higher, 'cause it would wind out before you got to the end of the straighta-way."

After shaking the car down in practice, McDuffie took to the mile track in qualifying. He drove it in deep, and to his surprise, the car stuck. At the final tick of the watch, No. 70 was on top of the board: 26.572 seconds for a speed of 135.480mph. No one else broke the 135mph mark, not even third-place starter Richard Childress, who also on McCreary tires. In his 404th NASCAR start, J.D. McDuffie finally earned his first pole.

"I will have the best starting behind me instead of in front and that should get my morale up on Sunday," said McDuffie, a sheepish grin on his face. "I guess it's kind of a surprise, but in practice we were running about the same times as everybody else. This is certainly a big day for me, no question about it." Among McDuffie's prizes for the pole was a brand-new refrigerated Busch Beer cooler wheeled out onto pit road, complete with a decorative tap.

Ima Jean could hardly believe it. "He come in that even-ing, and he held up his (index) finger. He said, 'I got the pole.' I said, 'You're lying.' I couldn't believe it." Ima Jean called Linda, who couldn't wait to tell her grandparents. "I remember running all the way from my house – it was a couple miles – to tell them, you know, that my dad won the pole and they said 'What' and I'm like 'yeah, he did' (laughs)."

Richard Petty, who managed just thirteenth on the grid after the local authorities handed him a speeding ticket the night before, recalled it well years later. "I know one time we was running somewhere (Dover) and J.D. won the pole, it scared him to death (laughs) he didn't know what to do starting up front!"

McDuffie started that Sunday's Delaware 500 alongside the fleet Bud Moore Engineering Ford of Bobby Allison, who won the Daytona 500 seven months earlier. For ten laps, No. 70 paced the field, outlasting four other drivers who pulled behind the wall. He ran fast, but the McCrearys couldn't hold up to the abuse of the steeply banked track. The McCreary tires were narrow – just eleven inches wide – and the track's high banking made it hard for the rubber to dissipate heat. Unable to cool, the tires simply came apart. "After eleven laps you could just about grab the rubber off in your hand and chew it," McDuffie said later. Early pit stops dropped No. 70 back in the field, and it wasn't long before he'd used up the ten tires in his pit stall. Finally, a dropped valve took him out of the race, leaving him a disappointing thirty-third. Bobby Allison dominated the second half of the race and cruised to an easy victory. After the race, he sought out the polesitter. "J.D.," he said, "I tried to outrun you every way I could, and I couldn't get around you."

Goodyear wasn't happy to see their tires outmatched in qualifying. After Dover, they threatened to leave NASCAR altogether. In the end, Bill France, Jr. instituted a new rule requiring each tire manufacturer bring 500 tires to each race. While the rule was officially made to ensure that every team could run any tire that was brought to the track, it quickly squeezed out Butlers, Inc. and McCreary. Unable to produce tires at that rate, McCreary pulled out of the sport soon after. Stacks of leftover McCreary's, constructively banned from the sport, ended up stacked in Wilbur Thomas' barn behind his home, where they remain to this day.

* * * *

But all was not lost. The ceremonial Busch Beer tap on McDuffie's pole-winning trophy had extra meaning that year, as it meant he now qualified for the inaugural running of a new exhibition race. The race, known as "The Busch Clash of '79," would be held at the Daytona International Speedway just days before the following year's Daytona 500. The only drivers invited to start the twenty-lap sprint race were the previous year's polesitters. McDuffie, one of just nine drivers to win poles all season, now had a chance to win $50,000 if he could beat just eight cars.

"I'm not going to do anything stupid out there," McDuffie told reporters the Thursday before the race. "I'm just going to do my best. These guys are the best in the world and I just hope I can show up good. Everybody's been kidding me about it – giving me last pace even before the race – but I'm just going to do my best. This is definitely the biggest race in my life."

That same day, all nine qualifiers drew for their starting spots by reaching into a metal tub of nine numbered cans of Busch Beer. McDuffie hoped to start first or last to avoid being shaken out of the draft. He drew fifth. Benny Parsons got the pole in the M.C. Anderson ride McDuffie had turned down. "I hope I can improve on this," McDuffie told reporters as he brandished the can. "I think I'll drink this right before the race," he joked.

The J.D. McDuffie Fan Club chartered a bus to bring forty fans to Daytona that day to cheer on No. 70. Also watching were those on the grid. "I guess everybody is overlooking J.D.," said eighth-place starter David Pearson before the race. "But, heck, he has started a race in front of all us before, hasn't he? He deserves to be here." So did Buddy Baker, who rolled off third. "Sometimes J.D. doesn't race his car as hard as some others because he's got to replace everything himself. But with only twenty laps to run he may let it all hang out. I think he's going to run better than everybody thinks he will."

The Clash marked the first time McDuffie drove an Oldsmobile, the model of choice at the time for many on the superspeedways. The car was another from "Tiger" Tom Pistone's garage and had engine parts from Benny Parsons. "If I was running my Chevelle, I would be giving up two or three miles an hour," McDuffie told Grand National Scene, "but now I won't be giving up anything body-wise."

The Olds handled well in practice but lacked speed on the Goodyears – even after the team changed engines. Unfortunately, this spelled disaster on race day. Seconds after the green flag, McDuffie had already lost touch with the leaders and was running by himself down the backstretch. No cautions flew in the short sprint race, and less than fifteen minutes later, he'd finished last, having pulled out with engine trouble in the final three laps. In an attempt to earn short-term speed, McDuffie had the heavy wheel bearing grease replaced with lightweight automatic transmission fluid, which burned out a bearing after only a few laps. Baker took the win. Still, the Sanford driver left with his car otherwise intact and $10,000 in his pocket.

A few days later, the same car finished twenty-fifth in the Daytona 500.

* * * *

J.D. McDuffie's years with the Baileys were some of the best of his career. From 1976 through 1980, McDuffie never missed a race, and always came home between eleventh and sixteenth in the final point standings. In 1980, he ran fastest in the second round of qualifying for Talladega. "I surprised myself," he said. "That's the fastest I've ever been in qualifying. I borrowed an engine from Benny Parsons just for qualifying. Man, those strong engines make a difference. It was all I could do to hang on, but I loved it."

Back on pit road, Ima Jean joined the other driver's wives – "The Fence Hangers" as they were called – and rubbed elbows with the many celebrities who were starting to take notice of NASCAR. "I met James Garner out in Riverside," she said. "He come up in scoring stands and I stuck out my pad and he autographed it for me, and he come back by and I stuck my paper out again and he wrote it again for me. I oughta grabbed him – he's a good-looking man (laughs)."

At Daytona, she also met John Schneider, who played Bo Duke on "The Dukes of Hazzard." "He said, 'Stand right there, I'll be right there,' and he come right back to me. He went to do something and come right back (laughs). Oh yeah, he said, 'I'm gonna show you all how to take a picture,' so he got me in the middle and put his arm around J.D. and said, 'this is the way you pose' and I said 'oh thank you.' I'd be glad no matter how I posed. I'm not nervous about things like that back then."

It was during this period that J.D. perhaps came closer than ever to scoring that elusive first win.

* * * *

Statistically, the Nashville Speedway, a 0.596-mile paved oval at the Tennessee State Fairgrounds, was McDuffie's best track. In twenty-nine career starts, he'd racked up four Top Fives, eleven Top Tens, and failed to finish only six of those races. Perhaps his success was because the track was a veteran, in its own right – constructed in 1904 and hosting NASCAR events since 1958. The corners once rivaled those of Bristol Motor Speedway, thirty-five degrees at their peak before 1972, but the eighteen-degree banks of the late 1970s were every bit as treacherous. To master Nashville required practiced hands.

Heading into the Sun-Drop Music City USA 420 on the night of May 11, 1979, McDuffie sat seventeenth in points, looking to rebound from a blown engine at Talladega. The next power plant was coming together in the Sanford shop, with help from daughter Linda. "I actually helped him build that engine," she said. "It was kind of a running joke, but you know that was something that I always teased him about. I was like 'maybe you should let me build the engines,' but he had a lot more knowledge than I did."

In Nashville, the father-daughter-built engine showed speed early, putting No. 70 ninth on the grid. Then, just thirty-two laps into the race, McDuffie wrestled the lead from rookie polesitter Joe Millikan. Many expected McDuffie to fall by the wayside as he had at Dover, but this time was different. For the next 244 laps, McDuffie waged war with Darrell Waltrip and Richard Petty, and spun battling for second with Cale Yarborough. He recovered nicely, leading as late as Lap 276 and closing on Petty for first.

With sixty laps to go, and rain in the area, Jimmy Byrd called McDuffie onto pit road to pit under green. The crew took two tires instead of four, but still lost two laps on the leaders. The plan was to force the leader's hand to pit early, putting No. 70 back up front before the rain stopped the race short of the finish. It almost worked. "And here comes the shower," said Byrd. "Well, everybody else got to pit under the caution. We were two laps behind."

Despite the setback, McDuffie still had a fast car under him, and after the rain went away, charged back to finish fifth at the finish. Though McDuffie was scored two laps down to race winner Cale Yarborough, Byrd insists No. 70 was much closer. "The last lap of the race, he was back to fifth place and he was probably about eight car lengths from being back in the lead...If he had just a few laps, it wouldn't have took many, two or three or four, I believe we would've won Nashville that night."

McDuffie led 111 laps that night, second-most to Richard Petty's 164. In his other 652 starts, he'd lead just fifty-one more.

CHAPTER 5
Phoenix From The Ashes

"Mr. Rumple really loved J.D. He really thought that man was gold on the ground. They just enjoyed each other."

—Ima Jean McDuffie, 2017

Sanford's exhibit hall at the Lions Club Fairgrounds was filled to capacity. Some of the guests had to stand beneath the hand-painted banners taped to the brick walls as they enjoyed chicken and barbecue from the Palomino Restaurant. At the podium, emcee Willie Hunt, a local comedian who worked at the local Harris Wholesale Company, introduced the man of the hour. Out walked J.D. McDuffie in a three-piece suit. The room erupted in applause. McDuffie shook hands with two of his fellow competitors, Bobby Allison and Darrell Waltrip, who joined him on stage. As the sound subsided, Hunt read a proclamation from Sanford mayor Roy Stewart.

WHEREAS, J.D. McDuffie has contributed to the City of Sanford, North Carolina, by acting as an Ambassador of Goodwill and bringing Sanford, North Carolina into focus on a national scale as he travels the NASCAR Grand National Stock Car Racing Circuit, and

WHEREAS, each week J.D. McDuffie is introduced to thousands of race fans from Florida to Michigan and from the Carolinas to California as being from Sanford, North Carolina, and is further recognized as an outstanding example of the caliber of people that compose the population of this fine city.

NOW THEREFORE, I, Roy M. Stewart, Mayor of the City of Sanford, do hereby proclaim February 29, 1980, as J.D. McDUFFIE DAY, and urge all citizens of our community to give full regard to the recognition that he has given to the City of Sanford.

DATED this the 8th day of February, 1980.

SIGNED Roy Stewart and City Clerk A.B. Harrington.

More applause. Soon after, Bobby Allison came to the podium. "He is the only guy with a cloud of cigar smoke in the car with him." The crowd laughed, and J.D. grinned around the cigar pinched between his teeth. Next was Broadway resident Vicky Holder, wearing a gold dress and red sweater, who glared at the driver from the podium. "He picked race driving over yours truly," she said. "Who would pick race driving over this luscious body?" She threw a pair of red underwear at McDuffie, saying he'd left them with her at Riverside. More laughter, especially from J.D. Other drivers couldn't make it, so J.D.'s brother Glen and members of the crew joined in. In the end, there was a toast. "J.D.," said Allison, "it's great racing with you." The crowd cheered. The first annual J.D. McDuffie Roast was a success.

Word of the event came from James Oldham, a close personal friend as well as the racing correspondent for the *Sanford Herald*. On top of founding the J.D. McDuffie Fan Club in 1972, Oldham had been one of McDuffie's most ardent supporters in the media. "Sanford has never supported their local professional race drivers like they should," he once wrote, "and there is one who was one of the most out-standing individuals in the sport and is now in the Stock Car Racing Hall of Fame in Darlington, S.C.," referring to Herb Thomas. In just a few years, the club had members all over the country and beyond. "The fan club had people from California, Canada and Florida, people from all over the place. They were just looking for somebody to relate to."

The roasts, which were held yearly from 1980 through 1983, were some of the club's most successful events. Darrell Waltrip was always the first to agree to come. Waltrip was the "roastee" in 1981, when the event took a surprising turn. Misinterpreting his new sponsorship from Mountain Dew as a plan to haul illegal moonshine, the local sheriff arrested Waltrip at the roast, and it was only when he got to the car that the mistake was caught. The outspoken Waltrip kept it all in good fun. "You know on the circuit, he was sort of booed and what not as a bad guy," said Oldham of Waltrip, "but he's one of the nicest Christian fellas you'd ever hope to meet."

The 1983 roast featured MRN radio reporter Jack Arute and another Winston Cup star, Neil Bonnett, who shared a story of a fishing trip with McDuffie. As the two drove their boat to the middle of a lake, the outboard motor fell off and plunged several feet down. McDuffie jumped over the side after it, came up for air, then went back down again. He was down there for several seconds, and Bonnett was worried that he'd drowned. He looked over the side and saw through the clear waters that McDuffie had not only found the motor but was trying to get it started. With a laugh, Neil yelled out, "You dummy, choke it!"

Each event included an autograph session and a raffle.

Nearly everyone in attendance left with a door prize, including coolers, caps, umbrellas, and radios. Everyone also made sure to take home their placemats, which featured hand-drawn caricatures of the drivers in attendance.

There were many other fan events back then. The first "J.D. McDuffie Family Fun Day" was held June 22, 1980, where the driver joined others in a baseball game. In 1982, the first "J.D. McDuffie Barn Dance" was held at the Bobby Joe Blue Farm in Vass, North Carolina. Providing the music was Chuck Fowler and the Mavericks, a band which participated in several McDuffie events. There was also a "Little Miss 70" contest for young girls organized by Freddie and Ruby Carlyle. More than 400 people paid the three dollars to get in.

The J.D. McDuffie Fan Club continued the same grassroots efforts which gave their driver his start. One fan sent letters from Czechoslovakia. Three fans from Cincinnati sent a yellow t-shirt with "J.D." on the front. On the back, signed in ink pen, "The Cincy Gang" wrote well-wishes:

"J.D. Good luck. Bring home a winner, Steve."

"Good luck in racing, always. Wendy."

"We're waiting for the big win. Lois."

All fans sent money, their membership dues going straight to McDuffie Racing for a radiator or a set of tires. But when Mack's Stores, Inc., a department store chain which sponsored one of the roasts, left the team at the end of the 1982 season, even these efforts fell short.

Heading into North Wilkesboro in October 1983, McDuffie's Pontiac had run without a primary sponsor in thirteen of twenty-five races and languished a distant twenty-sixth in points. Both Jimmy Byrd and Wilbur Thomas were leaving the sport with Byrd moving on to build house trailers. On top of it all, McDuffie had missed the field for the most recent race at the North Carolina short track and needed help if he had any chance of making it again.

Fortunately, help arrived from a most unexpected source.

* * * *

Like Sanford, the town of Elkin, North Carolina has a strong background in racing. Elkin was the birthplace of Barnet "Barney" Hall, perhaps the most famous voice in the history of NASCAR. By 1983, Hall was a booth announcer for MRN, bringing his radio audience the play-by-play from tracks across the country. As Hall prepared to make the call for that weekend's lead-up to the Holly Farms 400, he was approached by an immaculately dressed man from his home town. His name was Tom Rumple.

Rumple was the owner of Rumple Furniture, a retailer that had been in business in Elkin since 1957. To promote their business, the store had sponsored cars in the Winston Cup Series. The most recent in 1972 when Elkin-born driver Eddie Yarboro brought his Plymouth to Darlington. Rumple looked to do more, but tragedy struck on Christmas Day 1976 when the shop burned to the ground. Rumple, his son Don, and the rest of his family worked for years to get the business back up, reopening in 1978. Now, Rumple

looked to get back into the sport as a sponsor, and asked
Hall if there was a driver he recommended. Instantly, Hall
remembered the man he played poker with years earlier.
"Well, I'll talk to J.D. McDuffie," said Hall. "He's always
needing some help." Rumple met with McDuffie. He liked
what he saw. That same day, No. 70 had two sets of tires
and a man in the garage with a can of yellow paint. With it,
the man drew Rumple's logo in bold letters on the panel
above each rear tire.

Rumple and McDuffie became good friends, and the
store owner was considered a member of the McDuffie
family. "We always had a gentleman's agreement — a hand-
shake was good enough between us," said Rumple years later. "He'd never ask me for anything, but I'd say, 'Don't you
need so-and-so?' and he'd say, 'Yeah, I do,' and I'd get it for
him. He needed much more money than I could afford. He
was proud to be associated with Rumple Furniture Company,
and that made me feel real good." By 1987, Rumple would
pay between $20,000 and $25,000 a year to McDuffie Racing.

Rumple was equally eager to promote his driver. A
photo taken during a 1986 meeting of the J.D. McDuffie
Fan Club at the Martinsville Speedway shows McDuffie
standing next to Don and Tom Rumple, as well as Marsia
Goad, crowned "Miss Rumple 1986." In the picture, all
three are wearing dark velvet coats with the Rumple logo as
well as distinctive trucker caps. Don Rumple went down to
the Southern Emblem Company in Toast, North Carolina to
commission some caps for McDuffie to wear at the track. In
those C.W. McCall days, trucker caps were still a fixture in
the garage area, and Rumple commissioned Southern Em-

blem to make his own. The caps were brown with gold backing, the thick "Rumple" logo on a patch stitched proudly to the front. And though his driver had yet to score a Winston Cup victory, he had the company embroider a victory crown along the top of the bill. For the rest of McDuffie's career, he was rarely seen without one.

Rumple also looked to promote his driver at the Elkin shop by displaying a "show car." Many of today's NASCAR teams have such "show cars," typically an underused or out-of-date chassis, set aside to roll out during fan events at parks and grocery stores. The most famous "show car" belonged to Cale Yarborough, who drove to victory in the 1983 Daytona 500 driving a Pontiac LeMans that days earlier was parked in front of a Hardee's fast food restaurant. Always wanting to make the most of his equipment, McDuffie never had a "show car" of his own. The primary car Yarborough wrecked in qualifying was sold to McDuffie, who put a new body on it and made it his next No. 70. Still, Rumple was determined to make him one. He bought an old street version of a Pontiac Grand Prix from a junkyard, painted it dark blue, and decorated it to resemble the Rumple No. 70. For years, Rumple left it out in the parking lot beneath his street sign, drawing the attention of motorists traveling down US-21.

"Tom (Rumple) liked the idea of being a sponsor," said a teammate. "He wasn't gonna get his hands dirty. He was always impeccably dressed, and he was a nice guy."

One of McDuffie's greatest moments in the Rumple car came in 1986. That year, NASCAR added a new wrinkle to "The Winston," its second-annual "All-Star Race" at the Atlanta Motor Speedway. While the previous year's running was reserved for past race winners, 1986 would be preceded by a bonus 100-lap race known as the "Atlanta Invitational." The Invitational was exactly that – its field was determined by a fan vote among twenty-six drivers who made at least ten starts the previous year and were not already in the main event.

"I think this is a super idea," said McDuffie, who joined Rusty Wallace in announcing the event at a press conference. "I think that I have enough fans out there to help me get into that field of fourteen. I certainly hope so, because this is one race where I could make some money. If I am one of the fourteen, I will probably build a special engine and since the race is only 100 laps, I can afford to buy tires. If I am in the Atlanta Invitational, I intend to go all out."

On March 30, less than two months before the race, the J.D. McDuffie Fan Club was out in force, filling out ballots during the first four races of the season, and by mail. James Oldham went all-out during the campaign. "We sort of cheated a little bit and you know they went by the votes for J.D. and we sort of got the phone book out and put down names and what not to go and get him in the race there. But I'm sure other teams and what not did the same thing, I didn't really see anything wrong with it." The group lifted No. 70 from twelfth to second in the Invitational poll until he trailed leader Kyle Petty 31,070 votes to 34,137. By the time polls closed in May, McDuffie ranked eighth – still more than enough to make the fourteen-car field.

Heading into the race, McDuffie was eager to show everyone what he could do. "I have one of the best engines that I have had in quite some time and I intend to have four new tires instead of used tires that I am usually forced to run. I feel that the distance of the race will be in my favor. I will not have to run conservative like I do in a 500-mile race, so I will run all-out in an effort to win." He also thanked the fans for their support. "I feel that I owe the people that voted for me something, so they can look for me to give it my best shot and I hope that I can make them proud of me."

Unfortunately, McDuffie dropped a valve after thirty-seven circuits, leaving him next-to-last in the race.

* * * *

In 1988, McDuffie had a new lease on life. For the first time in seven years, he had a brand-new car of his own, the Rumple logos featured just as proudly on every corner. The car's chassis was built by the popular Hutcherson-Pagan Enterprises in Charlotte. The company's founder, Dick Hutcherson, had a brief but brilliant career in NASCAR with most of his fourteen victories won on dirt tracks. Once the car was delivered, it was McDuffie's job to finish it in his Sanford shop, including the assembly of its sheet metal body from parts provided by Morgan-McClure Motorsports. Pon-tiac upgraded the design of its Grand Prix that season, set-ting aside 1987's boxy 2+2 model in favor of a sleeker, more aerodynamic shape. McDuffie elected to give the new design a try. In just thirty-five days, McDuffie and team fin-ished the car, painted it blue, and had it ready with just days to spare. Ironically, he would still have to run a borrowed engine.

McDuffie was one of seventy-two drivers who arrived

in Daytona Beach, Florida to try and make the forty-two-car field for the season opener. Too slow to secure a starting spot on his speed in time trials, McDuffie had to race his way to a fifteenth-place finish or better in the thirty-four-car, 125-mile qualifying race. Just prior to the Thursday race, someone stole McDuffie's driving gloves from his dashboard. Without any time to get replacements, he decided to race without them. "What's the chances of me catching on fire?" a crewman recalled him say.

Truth be told, McDuffie had a love-hate relationship with Daytona's 2.5-mile tri-oval. He made the race twelve years straight from 1972 through 1983 but failed to qualify again until 1987. At the time, his most serious accident had also happened at the track. Four laps into the 1975 Daytona 500, three cars wrecked in front of him heading into the third turn. McDuffie slowed, but lost control and slammed head-on into the outside wall. The impact cracked his breastbone, bruised his chest and heart, and required fifteen days in the hospital. What happened three laps into the 1988 qualifier was even worse.

As McDuffie headed into the first turn, Ralph Jones lost control of his No. 92 Ford and slid into the left-front of No. 70, crushing the oil cooler. An oil fire started, and when Delma Cowart's No. 0 Chevrolet rear-ended the No. 70, the gasoline ignited, too, turning his Pontiac into a fireball. With his hands, arms, and left thigh covered in burning oil, McDuffie fought to stop his car on the apron. By the time he finally climbed out and fell to the infield grass, he'd suffered second and third-degree burns to both hands. The fire burned his eyelashes, singed his mustache, and filled his lungs with smoke. He also broke two front teeth. Paramedics rushed him to the nearby Halifax Medical Center, where he stayed for over a month. NASCAR flew Ima Jean to the hospital to be by her husband's side.

"I think it was tougher on her than me," said J.D. of his wife. "But we had to go on from there. She knew I was going to come back. I knew she would be all right." But she wasn't. On top of her husband's injuries, she was dealing with an article which quoted NASCAR Winston Cup director Dick Beaty, blaming McDuffie for his burns. The article stated the window net was improperly installed, causing it to stick in place. She contacted the writer and had him write another piece. "But he wrote it just like I told him," she said. "I know how things look."

McDuffie's burns required several skin grafts taken from his left thigh, then corrective surgery a year later. The surgery, performed at the North Carolina J.C. Burn Center on December 18, 1989, required he wear a brace on both hands every night until the Daytona 500 in February. Keeping the grafts in place were a pair of special leather gloves the driver had to wear for the rest of his life. Despite his excruciating rehabilitation, McDuffie's attitude had hardly changed. When a fan named Duffy Denemark stopped by to say "Hi," the driver welcomed him in past the "No Visitors" sign and the two talked for more than three hours. Other fans sent cards and letters, many with cash or checks for up to $1,000 from the "J.D. McDuffie Relief Fund." Jeff McDuffie made at least one attempt to get the No. 70 into a Winston Cup race, narrowly missing the cut at North Wilkesboro.

In the spring of 1988, when McDuffie was finally released and flown home on NASCAR's corporate jet, the city of Sanford once again rallied behind its favorite son, hosting a jubilee to benefit the Fund. Among the drivers in attendance was Rusty Wallace, who brought his Kodiak team's "show car." James Oldham and fellow fan club member Ronnie Gunter sold raffle tickets for five dollars each, the prize an all-expense paid trip to a race. The Fayetteville Speedway started to hold "J.D. Days" at the track, donating a dollar of every seat sold to McDuffie. The program was the brainchild of Patrick Purvis, the track's promotional consultant, who had followed McDuffie since his dirt track days.

Tom Rumple, who also stayed with McDuffie in the hospital, was as determined as his driver to return to the track. He surprised McDuffie with another brand-new Hutcherson-Pagan car, complete with new associate sponsorship from High Point Bedding. "It goes to a wonderful friend and a Prince of a person, J.D. McDuffie, compliments of Rumple Furniture of Elkin," said Don Rumple. "We hope to be back into racing with J.D. driving by July 24th." The driver couldn't wait. He was back at the end of May.

Though McDuffie would miss the field for his first attempt at the Coca-Cola 600, he made the very next round at Dover, besting two other cars in qualifying and finishing a solid twenty-fifth. He even led a lap that day – the 162nd and final of his Cup career. "I put that accident behind me," said McDuffie in preparation for his return to Daytona that July. "I'm going on now. I've had bad wrecks before and you just can't look back. You have to look forward." McDuffie made only one more start in 1988 – at Watkins Glen. It marked the first time since 1967 that he missed more races than he started. He made just twenty more over the next three seasons.

Just beneath *The News-Journal's* article about McDuffie's return to Daytona that July, another story didn't end so happily. Forty-eight-year-old Bobby Wawak, another independent driver, had enough. Minutes before McDuffie's qualifying race, a water leak sent Wawak's No. 57 spinning head-on into the wall at over 180mph. The crash nearly took his eyesight. After seventeen seasons and 141 starts, Wawak would never race again.

* * * *

Though the Daytona fire burned so hot that it melted the steering wheel, the damage suffered to the rest of McDuffie's car wasn't as bad as it first looked. Driver and team managed to piece it together in time for their return to the Daytona 500 in 1989. Again, McDuffie wasn't fast enough to lock himself in on speed. His qualifying lap was more than 15mph off the pole, putting him in the final row of the thirty-car qualifier. To make the show, half the field would have to finish behind him. This time, he had his driving gloves, but only 85% the use of his hands. When the race started, he lost touch with the leaders almost immediately. Near the halfway point, McDuffie was running by himself, and he seemed to be headed toward another disappointment.

Then, on Lap 16, Lake Speed crossed the nose of Rick Wilson as the two raced for third place. Both cars spun up the track, triggering a fourteen-car melee that eliminated most of the leaders. McDuffie was far enough back that he had a chance to spin clear of danger, suffering only minor damage from Rusty Wallace's Pontiac. "I whooped it this way and I whooped it that way," said the driver. While many of the wrecked cars couldn't continue, McDuffie re-started in ninth place. Despite a forty-one-second stop late in the race for additional repairs to the rear of his battered car, McDuffie finished fifteenth – exactly where he needed to finish to make his fifteenth and final Daytona 500. Once it was official, a factory man from Pontiac provided McDuffie's team with new bumpers to get his damaged car ready for Sunday.

Other drivers involved in the wreck sought out McDuffie, looking to buy his spot in the field. Among them was Kyle Petty, whose SABCO Racing team offered up-wards of $100,000 to McDuffie. Buying another driver's ride wasn't unprecedented. One of the times McDuffie sold his spot was in November 1987, when newcomer Charlie Baker wrecked his No. 93 Chevrolet for the season finale at Atlanta. As part of the arrangement, the No. 70 on the roof and each door was covered by a white square on which a big "93" was hand painted. In the end, Baker was involved in a mid-race crash, resulting in a thirty-third-place finish worth a paltry $1,350. Perhaps for this reason, McDuffie turned Petty down.

Kyle Petty ended up securing the starting spot earned by Eddie Bierschwale's family-owned team and finished tenth. McDuffie's rebuilt car came home twenty-fourth, seven laps behind race winner Darrell Waltrip. Two years later, this same car carried the names from Maurice Leg-gett's 1991 fund raiser at Darlington.

* * * *

Rumple Furniture stayed with the team into 1991, their logo moved to the rear "TV Panel," the place on a stock car where a passenger car's tail lights and trunk latch are located. There were still parties held at the Elkin shop where "Old Blue" rolled into North Wilkesboro for their twice-yearly races, but soon, McDuffie didn't have time to make them. He'd been too slow to make half the races he was attempting, which meant a quick turn-around to Sanford to get ready for the next race.

By the summer of 1991, the costs at McDuffie Racing were mounting. He had to pay a non-refundable $250 entry fee whether No. 70 qualified or not, plus an additional fifteen dollars for each crew member. A set of four fresh Goodyear tires cost $689, and since the tire compound differed by track, there was no incentive to stock up. Even though he worked on the engines, cylinder head porting and intake manifold matching required the work of an expert, costing upwards of $10,000 per set.

Standing against the tide with McDuffie and his family were the Baileys, the Rumples, the Fan Club, and a close-knit group of crew members.

CHAPTER 6
The Crew

*"He wanted to drive the car, and he did anything he
could so he could get in and drive it. That was his desire,
that was his ambition. And whatever it took for him to do
that, he would do that."*

—Mike Demers on McDuffie, 2016

Mike and Lesley Demers met in the ninth grade, married in college, then moved from Pittsburgh to Clarion,
Pennsylvania. The two shared, among other things, similar
backgrounds in the automotive industry. Frank Huggo, Lesley's father, was a charismatic salesman for the FRAM corporation. Huggo's work earned him several benefits,
including free race tickets. Ever since Lesley was nine, he
took her to races all across the northeast. Mike's father was
a mechanic, and he worked alongside him in his shop since
age twelve. When Mike and Lesley married, Huggo got
Mike a job at Clarion Auto Parts. For years, the two lived in
an apartment above the shop. Every time racing was on television, they and their two sons would watch.

In 1981, Mike struck out on his own and opened Son's
Auto Supply, a small automotive wholesaler in Westmont,
New Jersey. For five years, the two had hardly taken a day
off from work. Their first real vacation came in 1987. A
representative from Champion Spark Plugs got Mike and
Lesley into the pits for the NASCAR race at Pocono. It
was the biggest thrill of their lives. The representative introduced Lesley to Richard Petty, then she had her picture

taken, and she was hooked. "We need to be here every race," she said. "Sure," said Mike, "but how are we gonna do that?"

Mike and Lesley discovered that if they sponsored a NASCAR team, they would earn a sponsor's license, and with it, the ability to enter the garage for as many races as they liked. At first, this was easier said than done. Small businesses like Son's used to sponsor many of the sport's teams, but now they had to compete against the same big-money brands on their shelves in Westmont: STP, Havoline, Zerex. Most teams quoted prices too high to consider. Then, during a second trip at Dover, they noticed No. 70.

"We saw J.D.'s band of hooligans and misfits and everybody else, and you couldn't help but watch them," said Lesley. "And they never really did that well and sometimes were the first ones out, but that's when we wondered let's go down there and see what we can do to help him."

The Demers met McDuffie and joined up on the spot. "That was the first reason we did it," said Mike. "J.D. would take whatever we had, because we weren't a big deal, and he surely wasn't a big deal." With that, No. 70 began carrying decals for Son's Auto Supply, and the Demers got their sponsor licenses.

* * * *

The Demers used their new access to its full potential. A long-time fan of Dale Earnhardt, Lesley made it her mission to meet her hero. "I don't want to say I was stalking Dale [Earnhardt's] pit crew or anything, but I'd bake brownies or cookies – he had the yellow and blue car, so I would pick out all the yellow M&Ms and put them in the cookies and give them to the Earnhardt team." She, along with her friends Tom and Carol McDaniel, soon brought even more treats to the track, at one point erecting a portable gazebo by their conversion van for get-togethers. "I remember baking J.D. a blueberry peach pie that he said was out of this world."

Soon, the couple took on more roles at McDuffie Racing. Mike lent a hand in the garage area, saving the driver money by providing parts from Son's wholesaler suppliers rather than those at the tracks. He still treasures memories of pushing cars through inspection alongside the likes of Junior Johnson. "I've always been a motorhead," he said, "and it was just like a dream come true."

Lesley took on a "mother hen" role with the pit crew. Her first act was to buy them new uniforms. Everyone on the crew wore mismatched clothes, threadbare jeans, and in the case of the gas man, one of McDuffie's old driver uniforms found in the back of "Old Blue." Lesley bought twenty-four blue golf shirts from Land's End and had them customized: Rumple's logo on the front, sponsor patches on the sleeves, and a big No. 70 on the back. The number took the place of the Corvette that was at the center of Son's company logo.

Any modicum of regularity was a boon to the program. McDuffie's reliance on volunteers meant a different cast of characters would stand by most every week. Frank Leinard, a long-time friend of the driver, would drive from Ohio to North Carolina to help work the pits, his critical heart condition be damned. The gas and catch can men from 1991 would go on to become radio co-hosts of "The Duster and

Tex Show." And there was "Big John" Hunt (also known as "The Crane" by his teammates), a giant of a man who helped pit No. 70 during the west coast events in Ontario and Riverside. "I can still see him, walking through the garage with a tire and wheel in each hand," recalled Ima Jean.

Others were regulars from the Sanford shop. For two weeks of each month, Donald Mangum handled 911 calls for Raleigh's emergency communications service. He'd met J.D. and brother Glen in 1979, when they competed against local racers at the Lake County Speedway. The next year, when he turned eighteen, Mangum joined McDuffie Racing. On race day, it was Mangum's job to tow the three-wheeled fuel cart to the pumps and refill the gas cans. When the driver hit pit road, he would also jump over the wall with the half-sheet of plywood that was McDuffie's pit board, signaling the driver to stop. Most of McDuffie's pit boards read "Pit J.D. 70" or just the car number alone, though at least one had a woman in a bikini.

Mangum spent more time in the garage than pit road, though he also traveled to get parts for No. 70. When NASCAR downsized to a 110-inch wheelbase in 1981, it was Mangum who would make trips to Pontiac's warehouse in Charlotte. Unlike today's NASCAR, teams back then could purchase actual pieces that auto manufacturers used on street cars for their race cars. "I went down there with J.D. one time, and literally ten of everything, passing out front and rear bumpers and hoods and tops and trunk lids – back decks, then they fabricated the sides on the car. And then the sides weren't fabricated, the doors you'd put on there then come around and weld them to the front and back fenders."

Then there was thirty-year-old Leland Moore. Nick-named "Squid" by his teammates, Moore was no stranger to overcoming adversity. He was born with an enlarged heart, a collapsed lung, and even after sixteen surgeries was para-lyzed until he was five. By what can only be described as a miracle, Moore's underdeveloped arms and legs grew stronger, and he learned to walk and breathe normally. He then worked his way through school, earning a B.S. in busi-ness administration from the Florence / Darlington Tech-nical Community College, then a bachelor's degree in Transportation Management from Fayetteville Technical Institute. In the spring of '87, he started helping out at McDuffie Racing as shop organizer.

"I knew that I was like this," said Moore in a 1990 in-terview with *Winston Cup Illustrated*, "and the only attitude that I can take is to just live life while I can enjoy it and try to chase whatever dreams that I have. I feel thankful and blessed to have the opportunity to do this. So many people would give anything to be a part of racing...I think J.D. has been a little surprised that I could do it. There have been times that we would put in fourteen or fifteen hours a day getting the car ready, then driving to the track, then staying up without sleep the whole next day. But it's fun. If I didn't think so, I wouldn't be in it."

For all the crew's individual strengths, sometimes things didn't run smoothly. One time at Pocono, the tire changers forgot to tell their driver they were changing four tires instead of two, so the car left without lug nuts on one of the wheels. Another time at Watkins Glen, the crew put the left side tires on the right, causing the car to handle poorly. As a result, McDuffie's guiding principle was simple: "Take your time, do it right," Mike recalled. "If it took a minute, just do it right once so we don't have any issues, 'cause we had inexperienced people."

Other times, the mistake was on the driver. "I ran out of gas in Michigan while I was running in the Top Ten," said McDuffie. "I thought the engine blew and went into the garage area. My pit crew came running after me asking what happened. I told them it blew, they said no it didn't; you ran out of gas! The crew had the pit board up for fifteen laps, but I was so into the race I didn't even notice. That was the worst boo-boo I pulled."

By this phase of McDuffie's career, his crew chief changed from one week to the next. In 1991, Mike Demers, who started out cleaning the windshield, was the frequent choice. "Mike was instrumental too on keeping a positive attitude," said Lesley. Mike's experience running Son's brought some order to the team's operations, and his booming voice made up for the fact that McDuffie had only two radios on hand for team communications. "They don't need a radio," McDuffie once told him, "they'll be able to hear you."

* * * *

Since McDuffie traveled to the track alone, Mike and Lesley found themselves "on call," often resulting in sudden trips to the track. After McDuffie's fiery crash at Daytona in 1988, Mike and Lesley weren't expecting they'd be needed at the track in 1989, but when the No. 70 qualified for the race, the two had to change their plans. They tossed the keys to Son's Auto Supply to Bart Perkins, their new marketing employee, jumped in their conversion van, and drove down to Florida. Lesley remembers the trip vividly:

"I came home, got our stuff together, told our kids where we were going, drove all night through an ice storm down 95 through Virginia and there were cars all in the ditches...[W]e drove all night and we got to the racetrack Saturday afternoon when practice first started, the (Busch) race had just finished...I didn't sleep in the van on the way down and I had the blanket over my head because the ice storm was just horrific and we got to the track and met with J.D. and everyone was super excited you know and pumped and everything. We had no hotel, so we had to drive 100 miles south of Daytona to find a hotel to stay in and we were at the racetrack the next morning by six o'clock. When the race was over, we drove back to New Jersey and we were at work the next Monday morning."

Once the Demers got a taste for working behind the scenes, going in the grandstands just wasn't the same – especially when they arrived late at Bristol.

"It was about ninety-five degrees and we were all dressed in black because we were following Dale (Earnhardt) and I had my Earnhardt shirt on, and when we got there the ticket person said 'you guys have to go all the way to the front because that's where your seats are...So we went all the way below – we were below eye level of the track – and we've never been exposed to the chicken wing throwing thing they do in the south. So we were there and people were throwing chicken wings – the bones – down onto the sidewalk, so we were getting bombarded with chicken wings, and then Carol getting hit, like somebody had a box of Kentucky Fried Chicken and threw that and people were down and sweeping up the chicken bones…So it was like ninety-five degrees, 100% humidity, we're sweating, the race track is above our eye level, so whatever this bottom corner was, it was the race from hell."

* * * *

Mike and Lesley also took over the J.D. McDuffie Fan Club. Lesley sold memberships at the track and bought advertising space in *Winston Cup Scene*. When fans wanted autographs, she'd offer a club application, pointing out that McDuffie personally signed the back of every ten-dollar check. Though all fan club proceeds went to McDuffie, the club now had a number of perks, including photographs, Christmas cards, a copy of the NASCAR schedule, and letters from J.D. and Ima Jean.

The club's biggest perk were the Demers' own written newsletters. "If he made the race," he said, "we'd tell what calamity happened to us or if we finished decent or, you know, funny things that happened at the race track that anybody on the outside wouldn't know about." Years before the internet, these newsletters offered an intimate look at an aspect of racing the cameras didn't show. Most of the garage and pit road action described in this book owes its existence to their work. The following, from their account of the 1991 Darlington race, is reprinted directly from its newsletter:

Race day was bright and warm. The 70 was running good enough that J.D. was really 'racing' other cars in the field. Then trouble, no brakes. J.D. pulled behind [the] pit wall where the crew tried to bleed the brakes. Steam was coming from the brake caliper bleed valves. J.D. the driver, car builder, business manager, engine builder, truck driver and chassis man had forgotten to have the crew install vents to cool the brakes. Now the crew had to do the job on a hot race car. Some brake ducting was installed the second time J.D. lost the brakes. The extra time behind pit wall put the 70 many laps down but J.D. was running at the finish.

Mike and Lesley's newsletters also put the media to task for how their driver was represented. "When you read these articles you will be upset at the negativity expressed by the writer," they said in another newsletter in June 1991. "We are promoting a positive attitude towards J.D. by writing about all aspects of his life and racing. There are those who feel the 'independent' racer shouldn't exist. We only hope that a big sponsor could come forth for J.D. so all the negatism(sic) will be gone."

* * * *

As late as 1990, one of McDuffie's cars had the sponsors and door numbers painted on the car, practically unheard-of in an age where most NASCAR Cup Series stock cars were decorated with decals. McDuffie never liked applying such decals to his cars, so the job fell to Mike. He'd bought the vinyl-cut stickers at the local sign shop and placed them on the car. To facilitate this, fellow crewman Roger Lankford picked up sponsorship from Graphics Plus, whose logo soon appeared on the C-post of No. 70.

Demers gave his own logo for Son's Auto Supply the best spot – right above the air filter on the hood of the car. In 1989, he experimented with his logo to try and draw even more focus to it. "We did spend a lot of money on one decal which was like four parts, you know, it was orange and it had the sun and all this other stuff and beautiful to look at, impossible to put on, and everyone thought the car looked like a Mustang, so that didn't go over very well, so I said 'all right, the simpler the better – white vinyl here we go.' And that seemed to work for our needs."

One of the first promotions Demers came up with was a way to get other fans a sponsor license of their own. For a $1,000 donation, fans could get their names on both sides of McDuffie's car. There were a handful of takers, their names plainly visible in photos. McDuffie's Dover car in 1991 read KEN & NANCY STETTMEIER. At Pocono, it was TIM PATTY & CLIFF in June and H & M TRUCKING in July. For Watkins Glen, it read KATHIE & NEIL FRESON.

"Please tell us how to contact J.D. McDuffie," the Fresons wrote to the fan club on June 11, 1991. "We would be interested in joining a list of small sponsors to support his Winston Cup run at Watkins Glen this year. With your help, we may be able to do a little to enable an independent driver to compete with the big money teams."

With that, Demers applied another decal.

CHAPTER 7
Old Car, New Engines

> *"J.D. was a great guy. He worked on his own cars,*
> *hauled his own cars. He was a true independent and he*
> *raced hard every week and did the best he could with*
> *what he had. Really proud of him. He was a good*
> *friend."*

> —Car owner Richard Childress, 2017

Joining the logo for Son's Auto Supply on the hood of No. 70 was the logo for Medford Speed and Machine, based a half-hour's drive east of Son's in Southampton Township.

The family-owned shop was founded in 1964 by Jerry Glenn, a local drag racer who built and tuned engines. His son Jerry Glenn Jr. started helping him on nights when he was seven years old. When Jerry Jr. was old enough, he followed in his father's footsteps, competing in drags, then on dirt tracks, dropping Medford's powerful engines into his big block modified. He was also hired as a consultant to help one of his fellow competitors, who then became a customer.

"So, they asked me to come to the track to try and fix it," said Jerry Jr. of the deal. "He told me – this was thirty-something years ago – he said I'll give you $500 to come into the pits for four nights, he said, just watch and you know tell us some of the shit we're doing wrong. I went and got hooked, you know, and it was going two or three nights a week for the races and we started building motors for a lot of different people."

By the 1980s, Medford Speed and the Glenns had become local legends. Their power plants claimed countless wins on clay bullrings all over northern New Jersey. They even dabbled in off-shore boat racing. With their success, Medford moved to at least four progressively larger shops. The last was big enough to accommodate their next goal: fielding a NASCAR Winston Cup team. To this end, the Glenns purchased an old Ford Thunderbird from owner-driver Mark Stahl. They tabbed engineer Don Owens, a sales representative for machinist firm Sunnen Products, Co., who helped them acquire a professional engine dynamometer.

Then, in late 1990, the Glenns received a phone call. Another driver needed help with his engines.

* * * *

Jerry Jr.'s first memories of J.D. McDuffie were in 1985, during CBS' television broadcast of that year's Daytona 500. As Bill Elliott led the race by several seconds, head play-by-play announcer, Ken Squier, broke away to discuss McDuffie's plight with a five-minute segment. With "Twentieth Century Drifter" performed by singer-turned-racer Marty Robbins playing in the background, a reporter walked through the Sanford shop and interviewed both J.D. and his wife Ima Jean. Their separately recorded interviews spoke volumes about the harsh realities facing underfunded teams.

"I worry about him. I don't worry about the car. The car comes second," said Ima Jean, laughing nervously. "He's not a quitter, J.D.'s not. I would've quit a long time ago – I would."

"The last three years, I've been racing on borrowed money, you know, and you just can't do that," said J.D., trying his best to keep a smile. "I'm getting – I'm slipping a little farther back, but maybe I'll have some help this year where I can show up, you know. But – it is really tough."

"You see somebody coming in one time, nobody knows him, where he came from or what he's been driving," said Ima Jean, visibly concerned, "and before the race is over – before it started – he's got all this fantastic money just because maybe he knows one person. I don't really know how it works, but I always felt J.D. was left out. He never got a fair shake. 'Cause he's got the experience and he can *drive*."

"To run with the best in the world, you know," said J.D. "I could probably go out here run somewhere else and run right up front, you know, but you ain't got the caliber of competition there, you know. If I can make the top ten in this, I've really done something."

"I've told him to quit this year," said Ima Jean. "I begged him to quit. Really. But how can you keep going with zero, you know? But then you look at him. He can't *stand* that, he's gotta keep going. I understand his side of it."

"Yeah, I have to cut a lot of corners – buy used parts and run used tires," said J.D. "Knowing how to build the engines and everything myself, that's a big saver right there. I could never buy a fifteen to $20,000 engine. I'd be out of business in about two races, you know."

The segment concluded with one of those engines letting go during the qualifying race for that very 500. It couldn't have happened at a worse time. Over the off season, Restore Engine Restorer and Dutch Treats Cigars had signed on to sponsor the No. 70. Restore was originally going to sponsor Winston Cup rookie driver Terry Schoonover, but during the 1984 finale at Atlanta, Schoonover was killed in a hard crash on the backstretch. Not long after, the sponsors arranged a promotional photo shoot at the Sanford shop with McDuffie wearing new jeans and a silver Dutch Treats jacket.

Dutch Treats' involvement was particularly perfect: not only did McDuffie Racing need the money, but the driver enjoyed a good cigar. From his earliest days in the IRA, he was almost always seen with a cigar pinched between his teeth, and he always seemed to be grinning. Some say he preferred the Tampa Nugget brand, but really, he wasn't that selective. Fans sent him fresh ones over the off-season. NASCAR even gave him special permission to smoke in his race car, which was made easier by his white open-faced helmet and a push-in lighter installed through a hole the crew drilled into the dashboard. Sometimes his crew handed fresh cigars through the window during pit stops. Other times, they were taped to the dashboard, just as fellow independent Frank Warren did with sticks of Big Red gum – one stogie for each 100 miles. McDuffie was known to say that a good race was one where he smoked them all, because it meant he made it to the finish.

In early 1985, McDuffie's car carried the new blue-and-white paint job at Daytona, Richmond and Rockingham, but sadly, it was all in vain. One story was that the man who brought both sponsors to McDuffie didn't tell his boss, and when the man was fired, the companies wouldn't honor their contracts. Ima Jean was there when the Restore representatives arrived. She recalled that Restore wanted her husband to put their product in his race car engine. Her husband refused, saying it would gum up the motor. "And they put one in the motor and guess what happened? It gummed the engine up," she said. "Yeah, he knew better than they did. He was smarter than they were."

After the test, Restore never paid a cent, and Dutch Treats backed out. McDuffie kept the logos on the car for a few races, hoping something would come of it – maybe another sponsor who would follow through. When none came, he took them off. Just like that, No. 70 was back on a shoestring.

* * * *

The cars run in what is now the NASCAR Cup Series have evolved three times since 1991. Today's 3,300-pound cars are lighter than their predecessors, constructed of both steel and carbon fiber. No longer does leaded fuel mix with air in the carburetor. Instead, an ethanol E15 compound is worked through an electric fuel injection system. Electronics dominate the modern stock car, so much so that a driver sometimes has to reboot the car's onboard computer mid-race. Even the dials on the dashboard have been replaced by a customizable digital screen. About all that remains from two decades ago are their 110-inch wheelbase and fifteen-inch steel rims. As of this writing, an even more advanced car will replace the current model in 2022.

Until now, it's not been uncommon for a Cup team to run an old chassis. The outer skin of the car can be replaced with relative ease, making the same chassis beneath appear radically different. In 1998, Ernie Irvan drove a Pontiac at Martinsville that was once the Chevrolet that carried Jeff Gordon to the final win at North Wilkesboro in 1996. In 2000, Dale Jarrett finished seventh at the Sonoma Raceway driving a chassis Davey Allison raced at the same track nine years prior. And in 2011, Brian Keselowski (with some bump-drafting help from his brother Brad) raced into the Daytona 500 field in a car built for Evernham Motorsports in 2006. So old was Keselowski's Dodge, in fact, that when he was offered a brand-new engine for the 500, he had to decline because it wouldn't fit the old motor mounts.

In NASCAR's early years, factory drivers weren't allowed to run a car that was more than three years old. The motto "win on Sunday, sell on Monday" was taken as gospel, and the Big Three all had a vested interest in seeing the exact model car in victory lane that was on the showroom floor. For independents like McDuffie, unburdened by such contracts, they could run the cars Detroit deemed out-of-date. And so, just about every car that bore McDuffie's No. 70 already had a history. Junior Johnson's 1972 Chevrolet with the "correct" fenders was just one example.

During the summer of 1985, McDuffie drove for car owner Wayne Beahr, who acquired the Ford Thunderbird that Jody Ridley raced to his lone Winston Cup victory at Dover in 1981. As McDuffie reeled from the loss of the Restore and Dutch Treats sponsorships, Beahr hired him to drive the car for three races at Dover and Pocono. The car was renumbered from No. 35 to No. 70 for those races, granting McDuffie the owner's money and a share of the driver's purse. Beahr only asked for a small cut and the logo for his company Hanover Printing on the car. McDuffie agreed, but the car proved a handful. One time, the crew forgot to switch out a set of "warm-up" spark plugs, and McDuffie pulled in with bent valves. Eddie Wood of the prolific Wood Brothers Racing Team came over to help, but it was no good. The car finished no better than twenty-eighth.

Another car would come from Richard Childress Racing. Childress, himself an owner-driver with twelve years' experience, climbed out of the driver's seat in 1981, then two years later found his elusive first victory as a car owner with Ricky Rudd. In 1984, Dale Earnhardt and sponsor Wrangler Jeans signed with the Childress team, beginning one of the most successful partnerships in the sport's history. Earnhardt won twice in 1984, four times in 1985, then six of the following nine championships.

For the 1986 season, Childress entertained a manufacturer switch from Chevrolet to Pontiac, which he campaigned in 1981 and 1982. To this end, he built one of Pontiac's new rear-steer Grand Prix "2+2" models. To fans of "The Intimidator," the sight of Dale Earnhardt's #3 Wrangler Jeans-sponsored car on a 1986 Pontiac may seem strange, but it happened – although briefly. Painted and ready to go, the car never ran a Winston Cup race – at least not under Childress' banner. Childress decided to stay with Chevrolet and sold the Pontiac. As condition of the sale, the car could not be re-sold since Childress had installed his proprietary chassis geometry. He found a willing buyer in a Pontiac car dealer from Defiance, Ohio named Tom Winkle.

Winkle looked to follow in the footsteps of Rick Hendrick, who had turned his own Charlotte-area dealerships into a race-winning Winston Cup team with New York driver Geoff Bodine. As an outsider, Winkle looked to invest in an existing NASCAR team and offered the Childress Pontiac. He chose McDuffie Racing. So, midway into the '86 season, Donald Mangum picked up the car and brought it back to the Sanford shop. McDuffie repainted it bright orange with a slate-gray roof, the logo for Winkle's dealership featured prominently over the rear tires. Once completed, the only indication of the car's Childress lineage was its Wrangler blue-painted roll bars, which were later painted over in soft gray.

McDuffie waited to announce the partnership, waited even to tell his friends. He feared it would fall through like the Restore deal and others had before. But once he was sure the deal was made, he could hardly contain his excitement. "It means for the first time in years, I don't have to worry if the bills are paid," said McDuffie in an interview for *Florida Today*. "It means I'm going to run with new tires and I'm going to get some new equipment. Things should really be better. Maybe a little luck can go a long way."

Just as the Baileys upgraded "Old Blue," Winkle did the same for J.D. and Ima Jean's personal cars, a 1979 Chevrolet Malibu and a 1978 Chevrolet pickup. He presented them with brand-new Pontiacs from his lot: him a Pontiac Firebird and her a Grand Prix. There were also more cars in the race shop, which Winkle now leased – five cars in total, including the one from Childress. Winkle went on the hunt for a new engine builder and crew chief, even courting veteran "Suitcase" Jake Elder. He wanted to buy a two-car hauler and looked into paying to have McDuffie flown to races instead of driving. Winkle even made plans to sponsor a Busch Series car for Jeff McDuffie with eyes on him returning to Winston Cup in two to three years.

Additional sponsorship from AC Spark Plugs came in 1987, and the team commissioned t-shirts like the one David Slezak wore at Pocono. McDuffie participated in pre-season testing at Daytona for the first time. This allowed him to turn a lap of 200.927mph in qualifying for the Daytona 500, the fastest lap yet turned by his No. 70, and his first to cross the 200mph mark. Later that year, the McDuffie / Winkle partnership earned a best finish of sixteenth at Richmond. It was during this time McDuffie appeared in what may have been his only TV commercial. Speaking for a Daytona Beach-area insurance company, it showed McDuffie trying to buy insurance for his race car. After years of living on a shoestring, McDuffie now seemed closer than ever to becoming competitive in NASCAR's modern era. The writer for *Florida Today* agreed: "With a little luck and a lot more money, maybe J.D. McDuffie can hang on to his dying dream for years to come and keep a small piece of the racing work ethic alive."

Sadly, it wasn't meant to be. That same '87 season, Winkle hired a thirty-nine-year-old rookie driver named Steve Christman, who promptly finished fifth in his ARCA debut at Daytona. The same day McDuffie finished sixteenth at Richmond, Christman made his Winston Cup debut in an identical No. 62 AC Spark Plugs Pontiac. Though Christman only finished twenty-ninth that day, by the next round at Atlanta, Winkle and McDuffie suddenly parted ways. Winkle took back the McDuffie family's street cars along with all the equipment Winkle had purchased. Two

years later, when Greg Sacks drove for Winkle, his re-
claimed hauler still had McDuffie's name and number
printed on the inside of the rear doors.

As part of the separation, most of the AC Spark Plugs
sponsorship went to Christman. Most, that is, but not all –
AC remained as an associate sponsor for the rest of
McDuffie's career, and provided spark plugs, air filters, and
a representative at the track to "read" the plugs to make sure
they were jetting properly. McDuffie also got to keep the
Childress chassis, which was half as old as his only other remaining car. The car was now too heavy – 200 pounds too
heavy under a new NASCAR rule – but he managed to keep
it running. In 1990, the Winkle team closed its doors.
McDuffie Racing had outlived another one.

With the combined loss of Tom Winkle's financial
support in 1987 and the burns McDuffie suffered at Daytona the following year, the driver was now missing more
races than he was making. A key problem was engines,
whose technology was now moving in a different direction.
Then as now, NASCAR engines are routinely pushed to the
brink of failure. A previously used engine, even with new
parts, has a limited shelf life. McDuffie's were more used
than most. For five straight races in early '87, the engine on
No. 70 let go. The statistic was so appalling that it was
printed as part of McDuffie's biography in NASCAR's official press guide.

"Years ago," said Jerry Glenn, Jr., "people would buy
the used stuff from the teams and a lot of the stuff was
heavier, more stronger and it wasn't abused that much.
And when they bought that stuff, they were buying bombs,
most of the stuff was used up." When NASCAR mandated

carburetor restrictor plates in 1987 to slow speeds at its two fastest tracks, RPMs fell, making engines last longer. But this began a new race to make engines out of lighter parts which, once again, the independents couldn't afford. Now, even if McDuffie's engines lasted, they'd be made of such heavy parts that the weight would slow him down, costing him a spot on the track – or a place in the race itself.

Though McDuffie would never admit it, the old ways weren't working anymore. He needed help. By 1990, Mike Demers was among the crew members making phone calls. Those calls led to Medford Speed.

* * * *

In late 1990, the Glenns suspended their own Winston Cup effort to help J.D. McDuffie. By September, No. 70 had Medford Speed power plants under the hood. It must have been an adjustment for McDuffie, who had prided himself on maintaining his cars – particularly his engines. For years, he made the most of the two sets of heads and single engine block that Morgan-McClure provided each year, and only briefly let Butlers Inc. help with the power plants two decades earlier. Even when the Glenns handed him a new piece, his inner mechanic couldn't keep him from fine-tuning it.

"He asked us if it was okay if he took the heads off," said Jerry Jr. of one of the first engines they provided. "He wanted to mill the – cut some more off and get a little more compression in the motor. I know he'd done that." Sometimes, the adjustments went too far. The first engine Medford provided for McDuffie was the 1990 season finale at

Atlanta. It went in the Childress car, but it wasn't fast enough to make the field.

By that weekend, McDuffie had re-painted the Childress car again with a distinctive new look. He painted the top half burgundy, the bottom black, the two halves split by a white stripe around the middle. White trim ringed the inside of the passenger and driver's side windows. Large short-track style gold numbers on the doors and roof were later outlined with carefully cut strips of orange tape. McDuffie came up with the paint job after he spotted a particularly eye-catching Cadillac at a car dealership across town. It wasn't as new as his other cars – in fact, the Pontiac Grand Prix body style he was using was being phased-out for a new model in 1991 – but it was certainly the most eye-catching. A few potential sponsors asked about the paint job during the Atlanta weekend. It was decided the scheme would stay the following year.

CHAPTER 8
1991

*"I would say from 1986 on, it was Tom Rumple, Mike,
and Jerry Glenn and myself."*

—Marty Burke on McDuffie Racing, 2016

Mike Demers added two more sponsor logos to the
"rear decklid," the rectangular piece of sheet metal that
formed the top of the car's trunk. One, which joined in September 1990 for the fall races at Martinsville and North
Wilkesboro, was Run-A-Bout Auto Sales, a pair of used car
lots owned by minister-turned-salesman "Colonel" Don
Tyndall of Dunn, North Carolina. The other was misspelled:
"Classic Trophy's" was, in fact, Hatboro, Pennsylvania
award store "Classic Trophies." Classic, whose awards have
been presented to such celebrities as Bob Hope, Joe Na-
math, and the Blue Angels, was one of many businesses
owned by fellow McDuffie supporter Marty Burke.

* * * *

Burke was already involved in racing at the time he met
McDuffie. In addition to his business ventures, he'd been a
pit crew member since 1981. That year, he pitted the No. 64
Ford owned by future pace car driver Elmo Langley and
driven by fellow Pennsylvanian Tommy Gale. Langley, who
had just stepped out of the car after twenty-seven years as an
owner-driver, didn't spend long training him. "I guess ten
minutes before the race started," recalled Burke, "(Langley)

walked out and said 'You've gotta carry tires.' I'm like 'What do I do?' And Elmo was great, he said 'Follow me' because he was changing rear tires at the time and he said, 'you step over the jack and don't hit me with the tire.'"

Burke's experience with Langley also introduced him to the "race within a race" where independents battled to be best in class. By the 1980s, this group included James Hylton, Jimmy Means, D.K. Ulrich, Baxter Price, Henley Gray, Rick Newsom, and of course, J.D. McDuffie. Burke knew McDuffie well from these battles. "J.D. was always the one that was beating us," he said with a laugh.

Burke met McDuffie at Pocono, his home track, in 1985. By then, Burke had worked most every position on pit road except jack man, moving from Langley's team to Baxter Price and newcomer John Callis. When Callis failed to make the race, Burke went to McDuffie and asked if he could help. As with so many before him, McDuffie welcomed him to the team. Soon, Burke began to contribute sponsorship money, and Classic's name appeared on the car. Over the winter off-season, McDuffie visited Burke's Hatboro shop to sign autographs.

On pit road, Burke's responsibilities for McDuffie Racing continued to revolve around tires. He was often the rear tire changer and in charge of setting the "camber," the amount the wheel was leaned in or out to get maximum grip. This included finding a way to get tires in the first place. With sets of tires costing several hundred dollars, and several sets needed for each race, tires were a big expenditure for every team. While big teams could purchase as many tires as they wanted back then, McDuffie Racing didn't buy any unless they made the field. And if they ran out during the race, Burke would scramble up pit road and grab tires used by another car to see if they could make a few more laps.

When Burke couldn't buy any tires at all, more creative means were employed. Most often, McDuffie was hired by other teams to "scuff," or wear-in new tires for them. The exercise existed because teams found worn tires had more grip on certain tracks than new ones. It was a risk for both parties. In the 1988 race at Watkins Glen, McDuffie was scuffing tires for Junior Johnson's driver Terry Labonte, but ran off-course. Since the hot tires picked up debris in these run-off areas, those tires could no longer be used.

Mike Thomas, a crewman for Melling Racing, was another of McDuffie's supporters. During a race, Burke would roll his tire cart to where Thomas was helping Bill Elliott pit his No. 9 Ford. If Thomas had any new or scuffed tires to spare, Burke would cart them right back to No. 70. An ardent Ford supporter, Burke couldn't help but tease his Chevrolet-preferring boss. "I had to run to the Ford to get the fast tires for the Chevrolet."

One time at Richmond in the late 1980s, Thomas snuck McDuffie's car into Elliott's empty garage stall. He jacked up No. 70, put on Elliott's tires, and sent him out on the track to qualify. McDuffie made the race, outpacing even his old rival Richard Petty, then returned to the garage to have his old tires put back on. No one seemed to notice that McDuffie's car had switched from black-painted rims to Elliott's bright gold ones.

* * * *

On top of being a crewman and a sponsor, Burke also looked to race in Winston Cup himself. "At that time the Northern Invasion started, he said. "Geoff Bodine was one of the first successful drivers not from the southeast. I was young and could speak clearly and thought I might have some appeal to a potential sponsor."

When Burke first asked McDuffie if he could drive a second car out of the Sanford garage, McDuffie gave a firm "no." But, as the years passed, the two put together a plan with an eye toward the team's future. Burke would first find a way to fund McDuffie's team enough that McDuffie could field a second entry for Burke in the ARCA Racing Series. Based out of Michigan, ARCA (Automobile Racing Club of America) is a second-tier stock car division where short-track drivers gain experience on a mix of bullrings, dirt tracks, and NASCAR superspeedways. At the time, most ARCA teams didn't build their own cars, but instead ran older NASCAR cars sold by Winston Cup teams looking to upgrade their fleets – much like Cup Series independents. By running NASCAR-style cars on NASCAR tracks, developing drivers could learn a lot about the intricacies of elite stock car competition.

McDuffie dabbled in ARCA before, both as a driver and as an owner. For years, he'd shared his equipment with his friend Tom Usry. Usry, about two years McDuffie's senior, was a fellow Sanford dirt tracker who not only raced him in late models since 1961 but ran as a one-time NASCAR teammate for McDuffie Racing at Malta, New York in 1970. By the late 1980s, McDuffie was selling his old cars to Usry so he could run them in ARCA's superspeedway events. Usry earned several great finishes in his old No. 70s, including a fourth at Atlanta in 1986. He was headed for another Top Five at Daytona in 1989 when his car went for a terrible tumble exiting the tri-oval. Usry survived, but a broken neck ultimately ended his driving career.

Around the same time, Burke's own plans to drive began to materialize. He'd already taken laps running stock cars in the Buck Baker Driving School, and McDuffie instructed him while they were on the road. "He really took me under his wing," said Burke. "We normally bunked together at the races and we would talk about the racetracks and how to drive them." One of Burke's favorite memories had to do with the approach to Michigan, where today speeds entering Turn 1 reach more than 210mph. "Right before you go on the track," said McDuffie, "I'm gonna take a big hammer and hit you in the balls to make 'em swell up 'cause Michigan when you go into the turns you gotta do it wide-open." It got the point across.

Burke was excited but didn't want to rush things. "I would never have asked him to step out of the car – that would have to be his decision," he said. But, as the 1991 season began, the two began to put the plan into action.

The first step was to get Burke a car. At the time, McDuffie had three cars in his stable ready for the 1991 season. Two were the Hutcherson-Pagan-built Pontiacs, each upgraded over the off-season with Pontiac's new sheet metal for the Grand Prix model. One, painted a dark metallic blue, was to be used on the series' fast superspeedways. The other, coated in bright cherry-red, was for the short tracks. Like his third car, the burgundy Childress car, which sat unchanged from its 1990 appearance in a back corner of the garage, the cherry-red No. 70 was inspired by a car McDuffie saw on a lot. "I was driving past a new car dealer," said McDuffie, "and saw the color on a (Chevrolet) Lumina and I liked it, it is my car."

According to Burke, McDuffie sold him the burgundy Childress car in March 1991, the cost to be paid in five installments through the early summer. With this car, Burke would make his ARCA debut that June at his home track in Pocono. From June forward, McDuffie would run the blue and red cars, with Burke remaining as tire changer and sponsor for the season. Just as in the closing stages of 1990, engines would be provided by Jerry Glenn's Medford Speed Shop.

While the existence of this arrangement is disputed by both Ima Jean and Linda McDuffie, who claim Burke's payments were only for sponsorship and not the car, at least one article indicates there was a business relationship between McDuffie and Burke. On January 10, two months before the sale of the car, reporter Eddie Blain for *The Intelligencer* did a feature on McDuffie and Burke, and their concerted efforts toward the upcoming season. "It doesn't end with sponsorship alone," wrote the article. "Marty Burke, Classic Trophies' president, is also a long-time friend of McDuffie. McDuffie managed to steal away from his hectic schedule to spend time at Burke's home early in December." The article closed with, "This writer wishes nothing but the best for the Marty Burke / J.D. McDuffie efforts in the 1991 season."

* * * *

However, as the 1991 season progressed, McDuffie's sour luck intervened once more. The problems began at Daytona. In January testing, one of Medford Speed's engines lacked power while the other overheated. The car had been assembled at a friend's body shop in Delaware, but during SpeedWeeks, the team had to shave the left-rear fender to fit NASCAR's body templates, and their final engine blew in practice. When the Glenns were unable to put another power plant together in time, Dale Earnhardt and Richard Childress started a fund raiser in the garage for McDuffie to run Thursday's qualifying races. The group surprised McDuffie with a paper bag with $6,600 inside – enough money to lease an engine from another team.

By Thursday, the shaved fender on No. 70 was painted over, its mismatched gold and silver rims swapped out for a matching bright yellow set, and the car now carried associate sponsorship from Mansion Homes. McDuffie's qualifying speed placed him twenty-seventh on the twenty-nine-car grid for Race 2 of the Gatorade Twin 125s. With just one caution slowing the fifty-lap race, McDuffie came home twenty-first – on the lead lap, but just short of a spot in the Daytona 500. It was a tremendous effort, but unfortunately, without a share of the biggest purse of the season, 1991 would be a struggle.

For the next two races at Richmond and Rockingham, the blue car was the fastest to miss the race. Now 0-for-3, the team decided against their full-season effort and skipped the next race at Atlanta to focus on Darlington, where Maurice Leggett's fund raiser in Lumberton finally secured McDuffie his first start of the season. Bristol saw the season debut of the burgundy Childress car – the color described as a "deep wine" by *Winston Cup Scene* – but again it wasn't fast enough. The story was the same for the next two short tracks at North Wilkesboro and Martinsville, where the car's quarter-panels remained blank.

McDuffie wasn't making races, but he still had all three of his cars. That changed, however, on May 4, when the series rolled into Talladega.

Now as then, many NASCAR race weekends include a companion event for ARCA. Due to ARCA's technical regulations, the slowest NASCAR Winston Cup car at the time was about as fast as the best ARCA car. Thus, series president Bob Loga invited Cup drivers too slow to make the field a chance to run his ARCA race. The Cup drivers wouldn't even need to qualify for the ARCA race, taking positions at the back of the field. Even though they weren't formally entered in the race, each would still earn a share of the purse.

Such was the case at Talladega, where the blue No. 70 was again the second-fastest car to miss – DNQ number seven for the season. Thanks to Loga's invite, McDuffie started thirty-ninth in ARCA's field of forty. Now able to compete, McDuffie dashed into the Top 10, catching the eye of ESPN's cameras. Then disaster struck. On Lap 68, a five-car accident blocked the track at the start/finish line, forcing No. 70 to dart into the infield grass. Unfortunately, a large piece of debris fell directly in McDuffie's path, destroying the nose of his machine and sending him sliding into another car. Just a few feet away, a tragic wreck had unfolded after Carl Miskotten, Jr.'s Buick struck the tumbling Oldsmobile of Chris Gehrke. Gehrke, just twenty-five, lost his life in the crash.

As McDuffie worked to put his blue Pontiac back into service, the driver impressed his bright red "short-track" car into service on the 1.5-mile Charlotte Motor Speedway. Like the Daytona car, the red Pontiac didn't fit any of NASCAR's templates, only this time, a little sanding wouldn't be enough. "They said 'we told you before about it,'" recalled Burke. "But they were respectful of the fact that he was a one-man show and we can't take two weeks to carve up the car. We're not gonna win the race, it doesn't matter. But they made mention of it, they didn't make a big deal of it, but they wanted you to know who was in charge."

McDuffie finished third-from-last in the Winston Open, the qualifying race for The Winston all-star exhibition event on May 19. He was the second-fastest of six drivers to miss the following week's Memorial Day classic, the Coca-Cola 600.

The following race at Dover on June 2 started off kind to McDuffie's red car, as he beat four drivers for the final spot in the field. The team continued to make repairs to the car, including strips of red tape to cover the sanded left-rear fender. On race day, McDuffie stayed out of the way of the leaders, even as he lost several laps in the first half. Mike Joy, Buddy Baker, and Phil Parsons, who broadcast the race for The Nashville Network (TNN), mentioned McDuffie every so often. Then trouble found the driver once more.

On Lap 273, coming off Turn 2 on the steeply banked one-mile track, McDuffie was bumped by the closing Kenny Wallace, who was driving in relief of Kyle Petty in the fast No. 42 Mello Yello Pontiac. Petty had fractured his leg in a multi-car crash at Talladega in May. The contact from Wallace steered McDuffie straight into the inside wall, destroying it at both ends. The veteran was knocked out for a few seconds before he limped No. 70 back to pit road. The wreck left him thirty-first – and angry. But, as always, he didn't let others know it. "I don't know, I got bumped coming off two over there and got into the inside wall and banged it up pretty bad," he said to TNN's Glenn Jarrett. "It bent the rear end housing off." Jarrett asked McDuffie when his next race was. "We're going to Pocono."

Behind the scenes, driver and team now faced a crossroads. The Dover wreck happened just thirteen days before Marty Burke's planned ARCA debut. Burke had planned to come down to Sanford right after Dover, get the seat in the burgundy car adjusted, and load it on his own hauler for the trip to Pennsylvania. The two had even discussed the possibility of Burke running the Winston Cup race at the Pennsylvania track if the field was short – McDuffie in the red car from Dover and Burke in his burgundy Pontiac. But now with the red car out of service and more than forty NASCAR teams possibly showing up for Pocono, McDuffie wanted Burke to run ARCA instead. Burke refused. The purse disparity between the two series was such that they could earn as much as $4,000 in Cup versus $700 in ARCA.

"We didn't get into an argument, but I had to do a lot of 'convincing' that we needed to stay in the Cup Series," Burke recalled. "I know that he knew the smartest thing was for him to race my car in Cup, but he knew how badly I wanted to drive. Part of me is glad I convinced him, part of me is not. Who knows what would have happened?"

* * * *

And so, Burke found himself in a whole new role: as car owner. Burke did so *in abstentia*, refusing both the Owner Points and a formal owner's photograph with the car at Pocono. There were two reasons for this. First, Burke was only the car owner in the narrowest sense – he had bought the *car*, but not the *team*. Second, McDuffie needed to stay the listed owner so he could keep a Top 30 spot in Owner Points, making him eligible for another bonus check from NASCAR at the end of the season. Thus, the car was still fielded by McDuffie Racing.

As McDuffie said at Dover, he skipped the next Winston Cup race on the west coast in Sonoma, California, and prepared for the following round at Pocono. This time, McDuffie was guaranteed to start – just thirty-seven drivers arrived out of forty possible entries. Had the Dover wreck not happened, it's possible both Burke and McDuffie would have raced together in the burgundy and red Pontiacs. Instead, the last No. 70 carried a new qualifying motor from Jerry Glenn and a second set of correctly spelled Classic Trophies decals on the quarter-panels.

According to Mike Demers' newsletter, Glenn managed to make a Chevrolet manifold match with the Pontiac heads, but the experiment cost No. 70 straight-line speed. In qualifying, the Pontiac stalled out three-quarters of the way down the track's 3,055-foot Long Pond Straight, leaving him thirty-sixth on the grid. The team swapped out Glenn's engine for the team's backup with matched Pontiac parts, and while the car ran faster on the straights, it proved sluggish on the corners.

In Sunday's race, an improperly installed universal joint end cap caused such a bad vibration that McDuffie couldn't see anything with the rear-view mirror. He went to the garage on Laps 8 and 13 of the 200-circuit affair, spending nearly a quarter-distance with his team rebuilding the u-joint and yoke in the rear end. He ran a few more laps to make sure the problem was fixed, and in doing so climbed from thirty-seventh to thirty-fourth before calling it a day. That same weekend, McDuffie drove for another team in the ARCA race and finished nineteenth of twenty-eight starters.

No. 70 missed the next Winston Cup race at Michigan, but again ran well in ARCA that weekend, coming home thirteenth of thirty-two. McDuffie missed the field for July's return to Daytona, then set his sights on the second race at Pocono at the end of the month. Through it all, the burgundy car remained in one piece, ready to be used once more.

Unlike in June, qualifying for the second Pocono race was not a guarantee. Worse still, the No. 70 now fought a slippery clutch in practice which had to be replaced. The team borrowed fresh tires from Junior Johnson once more – this time from Sterling Marlin's No. 22 Maxwell House Ford – but the persistent cornering issues left him forty-first of forty-four drivers, one spot shy of making the forty-car field. McDuffie tried to change his approach, shifting early into Turn 3, but the car was still too slow. The crew finally had Marty Burke buy a set of new tires. This spelled the difference – although barely. As the next-to-last car to take time, McDuffie ran a lap of 60.4 seconds. Their final challenger, fellow owner-driver James Hylton, ran 60.58 seconds. By the narrowest of margins, McDuffie had made his fourth start in seventeen races.

The remainder of Mike Demers' account of the second Pocono race captured the struggles of McDuffie Racing during the summer of 1991. While McDuffie never "start-and-parked," that is, deliberately pulled his car into the garage to save his equipment for the next race, he did have to adopt a more conservative approach on the track:

Race strategy was the usual; stay out of trouble. The 3 car (Dale Earnhardt of Richard Childress Racing), 9 car (Bill Elliott of Melling Racing) and 11 car (Geoff Bodine of Junior Johnson & Associates) had given J.D. some good used tires; lack of horsepower would keep us from 'racing' today.

Numerous cautions help J.D. stay on the lead lap until Lap 54. J.D. knew he was the slowest in the field, so he was pitting just to stay at the rear of the pack. On the 65th lap the 70 started missing. J.D. pitted, and a noise was heard in the right-side valve cover. J.D. radioed to take the tool box into the garage area; he circled the track and pulled into a garage where most of the crew was waiting. After pulling the valve cover, J.D. found a broken rocker arm stud, the pushrod was gone, and the lifter was out of its bore. In less than 20 laps J.D. and crew placed the lifter in the bore, bought a new pushrod, pulled a replacement rocker arm stud from the spare engine and installed these parts on the 70. The repairs worked, and J.D. managed to stay away from trouble. We finished the rain shortened race in 25th position.

Burke was happy for McDuffie that weekend but couldn't help being a little disappointed. When McDuffie was struggling in practice, Bob Loga came by again inviting the No. 70 to run his ARCA race on Saturday. McDuffie explained that if his Pontiac wasn't fast enough to make the Winston Cup race, Burke would drive the ARCA event in his car, his long-awaited series debut. Burke had brought his helmet and uniform with him, ready to go. But by those eighteen hundredths of a second, Burke would have to wait once again. "You just don't know just what would've happened," said Burke. "But I was okay with that because I thought my time would come."

By all accounts, Burke wouldn't have to wait much longer. McDuffie's blue superspeedway car was almost completely repaired from the Talladega wreck in May. It wouldn't run in the series' return to the Alabama track in July, but likely would at Darlington in September. Until then, McDuffie would continue to run the burgundy car – the one Burke had just made his last payment on. "I'm going to Watkins Glen," McDuffie told his brother. "I feel like I can run pretty good on the road course."

Michigan would come the week after. Watkins Glen didn't host an ARCA event that year, but Michigan did. Perhaps then, Burke thought, he'd finally get behind the wheel.

CHAPTER 9
Smut

"Jimmy's such a quiet guy he probably didn't even cry when he was born."

—*a friend of Jimmy Means, August 1, 1978*

James Bradford Means had a lot in common with J.D. McDuffie. Twelve years younger and a few inches shorter, Means got his first taste of racing when he was fourteen. Caught in a rainstorm while working his paper route, he was invited in by one of his customers, who had a racing program on her coffee table. "It never left me," said Means later. "I read up on everything I could read up about racing and got the opportunity to help somebody with a late model car and went from there."

Means took inspiration from Smokey Yunick, arguably NASCAR's most famous mechanic. Yunick's books gave Means his start in racing, as well as his nickname. "He (Yunick) wrote a few books on how to build a small block Chevrolet and I read every book that he had out and I would quote him all the time, I think I was seventeen or eighteen, and I would quote him and the guys that I was helping on the late model sportsman car would say, 'well, you'll never be a Smokey, so we're just gonna call you Smut.' And Smut was a term (back) then that wasn't derogatory now, so I was the first Smut – I was a clean Smut."

When he began racing, Means' youth belied a tenacious spirit, both on and off the track. In 1974, Means was racing in the Late Model Sportsman Series at the same

Nashville Fairgrounds Speedway where McDuffie excelled in NASCAR. By July, he was still looking for his first win of the year. The 355-cubic inch engine on Means' No. 92 Chevrolet struggled to keep pace with those of NASCAR's big names, including Bobby Allison and Darrell Waltrip, who brought their top-flight equipment to the track. By 1992, Allison and Waltrip would score a combined 169 wins and four championships. In the summer of '74, Means led them both in Nashville's track championship. "I wish I knew," said Means when asked about his lead. "But I did total out this car I ran earlier and have a new car. I'd like to win, but Darrell (Waltrip) is about two-tenths of a second faster than the rest of us." It made little difference. At season's end, Means took the championship.

After he earned another track championship at Huntsville, Alabama and two runner-ups at Birmingham to NASCAR star Neil Bonnett, Means entered competition in ARCA, then moved up to Winston Cup. To save money, one of his volunteer crew members, Bill Gray, purchased the owner's license for Means Racing, and was the listed owner for the team's first two seasons.

Means made his Winston Cup debut in the 1976 Daytona 500. The twenty-six-year-old finished tenth in his thirty-five-car qualifying race, started twentieth in the 500, and stayed out under the first caution to lead Lap 13. Unfortunately, the engine let go on the restart, leaving Means a distant fortieth in the forty-two-car field. McDuffie made his 322nd start that day and finished seventh. By the time Richard Petty and David Pearson crashed each other in their legendary last-lap battle for the win, Means was already loaded up, heading back home to prepare for the next race. He would not lead another lap for six years.

In 1982, Means closed his Huntsville shop and moved his family to Forest City, North Carolina, 180 miles west of Sanford. He opened a new shop at 486 Withrow Road near Bracketts Creek, the ninety-foot building easily overlooked among a row of other faceless industrial structures. There, he toiled for hours on end, preparing his own cars with a handful of friends. In time, several old race cars would pile up in the back of the shop, making it easier for the crew to salvage them for still-useable parts. Means wanted to continue to run the No. 92, like he did in his Nashville championship, but since Billy Hagan's team ran the number full-time in NASCAR, he settled on No. 52. With that, Jimmy Means Racing went national.

"I'm the car owner, builder and driver," said Means in an interview with Larry Woody, "Your big-name drivers, they worry about climbing into the car at race time and driving it. That's all. Me, I spend all week working on my car, trying to scrape up enough money to buy a part here, a part there, get it all put together, haul my car to the track, drive it, then get it back to the shop to work on again for the next race." Over time, Means would come to love some of NASCAR's most demanding tracks, including Darlington, Bristol, and his old stomping grounds at Nashville.

As another of NASCAR's independents, only small businesses signed on to sponsor No. 52: Axe Equipment, Voyles Auto Salvage, Thompson Industries, and Howard's Machine Shops to name a few. The first to sign with any regularity was Mr. Transmission, a repair shop based near the Huntsville track on which he won years before. Next was Broadway Motors, a wholesaler and car dealership located three miles down the road from Jimmy Means Racing. Stud Murray, Broadway's owner, helped Means get started in Forest City, and for five seasons paid $500 a race to have his company's name on the sides of No. 52.

Like McDuffie, Means also developed a small, but potent fan base. Two decades before fans donated to put their names on McDuffie's No. 70 at Darlington, Means did the same at Talladega. The effort, spearheaded by long-time team supporters WIXC 1140AM in Florida, attracted at least thirty-four names and businesses. Means also followed McDuffie into the 1986 Atlanta Invitational. A fan vote pushed him from eighteenth in March to a qualified position in May. And in 1988, a fan named John Green, who was at his very first race, volunteered to fill fuel canisters for Means, then later earned his own uniform as the team's tire changer. "Twenty years ago, I was wishing for the chance to go see this racing at the track, never knowing, but dreaming, that I might have a small part in it," said Green in an article he wrote for the *Times-Daily*.

Perhaps the most famous member of the Jimmy Means Fan Club was one Dale Earnhardt, Jr., who befriended Means' son Brad as the two watched their fathers race from the infield. At the No. 52 trailer, the younger Earnhardt found a place where he could relax. "Dale couldn't be Dale in (Dale Earnhardt) Sr.'s hauler, you know, he couldn't be a kid," said Means. "They…always had the sponsors and were always a threat to win the race…and with my boy at the racetrack and Dale they could just hang out, you know, rather than being all business, he could be a kid at the race track." Those carefree days also made Dale Jr. a diehard Means fan. "I was always his hero when he was a little boy," said Means. "He used to pick up old spark plugs and lug nuts and bring them to me. I didn't use the plugs, but I did use the lug nuts." By the late 1980s, Means was also "scuffing" tires for Earnhardt's father.

Like McDuffie, hard luck came to define Means' career. More often than not, as one newspaper recalled, his car "picked up more dings and dents than a New York taxi." His best finish, a seventh, came at the Talladega Superspeedway, a track where he failed to finish fourteen times in thirty-three starts. "It was close to home and we had some good runs there," said Means, "but the best part of that place is when you drive out the back when the race is over, just making it out of there alive (laughs)." The championship proved just as challenging. In 1982, he came just twenty-eight points short of making the Top Ten in the championship. For the next eighteen seasons, he ranked no better.

But, like McDuffie, Means refused to let the hard times get him down. "Look at it this way," said Means. "You look at all the hundreds of farm teams in baseball and all of those players who would do anything to get just one day in the majors. Well, we've been in the majors for seventeen years. There are only about forty drivers who are able to start in a Winston Cup race each week and just think about how many millions of people who want to do it. We're not out there running junk, it's just that some other people have better equipment. But we are still in the pros...At certain times we have been able to run with the top names, in spite of our difficulties."

Those "certain times" came in 1987, when Means finally caught two big breaks. The first was sponsorship. On the heels of several good finishes, his agent brought a number of sponsorship proposals from national brands, including Turtle Wax and Eureka Vacuum Cleaners.

"I was younger and maybe a little more sellable than J.D. (McDuffie) or James Hylton or Buddy Arrington, when they was the major independents that I had to outrun. And I was the younger, you know, probably twenty years younger than those guys. And they look at all that. Not that I ran better. Buddy Arrington was hard to beat because he was so dang consistent. And Buddy was fortunate he had side help from the Pettys and maybe had some pretty decent money to take care of it, and he was a really good points racer. Maybe just the fact that I was a little bit younger and this guy was able to sell me...and I was a family man and clean cut and had a good – no record, no felonies (laughs), they did that even back in the day they did a background check on you just to see what kind of person – a corporate person's not gonna get involved with you if you're not squeaky clean."

The new sponsors brought Means an estimated $75,000 per year – more than he ever received previously. With this funding, the driver was able to afford new parts, and thus enjoyed one of the best performances of his career.

* * * *

In 1987, one year before its expansion into a three-quarter-mile D-shaped oval, today's Richmond Raceway was a 0.542-mile bullring, its bumpy pavement ringed with dirt and bare steel guardrails. In twenty-two previous starts at the track, Means earned a best finish of tenth in 1977, but thirteen times came home inside the Top 20. On September

13, Means' No. 52 Eureka Vacuum Cleaners Pontiac started twenty-fifth in the thirty-two-car grid and wasn't considered a threat to win the 400-lapper. Then he took the lead on Lap 64. Took it again on Lap 113. Claimed it a third time on Lap 183. And a fourth on Lap 240. It wasn't until Lap 245 that Dale Earnhardt was finally able to wrestle the lead away from No. 52.

In the closing stages, Means ran out of new tires, but still fought to preserve a top-ten finish. When the white flag flew, Means rekindled memories of Huntsville when he slid into Neil Bonnett off Turn 4 in a frantic battle for position. Means kept control, but Bonnett slapped the wall, and the race ended under caution. Earnhardt took the win but Means finished ninth – his best finish in nearly four years.

Among those who took notice of Means that day at Richmond was car owner Rick Hendrick. In 1987, Hendrick was without one of his top drivers. The previous year, rising star Tim Richmond finished a strong third in points, racking up seven wins. But an illness, originally called "double pneumonia," kept Richmond out of his No. 25 Folgers Chevrolet for much of the season. After a brief return that summer in which he won twice more, Richmond climbed out of the car for the final time, and ultimately died of AIDS. In Richmond's absence, Hendrick had fielded the No. 35, a full-time ride for Benny Parsons with Richmond's crew, satisfying Folgers' contract, but he looked at other options to put the No. 25 on track. September drew him to Jimmy Means.

On September 30, Hendrick offered Means a one-race deal to run for him at the team's home track, the Charlotte Motor Speedway, for the 500-mile event on October 11,

1987. With the blessing of Eureka, Means would drive a fast red Folgers Chevrolet, the No. 25 swapped to the driver's familiar No. 52. Dennis Connor, who would go on to win Hendrick three championships in NASCAR's Camping World Truck Series, served as Means' crew chief. With a brand-new driver's uniform with "Jimmy 'Smut' Means" embroidered on the chest, the Alabama driver climbed aboard for qualifying, jammed the pedal down, and put up the fifth-fastest lap – the best qualifying run of his entire career. "It's a chance of a lifetime," Means said. "It's a chance to show what I can do when I have the right equipment."

That Sunday, Means rolled off just one row behind his teammates Benny Parsons in second and 1986 Daytona 500 winner Geoff Bodine third. At the start, he dropped back a couple positions, holding fast to a Top Ten and perhaps his first win in his 316th start. Sadly, it didn't end that way. On Lap 21, two of the leaders wrecked, triggering a multi-car pileup. Means turned left and tried to slow down, but another driver hit him from behind, pushing No. 52 into the ensuing pileup. Unable to avoid it, Means was collected, destroying the right-front and right-rear of his Chevrolet. Just as in his Winston Cup debut, a promising start ended with an early exit, leaving him fortieth of forty-two.

Dale Earnhardt, Jr., who watched it all happen from his family's condo at the track, couldn't believe it. "I cried and cried and cried," he said. "I just couldn't believe it. A man dug so hard for so long to have a chance like that. How could this world be like that? It hurt me for a long time." Means, ever the optimist, shrugged it off and walked away. "It's a shame something else didn't come of it," he said later. "But that's life."

Curiously, Rick Hendrick had also offered J.D. McDuffie a ride in the Folgers car at Talladega earlier that year. "He was very quiet when he told me that," recalled Marty Burke. "He called me over and said 'I've got something to tell you,' and I said 'What's that?' and he said 'You gotta come to Talladega,' and I said 'Why?' and he said 'I might be driving a Hendrick car,' and I said 'What?' and he said 'Yeah they called me and they said they're trying to get it ready and they want me to drive it.' And I'm like 'I'll be there.'" Unfortunately, the deal didn't come together in time. "They didn't get the car done. They called him the week before and they didn't get the car done...But yeah, that would've been neat to see."

* * * *

After the Charlotte wreck, Jimmy Means went back to work in Forest City. Eureka stayed with him as a sponsor through 1988. "We liked the spirit and persistence shown by Jimmy Means Racing and that helped us decide to sponsor him for the full season this year," said Eureka's advertising manager Dick Smith. "We're far from a full sponsorship, but it's substantial enough that it's more than I've had in the last twelve years," said Means. "We've made the shows. We just need to get our engine problems straightened out. There's no way to go but up from here." The sponsorship secured him three new cars for a fleet of five. The cars, crammed next to each other in the small Forest City shop, were each worked on by just four full-time employees.

On June 16, 1988, Alka-Seltzer signed as an associate

sponsor for No. 52. In early 1989, Means' son Brad came up with a brand-new paint scheme. His Pontiac would be painted a soft powder blue, the Alka-Seltzer logos featured proudly in blocks of dark blue and bright red ringed in white. By 1991, the car also carried door and roof numbers printed in a mirror-clear silver foil. The result was the eighth-most recognizable car on the circuit, and one of Alka-Seltzer's most successful ad campaigns.

"NASCAR racing offers us a number of good promotional opportunities," said Carl Oberle, Alka-Seltzer's group product manager, in the team's 1991 press release. "And one of the most productive has been sampling Alka-Seltzer to race crowds from our little red fire trucks. When fans spend a long day at the track cheering on their favorite drivers and enjoying food and drink, it can create a situation in which someone needs the fast, effective relief of Alka-Seltzer."

"Because of my association with Alka-Seltzer," said Means, "this had been the first time in almost twenty years that I can concentrate on racing and not have to worry about where the [money] to pay the bills will be coming from...Again this year I'm looking forward to putting all my efforts into what I'm doing behind the wheel, instead of trying to do everything myself."

Soon, the car was everywhere. Dale Earnhardt, Jr. wore one of the team's blue crew caps, featuring Alka-Seltzer's diminutive mascot "Speedy" brandishing a white racing helmet. Other fan shirts and hats by Spectator Sports Services, as well as a pocket road atlas by Rand McNally, both featured the distinctive-looking Pontiac. In grocery stores, little plastic displays in the shape of the No. 52 race car held packets of product. A proof of purchase and seven dollars in 1991 would score you a "Thunder and Thrills" racing videotape by ESPN, featuring an introduction by Means from pit road at the Charlotte Motor Speedway. "Jimmy Means is a very popular driver," Oberle continued, "and it's amazing how many fans come back to the Alka-Seltzer's fire truck, not only to thank us for Alka-Seltzer's fast relief, from upset stomach with headache, but also for sponsoring Jimmy."

In 1990, Means and Alka-Seltzer managed to parlay this popularity into a cameo in Paramount Pictures' racing film "Days of Thunder," starring Tom Cruise. Means and Cruise even shared a scene together. "There was a scene where Cruise is on the outside pole and I'm on pole and I'm talking to Cruise on the radio," said Means. "I said 'You do what you wanna do and don't dodge me, I'll dodge you. So just drive the car you know and do what you wanna do.'" Though the scene was cut from the film, the Blu-Ray edition has a picture of Means racing Cruise on the back cover.

* * * *

Throughout their careers, Jimmy Means and J.D. McDuffie were often mentioned in the same breath. Their similar backgrounds, both as independents and as champion short trackers, built a fast friendship and a friendly rivalry. "Well, we run the best against each other – independents run the best against each other (laughs) – nobody rolled over," said Means. "So back then in those days you had four, five, eight guys who had money and twenty-five independents, and we strived to be the best independent. We wanted to beat one another...I think we had a race within a race. No, we didn't outrun the big guys – Yarborough or Petty or Pearson or whatever, but when we left there, you know, we were best in class and we held our heads high."

In 1978, McDuffie trusted Means to help shake down his car at Darlington. "J.D. come over there and said, 'Jimmy will you drive my car,' he said, 'I can't seem to get around – can't seem get up to speed.' So I said 'Yeah sure J.D.' So here I am maybe 120 pounds sitting in J.D.'s car and he's maybe 200, 210, so I go out there and ride the thing a few laps, come back in, and said 'J.D. this car drives great, you need brakes on this thing.' In my estimate, that's all he needed. So, it was just where he had confidence in me, you know, they trusted me to give some feedback on his car."

"I loved J.D. to death. He just – nobody with a bigger heart than what he had, and his heart was for racing, you know, he didn't want the glitz and the glitter, he wanted the money, so he could keep racing. And we all did, that's what – we raced off the purse. You had to make the races. And it was devastating when I missed a lot of races, he missed a lot of races, kind of hard to get to next week when you don't make the race previously."

In 1991, Means faced many of the same struggles as his friend. Through the first seventeen rounds of the season, Means failed to qualify three times and finished no better than twentieth, leaving him a distant thirty-fourth in points. He also stepped out of the car twice – at Dover and Sears Point. Sears Point, a twisting 2.52-mile road course in Sonoma, California, proved challenging for Means. Just before opening practice for the 1989 inaugural, local racer Ron Esau warned Means not to let his left-rear tire touch the grass in Turn 10, a hard right-hander. Unfortunately, that was exactly what happened. On his first lap, Means put a wheel off and lost control, sending his car into a flip off the tire barriers. "When someone asks," an uninjured Means told reporters, "tell them I dodged a deer that was on the track." The crew managed to repair the car, but the wreck ultimately cost him a spot in the field.

At Dover and Sears Point, Means handed the wheel to Texan driver Bobby Hillin, Jr. Hillin entered the '91 season without a ride, but had so far managed to make every race by driving for multiple teams. When Hillin was again without a ride in May, Means put him in No. 52. Despite a fuel pickup problem which required extra stops, Hillin finished a respectable nineteenth at Dover and twenty-first at Sears Point. Five days after the road course, Hillin was tabbed as relief driver for Kyle Petty until Petty returned from his Talladega injury. The only race Hillin wouldn't drive the No. 42 Mello Yello Pontiac was Watkins Glen.

As it turned out, this didn't change Means' plans. He was already planning on running the No. 52 at The Glen.

A young J.D. McDuffie during the 1940s.
(James Oldham Collection)

From the start, even before he raced in NASCAR, J.D. McDuffie drove No. 70, a number "easy to draw and easy to remember." (James Oldham Collection)

J.D. McDuffie (right) and crew member Lewis Hunter (left) prepare a Keith Motors Buick for the Northern Tour, circa 1967. (Wilbur Thomas Collection)

J.D. in a soon-to-be-banned Junior Johnson Chevrolet
(Wilbur Thomas Collection)

The McDuffie family, circa 1975. J.D. (left), wife Ima Jean
(right), along with children Jeff (bottom-left) and Linda
(bottom-right). (James Oldham Collection)

J.D. McDuffie wins his lone pole position at Dover, 1978.
(Bryant McMurray)

"Winding" Wayne Andrews, one of J.D. McDuffie's dirt
track rivals in the IRA. (Wayne Andrews Collection)

Jimmy "Smut" Means stands next to his 1991 Alka-Seltzer
Pontiac. (Jimmy Means Racing)

A promotional photo taken for the ill-fated Restore Engine
Restorer and Dutch Treats sponsorship. McDuffie ran this
paint job for a few races in 1985, even after the deal fell
through. (Charlie Berch Collection)

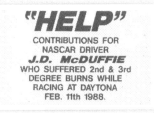

A fund-raising decal made by the J.D. McDuffie Fan Club after his fiery crash at Daytona in 1988. (Mike and Lesley Demers)

J.D. McDuffie (right) and Mike Demers (left) debrief in the Willett Road shop shortly after McDuffie's return to racing, 1988. (Lesley Demers)

Wearing polos and jeans, the McDuffie Racing crew pits No. 70 at Watkins Glen, 1988. (Mike and Lesley Demers)

J.D. (left), Marty Burke (middle), and Jeff McDuffie (right) survey damage after a tangle at Dover, 1991. (Mike and Lesley Demers)

The names of more than fifty fans and businesses were on
No. 70 for McDuffie's first start of 1991 at Darlington.
(Mike and Lesley Demers)

J.D. McDuffie, his cigar
at the ready, prepares to
start the 1991
TranSouth 500
at Darlington.
(Charlie Berch)

Victory Lane, at last. J.D. McDuffie (right) after winning a celebrity race at Shangri-La Speeed-way in Owego, New York on the night of August 10, 1991. (Dave Boland)

(Below) J.D. McDuffie adjusting the tie rod nut on race morning at Watkins Glen. It was this wheel which came off No. 70 on Lap 5, triggering the wreck. (Mike Demers)

J.D. McDuffie with photographer Janine Pestel (right),
shortly after being given a plaque made from one of
Pestel's photos. Note "Old Blue" at far left. (Mike Demers)

Charlie Berch's photograph of McDuffie (left), Dave Marcis
(middle), and Richard Petty (right), representing the top
three finishers at the Albany-Saratoga Speedway in Malta,
New York, scene of McDuffie's career-best third-place
finish on July 14, 1971.

The final picture taken of J.D. McDuffie, just before he
climbed aboard No. 70 at Watkins Glen on August 11,
1991. (Janine Pestel)

Early laps of the 1991 Budweiser at the Glen. Polesitter
Terry Labonte's No. 94 leads the No. 6 of Mark Martin into
Turn 5. (Charlie Berch)

McDuffie negotiates Turn 5. After this picture was taken,
just as the fourth lap was completed, Charlie Berch loaded
color slides into his camera. (Charlie Berch)

Charlie Berch took these seven pictures of McDuffie's accident as it unfolded directly in front of him at Turn 5. In the final picture, Jimmy Means signals for help, the first sign that McDuffie is injured. (Charlie Berch)

The Budweiser at the Glen resumed and ran to completion.
Brett Bodine's No. 26 Buick breaks down and pulls off at
the old chicane entering Turn 5. (Terry Letton)

Ernie Irvan (No. 4) races Davey Allison (No. 28)
into the corner en route to victory. (Terry Letton)

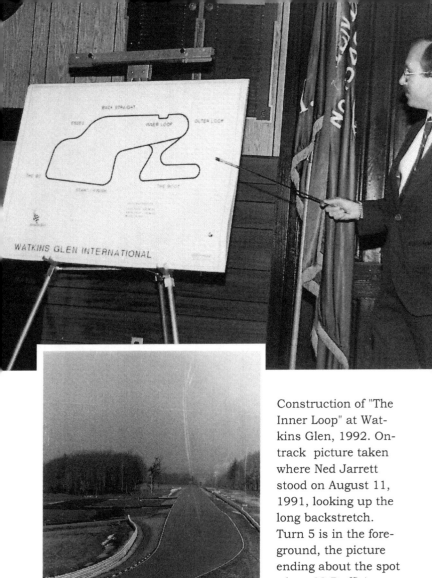

Construction of "The Inner Loop" at Watkins Glen, 1992. On-track picture taken where Ned Jarrett stood on August 11, 1991, looking up the long backstretch. Turn 5 is in the foreground, the picture ending about the spot where McDuffie's car left the track. Note the downhill slope of both the track and runoff area. (Charlie Berch)

"Old Blue" dwarfed by two modern haulers belonging to
A.J. Foyt Enterprises (left) and Hendrick Motorsports
(right), circa 1988. (Mike and Lesley Demers)

"Old Blue" at the headquarters of Bailey Excavating in
Jackson, Michigan, carrying John Bailey's pavement late
model, 2016. (Jacob Bailey)

J.D. McDuffie's two shops are still standing. The "Tune Up Shop"
on Wilbur Thomas' property in Broadway— (Brock Beard)

—and the inside of the Willett Road shop, today owned by
Sanford Transmissions. Both pictures taken September 2017
(Brock Beard)

In 2016, Front Row Motorsports dedicated their No. 38 to J.D. McDuffie, complete with sponsorship from Bailey Excavating and Rumple Furniture. Landon Cassill drove the car to a 30th-place finish. (Front Row Motorsports)

CHAPTER 10
The Glen

"It's a lot like running from the law – you don't know where you're gonna turn next."

—NASCAR driver Mickey Gibbs on road racing, 1989

Well before it joined the schedule, Watkins Glen International shared a great deal in common with NASCAR. Both were birthed in postwar America as outlets for the nation's rekindled love affair with the automobile.

Bill France, Sr. founded NASCAR on February 21, 1948 during a meeting with fellow promoters at the Streamline Hotel in Daytona Beach, Florida. The signature event on the NASCAR "Strictly Stock" calendar was one France competed in as a driver a decade earlier: a 166-mile race around the city's namesake. For forty laps, drivers would literally race down the tightly packed sands of Daytona Beach, their cars just inches from the surf. Next came a hairpin turn to the left onto a parallel stretch of Highway A1A, where they'd speed two miles north toward another hard left-hander. The best seats were in France's grandstands behind the turns, where heavy Fords and Oldsmobiles would often dig their skinny tires into the rutted sand and crash spectacularly.

That same year, 1100 miles north in the Finger Lakes region of New York, law student Cameron Argetsinger looked to satisfy his own need for speed. Growing up, Argetsinger loved to stay at his grandparents' home on Lake Seneca near the sleepy village of Watkins Glen. As an adult, he also loved to race his MG TC around the winding roads through the adjoining state park. To satisfy his love for both the region and racing, Argetsinger plotted out a 6.6-mile course on the roads. Though he later admitted that he originally mapped out the track for his own personal enjoyment, Argetsinger later chose to dream bigger: invite other racers to tackle his literal "road course" in a Watkins Glen Grand Prix.

At first, Argetsinger's "track" was a flight of fancy – not to mention a logistical nightmare. Many of the roads weren't even paved: the meandering loop shifted abruptly from concrete to gravel to dirt. Even worse, a stretch of tracks belonging to the New York Central Railroad divided the course neatly in half, requiring drivers make a 100mph sprint through an underpass on one side, then dash across the tracks on the other. But Argetsinger persuaded the village elders to agree, and with the help of Alec Ulmann, activities chairman of the Sport Car Club of America (SCCA), the first Grand Prix was set for October 2, 1948.

To deal with the problem of rail traffic, racers were first instructed to stop at the crossing and listen for approaching trains before they completed the final quarter of the course. But by the time the day came, Mayor Allen Erway had called in a favor with the railway. With that, the first postwar road course race in the United States passed into history as "The Day They Stopped The Trains."

Frank Griswold claimed a close victory in the eight-lap event, his No. 35 Alfa Romeo 8C 2900B edging famous road racer Briggs Cunningham in his No. 9 "Bu-Merc Special" – a Buick with a custom-built Mercedes body bolted onto it. Cameron Argetsinger's MG came home in ninth.

A map by *New Yorker* cartoonist Sam Cobean, who lived in the vicinity of Turn 3, shows the quaintness of the original course. The starting line was in front of the court house on Franklin Street, where several blocks served as the pits. Some corners were named for nearby buildings. "School House Corner," near its eponym, led to the signature spot on the track: a narrow stone bridge over Glen Creek. The bridge, today known as "Cornett's Stone Bridge," instead memorializes a spectacular racing crash. On the second lap of the 1948 race, Denver Cornett rolled his MG off the bridge and into the creek. Cornett survived his spill, as did William Milliken, whose Bugatti 35A tumbled into hay bales coming off the penultimate corner, known thereafter as "Milliken's Corner."

But two years later, these crashes turned deadly. On September 23, 1950, advertising agent Sam Collier was leading on the second lap of the Grand Prix when his No. 54 Ferrari left the course, rolled, and crashed, killing him instantly. Then in 1952, Fred Wacker's Allard roadster slid off the track on the Franklin Street homestretch and drove into the crowd. Several spectators were injured, and seven-year-old Frank Fazzari was killed. The race's organizers attempted to move the event to a smaller 4.6-mile course, but further safety concerns ultimately ended sanctioned racing on New York's public roads.

In 1956, Bill France, Jr.'s "Strictly Stock" division – now the Grand National Series – was still making yearly trips to the beach for forty laps of bone-jarring races on the sand. In the small town of Dix, five miles south-west of Watkins Glen, a new permanent facility was constructed on

550 acres of rolling farmland and groves of maple, cherry, and hemlock trees, the best of five potential sites.

Nine years after he brushed the hay off his wrecked Bugatti, William Milliken designed the 2.35-mile road course. The track would have eight corners, many of them replicating features of Argetsinger's original track. The starting line led directly into Turns 1, 2, and 3, an uphill sequence of three alternating corners, or "Esses," which flowed right, then left, then back right again, resembling the jaunty "White House S" of the old Grand Prix. A 2,300-foot-long "East Leg" straightaway followed due south, rising fifteen feet to the track's highest point, then dropping at the braking zone to the south. There, the track fell into Turn 4, a "Loop," or long 180-degree turn to the right, which corkscrewed down with the change in elevation. The turn dumped out onto the "West Leg," another short chute to the north that was kinked at its midpoint. This "kink" at Turn 5 was a high-speed corner that then spilled into the "Big Bend" of Turn 6. Named for the steep downhill path that led into "Milliken's Corner," this right-hander forced heavy braking and hard steering. A jerk to the left followed at Turn 7, another to the right at Turn 8, and drivers were quite suddenly back at the starting line.

By 1957, track officials began to add a single row of steel Armco barriers at certain spots around the track, like those used on mountain roads. The barriers, which would later be stacked up to four rows high, were painted light blue. The color was a mix of the leftovers from painting the buildings in the infield white with blue trim – the United States' official colors in international motorsports. On August 4, 1957, NASCAR and Watkins Glen crossed paths:

Bill France, Sr.'s racing series hosted the first professional-ly sanctioned event at the new track.

* * * *

Many of NASCAR's pioneers were moonshiners who slung their modified cars left and right through twisty mountain roads across the south-east. But on race day, those same cars and drivers ran exclusively on ovals.

It wasn't until the series' sixth season in 1954 that its drivers first competed on a road course. Even then, the 200-mile race around the temporary track at Linden Airport in northern New Jersey was kind of an oddity. That day, NASCAR relaxed its restriction preventing foreign name-plates from competing. Linden would match one row of twenty-two full-bodied American marques against a cadre of twenty-one international sports cars. Earlier that season, third-place starter Al Keller had already scored his first NASCAR victory in a burly Hudson Hornet, but at Linden he now squeezed into a tiny Jaguar XK120. Keller's light-weight red-and-white machine took the lead near halfway and motored to victory, besting not only Fords and Plym-ouths, but twelve other Jaguars, five MGs, an Austin Hea-ley, a Morgan, and a Porsche.

While it wasn't until 2008 that another foreign manu-facturer would win in NASCAR, road course racing contin-ued to keep its tiny space on the schedule. The next left-and-right affair in 1955 was also the first NASCAR event held on the west coast: the oil-and-sand surface of the 2.5-mile Willow Springs International Raceway in Lancaster, California. NASCAR scheduled the November 20 race the same day as a dirt track event on the other side of the country in Charlotte. When Lee Petty, Herb Thomas, and NASCAR's other top drivers elected to run the oval, the Willow Springs win went to an outsider: open-wheel star Chuck Stevenson. It was Stevenson's second and final NASCAR start before he returned for five more attempts at an elusive Indianapolis 500 victory.

The 1956 return to Willow Springs was a stand-alone date with Californian driver Marvin Panch, second in the inaugural, taking the checkers ahead of teammate Glenn "Fireball" Roberts. On December 30, Roberts won what would be the only NASCAR event held on the 1.6 miles of turns named Titusville-Cocoa Speedway, another temporary course at an airport in central Florida. Panch and Roberts went on to have great success in stock car racing, each winning the prestigious Daytona 500 in consecutive years.

In between the two Willow Springs races, two-time and defending NASCAR champion Tim Flock took the checkers at the sprawling 4.1-mile permanent road course in Elkhart Lake, Wisconsin. Today, the track, known as Road America, still hosts the Xfinity Series, NASCAR's second-tier division. They wouldn't host a Cup Series race again until 2021. In 1957, Road America lost its mid-August date to Watkins Glen.

Once again, the oval-track stock cars were at odds with the new road course. Their fuel pick-ups were set up for left-hand turns only, and each right-hand turn ran the risk of starving the engine. With rights outnumbering lefts three-to-one, the decision was made to run the track in the opposite direction. The change favored the veterans. Buck Baker won the inaugural "The Glen 101.2" in dominant fashion, leading all 44 laps from the pole. It was Baker's sixth of ten wins that season, paving the way to his second-consecutive Grand National championship.

NASCAR didn't return to The Glen until 1964. This time with the fuel system issue repaired, the cars ran the course in its proper direction. Taking the checkers from the pole was third-year driver Billy Wade, driving for long-time car owner and D-Day veteran Bud Moore. Wade became the first NASCAR driver to win four consecutive races. In 1965, Marvin Panch scored his first road course win since Willow Springs 1957 when his Wood Brothers entry led fifty-three of sixty-six laps of the race.

By the end of 1966, Panch had retired, Wade had lost his life in a testing crash at Daytona, Baker had claimed the last of his forty-six career victories, and NASCAR had left Watkins Glen.

* * * *

In NASCAR's absence, SCCA-sanctioned sports cars continued to compete at "The Glen," but Formula One now dominated the schedule. The track was already home for the United States Grand Prix since 1961, when Innes Ireland's Lotus bested Dan Gurney's Porsche by 4.3 seconds.

In 1971, track officials reconfigured Watkins Glen at the cost of $3 million, lengthening it into today's eleven-turn, 3.377-mile "long course." The changes concentrated on the west side of the course, from the exit of the "Loop" to the entrance to the "Esses." The changes are best de-scribed if the track were a length of string. The "kink" of Turn 5 had been tugged right, pulling Turns 6 and 7 into a

1,214-foot downhill straightaway. This straight stretch of road, now bisected by the new starting line and flanked by a new pit road, led into "The Ninety," Turn 8 on the old course and Turn 1 on the new.

The "Esses" – now Turns 2, 3, and 4 – remained unchanged, as did the 2,300-foot back straightaway toward the "Loop," now Turn 5. At the exit of Turn 5, drivers now veered left onto a new complex of four tight corners. Known as "The Boot" for the appendage's resemblance to a foot, Turns 6 through 9 were each linked by straights between 700 and 1,733 feet in length. Turn 9 dumped cars back onto the old "Chute," where two final ninety-degree bends at Turns 10 and 11 still separated them from the starting line.

The first Formula One race on the "long course," held October 3, 1971, was won by twenty-seven-year-old François Cevert. The charismatic Frenchman scored his first Grand Prix victory that day, securing him a career-best third in the season standings. Cevert's teammate Jackie Stewart officially took home his second World Championship that day and looked forward to passing the torch to his protegé. Two years later, Stewart came to Watkins Glen with his third title already in hand, set to retire after what would be his 100th Grand Prix.

On the morning of October 6, 1973, Cevert was pushing his blue Tyrrell hard, trying to snatch away pole position from Ronnie Peterson, when he lost control in the uphill Esses. His No. 6 clipped the steel traffic barrier on one side, then slammed another nearly head-on, sending his car tumbling over it. Track officials didn't attempt to remove him from the car. The twenty-nine-year-old Cevert was dead, his body nearly scissored in half by the impact.

Stewart and the rest of the Tyrrell team withdrew from the event.

When Formula One returned to The Glen the following year, tragedy struck yet again. On October 6, 1974, twenty-five-year-old Helmuth Koinigg was making just his second Grand Prix start. The young Austrian impressed in his debut the previous month with a tenth-place finish in the Canadian Grand Prix at Bowmanville, Ontario and was looking for more. On Lap 9 at The Glen, he was fighting his way up from the back of the pack in his Surtees TS16. Heading into the braking zone of Turn 7, the hairpin "Toe" of "The Boot," his suspension failed, sending his No. 19 speeding off the course. Unable to slow in time, Koinigg's car smashed head-on into two rows of traffic barriers. In an instant, the low-slung car acted like a wedge, lifting free the loosely fixed barriers, shearing away the roll hoop, and jamming the chassis under it on the other side. When crews came to the scene, Koinigg's helmet was off. His head was still inside.

Cevert and Koinigg were already the sixth and seventh fatalities suffered at Watkins Glen since its opening in 1956. The first came in 1960, when motorcyclist Tommy Seagraves crashed his Harley-Davidson during an American Motorcyclist Association (AMA) event. By 1976, that list had grown to eight after Mark Freed's car rammed through four barriers during a "closed-circuit" SCCA-sanctioned race. Freed joined four other SCCA competitors who all died at The Glen in a six-year span from 1962 through 1967: A.M. "Bud" Faust, Harold Woods, Edward Mathias, and Martin Krinner. Faust and Mathias struck one of the trees surrounding the track. Woods was killed at Turn 5, the

180-degree "Loop" bend at the end of the track's longest straightaway.

In 1975, Formula One driver Jody Scheckter, then the spokesman for the Grand Prix Drivers Association, threatened to boycott that fall's race. Scheckter alleged that Watkins Glen was asked to make changes to the track two years earlier but had done nothing. Of particular concern were the Armco barriers, which by then ran around much of the track on both sides. In many places, the barriers were placed as close to the racing surface as possible to reduce the chance of head-on collisions, so a car could only glance off them. But after the deaths of Cevert and Koinigg, Malcolm Currie, the executive director of Watkins Glen Grand Prix Corporation, the group in charge of the reconfiguration, began to second-guess the decision.

"Now the thinking is to move the guard rail away from the track, so a driver has a chance to correct before he hits anything. This theory also incorporates flat and steep areas where the drivers would have room to correct and catch fences at the end of turns or fast straight-aways." Currie also urged patience as the track adjusted. "But the thing you must remember is that we have about seven miles of guard rail to take care of, and it would take a substantial amount of money to move it all and recontour the land." In the end, a series of tight left and right-hand turns known as the "Scheckter Chicane" was added between Turns 2 and 3 leading into "The Esses" to slow cars down. The rest of the track, including Koinigg's Turn 7 and the "Loop" at Turn 5, remained unchanged.

Formula One left in 1981, and the track fell into bankruptcy, then disrepair, holding only a handful of SCCA races to empty grandstands. In 1983, the track was purchased by two parties. The first was Corning Enterprises, a wholly owned subsidiary of Corning Glass Works. The other was the International Speedway Corporation, belonging to NASCAR's France family.

One of the first measures taken was to close the roads which ran through the track property. Open to through traffic since the track was built on top of them, they were finally closed on October 29, 1983. The unused portions of these roads remain woven through the infield today. The next was to remove the "Scheckter Chicane," which again allowed drivers to accelerate uphill into "The Esses." As NASCAR's Bill France, Jr. weighed the option of adding the track to his circuit, a preliminary Camel GT event was used to test the track surface. Satisfied with the results, on October 16, 1985, NASCAR announced it would return to New York. The first "Budweiser at the Glen" ran the following August.

* * * *

During "The Glen's" absence, NASCAR road racing became even more specialized. From 1967 to 1985, the only time the series turned left and right was at the Riverside International Raceway, a sprawling nine-turn, 2.62-mile Y-shaped track in the desert north-east of Los Angeles. Like Watkins Glen, NASCAR brought the first nationally sanctioned race to the track in 1958. But unlike The Glen, many of Riverside's first winners were road course specialists from other motorsports, especially USAC open-wheelers: Parnelli Jones, A.J. Foyt, and most notably Dan Gurney.

From 1963 through 1968, Gurney won five of seven Riverside races, and each time cruised to a margin of victory of
over twenty-seven seconds. Richard Petty didn't win there
until 1969.

What now held back NASCAR stars on the road courses was a difference of philosophy. Teams and manufacturers modified their cars to tackle the circuit's fast new
superspeedways. First came an "aero war" in the late 1960s
with sleek new cars like the Ford Torino Talladega and the
Plymouth Superbird, the latter constructed with an arrow-
like nose and huge rear wing. Then in 1981 came smaller,
shorter wheelbase models like the Buick Regal and the Pontiac LeMans. While NASCAR's nimble little cars proved
even faster on the superspeedways – at one point turning
qualifying laps of over 212mph – their skinny tires, small
brakes, and truck arm suspension made them a handful on
road courses.

Other parts on a NASCAR stock car just weren't up to
the task of road racing. "Riverside, California in the early
'70s," recalled Jimmy Byrd. "I think they blew fourteen engines in the first few laps of the practice." At least one driver that day, Hershel McGriff, attempted to circumvent all
the upshifts and downshifts by running an automatic transmission. The experiment proved a complete failure. The
transmission let go after only a few minutes, splattering a
trail of slick fluid over half the track's length.

NASCAR's struggles distinguished the series from
Trans-Am, a stock car division which competed on road
courses exclusively. To make a Chevrolet Camaro or Ford
Mustang handle left and right turns, Trans-Am teams modified their cars with lightweight bodies, wide tires, and big

brakes. This allowed drivers to sling the cars around road courses – and even tight street courses – with comparative ease. In the 1980s, NASCAR attempted to create its own L-R car (short for "left-right"), a lightweight stock car which took inspiration from Trans-Am. But the program stalled out by the end of the decade. NASCAR and Trans-Am have continued down separate paths ever since.

As a compromise, NASCAR's rulebook allowed teams to make minor adjustments to the current oval track car for road racing. A few of Jimmy Means' methods are still used today: "We didn't have a purpose-built race car for road courses...we took our short track car and made it a road course car...Change batteries from the left to the right, change track bar mounts which you don't do today, but you could back then. So, there's things that we did to try and get right side weight in the car because you're basically turning right not the left, and the driver's sitting on the left." Since these changes could only make a car handle better, not perfectly, drivers had no choice but to merely get through Riverside, Sears Point, and Watkins Glen: fight your ill-handling machine around the track, leave with whatever finish you could, and move on.

This scrounging for a mid-pack finish created a complex in the minds of some drivers. Buddy Baker, one of NASCAR's greatest superspeedway racers, was the first to break the 200mph mark in a stock car, and in 1980 won the fastest Daytona 500 on record. He wasn't a fan of road courses, however, and his crew chief Harry Hyde knew it. "Running Buddy Baker at Riverside's like running a plow mule in the Kentucky Derby," he said. In 1986, when Baker entered his own car in the inaugural Budweiser at the Glen, the veteran decided to do one of the few things the NAS-CAR rule book allowed on road courses. He handed the wheel to a "road ringer," in his case, three-time Indy 500 winner Al Unser.

The theory behind hiring a "road ringer" dates back to the days of Gurney and Foyt – put an expert road course driver in your NASCAR stock car, and you'll dominate the field. But this assumes two things of the "ringer:" first, that he can adjust to NASCAR's unique cars; and second, that he can overcome the limitations of the car. In time, the task gradually became more daunting. At Riverside in 1973, Mark Donohue wheeled a Roger Penske-prepared AMC Matador to victory. When NASCAR returned to The Glen in 1986, a "ringer" hadn't won a Cup Series race since.

* * * *

On August 10, 1986, "The Budweiser at the Glen" took the green flag. Among the thirty-six starters, including eventual race winner Tim Richmond, just one had raced a stock car at the track: Forty-eight-year-old Richard Petty. Petty, NASCAR's top winner, finished twenty-first of twenty-six in 1964 when he, too, wrecked in Turn 5. He made just ten laps. "At this track, we're all rookies," said Petty before the start. "This is our experimental race. We'll learn a lot and when we come back next year we'll add on to what we learn." Petty wasn't exaggerating. The reconfiguration confronted the field with a brand-new challenge.

Unlike other road races held at the facility, The Budweiser at The Glen would be contested on the "short course." Used during the 1971 Six Hours Race – held after the straightening of Turns 10, 11, and 1, but before the completion of "The Boot" – the NASCAR course was just 2.428 miles in length. Without "The Boot," each of the ninety laps involved speeding down three long straightaways into three heavy braking areas: the 1,214-foot downhill sprint into "The Ninety" at Turn 1, the 2,300-foot rise, then fall into Turn 5, and the 2,040-foot "Chute" into the hard left-hander at Turn 10.

All three braking areas had large grassy areas to catch spinning cars – a remnant of the original Scheckter proposal. The relative sizes of these "run-off areas" was determined by the traffic barriers at the edge of each, where two perpendicular Armco barriers met at right angles at the farthest point. Unlike the other two main braking zones, Turn 5 had a large grassy area to catch spinning cars. A grove of trees had been cleared to allow for nearly 200 square feet of open space. At the far end, where two perpendicular barriers met, a row of used passenger car tires were piled in front of the Armco, a standard practice at road courses to lessen the force of an impact. Behind the Armco was a catchfence consisting of chain-link and eleven high-tension wires, all of it supported by several equally spaced posts sunk into the ground. The multi-layered barrier was a necessary safety feature: unlike Turns 1 and 10, Turn 5 also dropped fifteen feet from entrance to exit, meaning the run-off also ran downhill. If a car found trouble here – particularly coming *into* the corner – it would more than likely find the wall.

The first NASCAR driver to find this out was Bill Elliott. During Friday's qualifying session at The Glen, Elliott's No. 9 Coors Ford sped down the long back stretch, the driver determined to best Tim Richmond's pole speed of

117.563 mph. Heading into Turn 5, Elliott braked, but lost control, sending him skidding backwards across the grass. The car struck the barrier with such speed that it nearly left the track completely, knocking down a section of protective fencing. When the dust settled, the car was perched atop the Armco barrier and a pile of scattered tires. Uninjured, Elliott recalled the incident. "We were very quick down the back straight and thought we were getting into the corner OK," he said. "If you don't get in there just right, you've got trouble. I guarantee you I gained at least ten miles an hour when it got into the grass." The Melling Racing crew managed to piece No. 9 back together in time for the race, though the passenger side still bore the scars.

Three years later, Geoff Bodine's No. 5 Levi Garrett Chevrolet was speeding toward the same corner, coming around to complete the final lap-and-a-half of the 1989 Budweiser at The Glen. Heading into the braking zone, something blasted out of Bodine's right-front wheel, followed by a huge cloud of white smoke. Bodine fought for control, but by the entrance of Turn 5, the rear tires lost traction, sending him into an uncontrollable high-speed spin. Bodine's No. 5 never slowed as it skidded backwards off the track and onto the grass. It had just enough time to turn 180 degrees and slam head-on into the barrier. The tires, barriers, and the fence behind grabbed Bodine's car like a catcher's mitt, stopping him so suddenly that his head jerked forward, nearly striking the steering wheel. Fortunately, the wheel wasn't there – the impact had bent the steering column upward, hoisting the wheel to a position more than a foot higher than normal. Bodine escaped injury, but the car was destroyed.

The following year brought perhaps the most serious NASCAR wreck the track had yet seen. Heading into the 1990 Budweiser at the Glen, west coast competitor Troy Beebe had a good chance of making his first start at the track – he only had to beat one car to qualify. During practice, Beebe's No. 90 Tops Friendly Markets Ford found trouble before he even got to Turn 5. While negotiating The Esses, Beebe lost control, suddenly blocking the track for an approaching Dick Trickle and Mark Martin. Trickle had a split-second to react. He cut right to avoid Beebe, but the hole closed-up, collecting both Trickle and Mark Martin behind. Knocked unconscious by a direct impact to his driver's side door, Beebe had to be cut from his car and airlifted to a hospital in Pennsylvania. He spent two hours in the trauma unit before he finally recovered. Trickle and Martin escaped with cuts and bruises and qualified for the race in backup cars. Beebe, still recuperating on race day, went home with his only car in tatters.

J.D. McDuffie made all three races, finishing twenty-fifth in 1986, thirty-fifth in '89, and a track-best twenty-second in '90. In fact, he'd never once missed the field at Watkins Glen. The 1990 finish was also his best finish all season – though he made just eight races of the twenty-nine scheduled that year. McDuffie always enjoyed road courses, not only because a driver could get away with less horsepower, but because they could make a mistake in one corner and make up for it in the next. In 1986, he was running ninth in the late stages at Riverside when Tim Richmond spun him out. As it came time to return to New York in 1991, J.D. McDuffie certainly had reason to look forward to it.

CHAPTER 11
Radial and Radius

*"Accidents can happen anywhere, you've just got to take
them as they come (and realize) they're a part of racing."*

—*J.D. McDuffie, January 12, 1989*

Thursday, August 8, 1991. For the first time, the Budweiser at the Glen weekend would start at noon the Thursday before the race. Track president John R. Saunders added
the fourth day to the weekend's festivities free of charge,
thus giving the 120,000 fans a better chance of setting up
their campsites during the day. Those who filed in that afternoon realized this was the first of a series of changes.

Looking to reel in the track's historically rowdy fans,
Saunders designated the infield spectator area inside the
course "family only" with a strict 11:00 P.M. curfew. Those
looking for late-night excitement would have to go into
town to The Savoy, the club on West 4th Street, where the
bands Rogues and Savannah would be performing on Saturday and Sunday. The track also banned spectator parking
in the infield, bicycle traffic, cruising, the use of large box
trucks, and began to dissuade fans from erecting scaffolding
to get a better view. A six-foot height would be tolerated in
1991, then none at all in '92.

A lot had changed, and yet much was still the same. As
fans staked their claim on the grass, flags and banners soon
waved over grandstands and mobile homes alike. One of the
biggest was a towering shrine to the current Winston Cup
point leader. Next to a big black Chevrolet "bowtie" and

beneath the American flag, a sign in black spray paint read "Dale Earnhardt: God of Thunder No. 3."

* * * *

Watkins Glen could not have come soon enough for Ricky Rudd.

Rudd came into the race second in the Winston Cup championship standings, 160 points – more than a full race's worth of ground – behind Earnhardt. Two weeks previous, Earnhardt had taken the checkered flag in the DieHard 500 at the Talladega Superspeedway, his third win of the season and fifth on the series' biggest and fastest track. Now, coming into New York, the shoe was truly on the other foot. In seventeen years on the circuit, Earnhardt had never once won on a road course. Rudd, on the other hand, was The Glen's two-time and defending winner.

Rudd should have been going for a road course sweep in 1991. In June at Sears Point, Rudd chased down race leader Davey Allison heading into Turn 11, the slowest corner on the track, with two laps to go. As the two hit the brakes, Rudd's bright orange Tide Chevrolet nudged the rear bumper of Allison's jet-black Havoline Ford, sending Allison into a spin. Rudd took the white flag and appeared headed to the checkers the next time by. Instead, NASCAR gave him the black flag, citing him for aggressive driving. When the dust had settled, a five-second penalty was assessed on Rudd, giving Allison, who recovered from his spin, the victory.

Watkins Glen was Rudd's chance for retribution. He even brought the same No. 5 car from Sears Point. What he didn't need was a setback – or a curveball. Unfortunately, in Thursday's first practice session, he got both.

In 1989 Goodyear – NASCAR's exclusive tire manufacturer at the time – elected to shelve its traditional bias-ply tires in favor of radials to reduce the number of flat tires. To understand the difference between the two types of tires is to understand what happens when a stock car driver makes a high-speed turn. Turning shifts the car's weight onto the left or right-side tires, causing the tires to bend and change shape as they take on the load. Under the same circumstances, bias-ply and radial tires bend in different ways.

A bias-ply tire bends the best since the sidewall and the tread form a continuous curve – when one bends, so does the other. This bending allows the "contact patch," the surface area of the tire which touches the surface of the track, to stretch larger if needed. This is why bias-ply tires are considered more "forgiving," that is, better able to stick to the track even when the tire is being pushed to its limit. Bias-plys are still used in lower divisions of stock car racing, including the NASCAR K&N Pro Series, where drivers are often less experienced and more prone to accidents. Veterans can also use bias-plys to make their own daring moves on the track, knowing the tires will help make the move stick. The problem is that bias-plys, while cheaper, are also weaker. Increasing speeds had added more weight to the tires, stretching the rubber past the breaking point and making them more prone to failure.

A radial tire, on the other hand, sacrifices flexibility for strength. This is accomplished by constructing the sidewall and the tread separately to stiffen and strengthen each, allowing the tire to carry more of the car's weight. The separation between sidewall and tread also forms a barrier which sets a limit on how much the tire can flex. With this barrier in place, a driver making a corner on radials can only rely on the tread to catch the weight of his car, resulting in a much smaller contact patch. If the driver stays within the tire's limits, the tire will grip. If he's too aggressive, the contact patch will shrink so much that the car can't stay on the track.

NASCAR introduced radials gradually over several seasons, starting at the short tracks. The 1991 season saw the change come to the road courses: bias-plys at Sears Point, followed by the first use of radials at Watkins Glen. This presented a problem. Since the cars weren't purpose-fully designed for road courses, drivers already had to be particularly aggressive on bias-ply tires just to keep pace. But with the reduced flexibility of radials, the same moves wouldn't work. In fact, they could be dangerous.

Rudd was the first to find this out during Thursday's opening practice. As he dove into Turn 5, his Tide Chevrolet lost traction, spun out, and smashed into the tire barriers, tearing the rear panel and front valence from his car. Rudd's Hendrick Motorsports crew first wrote off the car as a total loss and prepared their backup car for another run on the track. "You just don't get a lot of warning," said Rudd in an interview with *Winston Cup Scene*. "Normally, with a bias-ply tire, you get a lot of warning. Now when the car breaks loose and you get off the throttle, you're not always going to be able to turn the car. The radials stick better, there's no question about that. But when you start to go, there's no going back."

Meanwhile, more drivers found trouble in Turn 5. Next was the No. 33 Skoal Bandit Oldsmobile of "Handsome"

Harry Gant. Gant, just over a year younger than McDuffie, was just weeks away from a career renaissance. In September 1991, he would win four races in a row – six if you include victories in the Busch Series – earning him the nickname "Mr. September." The following August, he won his final race at fifty-two years, seven months, and six days, setting an age record that stands to this day. But at Watkins Glen, Gant spun off at the same spot as Rudd and hit the tires flush with the passenger side. "You spin out faster with the radials," said Gant. "It's just a lot quicker tire. You have to get used to that and this is the first chance we've had to do that on a road course."

Alabama driver Hut Stricklin followed suit when his No. 12 Raybestos Buick backed into the tire barriers, destroying the rear clip. "I came off turn five and I was a little sideways," he said. "I tried to get back on the gas and when I did, there was no saving it. The problem is, I think, you are more sideways than you think you are. I think we might be seeing a lot of this in the race."

Even Davey Allison, Rudd's Sears Point nemesis, wasn't immune. Unlike the wrecks that preceded his, Allison lost control in Turn 10, where two drivers blew engines earlier in the session. Allison blamed his wreck on driver error, not the radial tires, yet reports indicate that track crews might have missed some of the oil, or put down too much "oil dry," the kitty litter-like substance sprinkled on asphalt to absorb fluids. "My wreck was the result of the driver screwing up," he said. "I went back out, ran a couple laps under caution to warm up the car and then in turn one, I eased on the gas, shifted from second gear to third and crashed. I don't have the faintest idea what happened."

Allison's crew decided not to go to a backup and instead patched together a new nose piece for No. 28.

For the thirty-year-old Allison, this was a literal insult to injury. Two weeks earlier at Talladega, he broke his right hand. It wasn't the result of an on-track incident, but a momentary lapse of judgment. With three laps to go in the DieHard 500, Allison made his move on race leader Dale Earnhardt, certain the three Fords behind him would help him draft by into the lead. When two of them chose to follow Earnhardt, Allison slipped down in the order, eventually winding up ninth. Furious, Allison climbed from his car and punched the side of his car hauler. The resulting injury required both an adjustment to his seat and a flexible cast to help him grip the steering wheel and shift gears around The Glen. By the time he arrived in New York, Allison was in better sprits – two days after Talladega, his wife Liz gave birth to their second child, Robert Grey Allison.

* * * *

The next day on Friday, August 9, a persistent rain held back the day's events. Despite a coveted late summer date, the Budweiser at the Glen has always been plagued by bad weather. Rain pushed the 1987, 2009, and 2011 races to Monday while the 1992 race was shortened to just past half distance. In 1994, rain limited practice so much that, on race day, seven cars suffered mechanical issues in the first eight laps. And in the nine races from 2000 through 2008, pole qualifying was rained out five times. The 1991 race came close to joining that list. A morning practice was washed-out, but the cars made it out on track to practice again at 3:30 P.M.

When the session opened, Ricky Rudd took a couple laps in his backup car, but wasn't satisfied with its speed. The decision was then made to repair the wrecked car from Thursday. The rear clip was rebuilt by cannibalizing parts from the backup. And, in a curious show of sportsmanship, Richard Childress Racing provided a new front valence. There wasn't enough time to repaint the nose – Rudd's bright orange Chevrolet would run the rest of the weekend with Earnhardt's black front bumper.

Out on the track, teams continued to find the tire barriers and guardrails. Rudd's teammate Ken Schrader came to The Glen fresh off a road course victory of his own the previous Sunday, when he dominated the ARCA event at Heartland Park Topeka in Kansas. But his No. 25 Kodiak Chevrolet slid off course and banged the fence in Turn 5, knocking the toe-end out of alignment. The team managed to make repairs.

Not so fortunate was Michael Waltrip. During the late-afternoon session, Waltrip discovered getting out of Turn 5 was just as treacherous as getting into it. Coming out of the turn, Waltrip's bright yellow No. 30 Pennzoil Pontiac lost control and slid into a grassy wedge that separated the entrance to "The Boot" from the short chute. There, another tire barrier came up fast, which Waltrip smashed into with the passenger side. "It was a loud, fast, and violent hit," said Veronica Holland, a fan who witnessed the wreck from the infield. "No parts and pieces went flying to dissipate the energy."

After the hit, the six-foot-five-inch Waltrip was slow to get out of his car and was sent to Corning Hospital, eighteen

miles to the south, where CAT scans revealed he'd fractured his right shoulder blade. "I feel good," he said after he
was discharged later that day. "I can move my shoulder and
it doesn't hurt a whole lot. It hurts some, but we'll see how
it goes tomorrow. I do plan to race on Sunday." Waltrip was
okay, but his brand-new road course car was totaled. The
sheet metal along the passenger side was crushed so tightly
against the frame that the right-side tires protruded out several inches. As the Bahari' Racing team prepped Waltrip's
backup – the car with which their driver finished fourth at
The Glen the year before – the team prepared an alternate
strategy. Scott Pruett, on hand to run a companion race,
would stand by as relief driver.

* * * *

In the closing darkness, first-round qualifying for the
first twenty of the forty starting positions followed practice
around 5:30 P.M. The pole position went to series veteran
Terry Labonte, his first since the First Union 400 at North
Wilkesboro on April 17, 1988, ninety-six races previous.
His lap of 121.652mph set a new track record, besting Dale
Earnhardt's 1990 record of 121.190mph. He also ran the
fastest speed down the backstretch of over 175mph, a full
two miles per hour faster than any other qualifier. "It's been
so long since I won a pole, I don't know what to say," Labonte remarked.

The 1991 season saw Labonte reunite with team owner
Billy Hagan, with whom Labonte claimed the 1984 Winston Cup. Up until that day, the pairing had yet to yield
much fruit. Labonte's No. 94 Sunoco Oldsmobile entered

the race a distant twenty-third in points. Like Rudd, Labonte looked to the road courses for a rebound: his season-
best sixth-place finish came at Sears Point in June, and he
won the inaugural 150-mile Busch Series race at The Glen
later that month. "We learned some things in that race," said
Labonte. "So, when I went back to the shop, we made some
changes on our Winston Cup car for here and it helped."

Joining Labonte on the front row with a lap of
121.397mph was the No. 6 Folger's Ford of Mark Martin.
Fifth in points coming into The Glen, Martin was making
the most of his second chance. He attempted to break into
Winston Cup as an owner-driver in 1981, but three difficult
seasons bumped him back to the short tracks of the American Speed Association (ASA). Then, in 1988, Martin signed
with Jack Roush, who was looking to expand his road racing team into Winston Cup. The chemistry yielded near-
instant results with Martin in position to win both the 1989
and 1990 championships. Martin had yet to win in 1991 –
or at The Glen for that matter. One year after he was collected in Troy Beebe's crash, Martin was fastest in Thursday's opening practice, the only car to break 120mph that
day. He briefly held the track record until Labonte bested
his time.

Expected to join Labonte and Martin at the front was
Rusty Wallace, winner at The Glen in 1987 and 1989. In
many ways the equal to Ricky Rudd on the road courses,
hopes were high that Wallace would challenge for his fifth
top-five start in six races at the track. After all, he was now
back with Roger Penske, the man who at Atlanta eleven
years earlier fielded Wallace's first Winston Cup car, a
Chevrolet he wheeled to a stunning second behind Dale

Earnhardt. Wallace's 1991 ride was a sleek black-and-gold Pontiac Grand Prix with sponsorship from Miller Genuine Draft, the beer brand that Wallace carried over from his championship-winning ride at Blue Max Racing. But after putting up the second-fastest time on Thursday, Wallace's No. 2 sputtered around the course in qualifying with a misfire in the engine. His first-round speed of 117.164 mph was nearly a full mile per hour off a spot in the Top Twenty. Frustrated, the Penske Racing South team spent the rest of the afternoon trying to figure out what went wrong.

Schrader and Allison bounced back in qualifying by starting sixth and ninth, respectively, in their rebuilt cars. Gant's crew banged out the dents in time for their ageless driver to lock-up fifteenth. Joining Wallace outside the Top Twenty were Hut Stricklin's Buick with a new rear clip, the Chevrolet Frankenstein of Ricky Rudd, and Michael Waltrip, who chose not to run. All four would have to re-qualify the next day, and with the first half locked-in, none would start better than twenty-first on Sunday.

No one crashed in qualifying, but Morgan Shepherd came close. The forty-nine-year-old's No. 15 Motorcraft Ford slid up the track in Turn 5, and he just barely managed to keep it on the pavement. The slip didn't cost him a car, but it did cost him time. By a fraction of a second, he was twenty-first, the fastest car not locked-into the field. This was just the latest episode of a roller coaster week for the North Carolina veteran. The previous Tuesday, he was at Ford's plant in Lorain, Ohio, driving the first 1992 Thunderbird off the assembly line. Then, on the way to The Glen, his motor home blew an oil seal. Then the fan belt broke. He barely got to the track in time. Perhaps, then, it was appropriate that Friday was "Morgan Shepherd Day" in nearby Montour Falls, New York. The town's yearly fan festival brought more than 5,000 to see Shepherd, who had been active in NASCAR since 1970. "This is an honor for me," said Shepherd, "because I've never had a town name a day after me."

The big story from first-round qualifying involved Wally Dallenbach, Jr. Dallenbach made his Winston Cup debut early in the 1991 season driving for veteran owner Junie Donlavey, but by then was already a road racing standout in Trans-Am. Friday at Watkins Glen, it was announced that Dallenbach would join Roush Racing in 1992 as Mark Martin's teammate. A sponsor had yet to be signed, so he was only confirmed for a part-time ride, but Keystone Beer soon joined for a full-season run. To get Dallenbach ready, and to take advantage of both he and Roush's road racing prowess, Roush gave Dallenbach one of his Fords for him to run at The Glen. Carrying Donlavey's No. 90, but with Roush's team logos and associate sponsorship from Valvoline, Dallenbach ran eleventh in Thursday's practice, then put the white Ford fifth on the grid. Dallenbach wouldn't qualify that well in Winston Cup again until 1997 – four years after he left Roush.

Sixty-seven years young, Donlavey had been hiring drivers to run his cars since NASCAR's second season in 1950. That weekend at The Glen, he didn't have anyone signed to replace Dallenbach in 1992 but had made at least one offer. That summer, Marty Burke contacted his brother-in-law, who was vice president for Motorola, about sponsoring J.D. McDuffie the following season. Since Motorola had a partnership with Ford, Burke sought out Ford teams who were looking for a sponsor. Burke contacted Donlavey, knowing he was the only Ford team who was figured to be in the best price range. "I'd love to have J.D. in the car," Donlavey told Burke, then right away quoted his price. "It's $25,000 a race." Burke spoke with his brother-in-law, looking to get $35,000 a race for McDuffie in 1992. That way, Burke could run the No. 70 the following season while McDuffie ran Donlavey's No. 90.

Burke began to put together a sponsorship portfolio to present to Ernie Saxton, who had previously done public relations work for driver Sterling Marlin. Included would be a thirteen-minute "J.D. Promo Tape" Mike and Lesley Demers put together, a VHS cassette showing the times McDuffie was mentioned on television during that summer's races at Dover and Pocono. When he told McDuffie about the offer, Burke couldn't help but tease the driver, saying "I'd do everything I can to get you into a Ford." But McDuffie was on board. He hinted at this to Maurice Leggett before he left Sanford days earlier. Leggett, a Ford enthusiast, thought he was joking. He wasn't. There was a meeting with a PR firm scheduled right after Watkins Glen.

* * * *

Saturday, August 10 saw another two Winston Cup drivers come to grief in Turn 5. The first was Dave Marcis.

Like McDuffie, the fifty-year-old Marcis was an owner-driver with more than two decades of experience. Unlike his competitor, the Wisconsin native found victory lane five times – four of them while driving for championship team owner Nord Krauskopf. He also had a long-standing relationship with Richard Childress Racing through mutual friend Dale Earnhardt, who, with increasing frequency, provided Marcis with cars and equipment to keep him on the track. Marcis, in turn, helped McDuffie.

In 1990, Marcis broke his leg at Daytona after a crash in practice with Darrell Waltrip. Marcis' crew got in touch with McDuffie, who was on his way home in "Old Blue" after he failed to qualify. The two arranged for Marcis to start McDuffie's No. 70 – renumbered No. 71 – to keep him in driver points. McDuffie would then take over and run the rest of the race, taking home the prize money for his trouble. The arrangement turned out to be a good one. On Lap 1, a twenty-three-car wreck took out most of the leaders. Marcis made it through and the driver change was made. McDuffie came home twentieth and left with $8,570 in his pocket.

Like McDuffie and his cigars, Marcis' signature was his wingtip shoes he wore in the race car. Marcis also wore a Goodyear hat on pit road, though his feelings for the brand were certainly tested when his No. 71 Big Apple Markets Chevrolet slammed head-on into the Turn 5 tire barriers during "Happy Hour," the final Winston Cup practice.

Marcis walked away from the wreck with a stiff neck and a totaled race car. He brought a backup car just in case, but unlike those of the bigger teams, it wasn't at all ready to go road racing. The transmission and weight distribution were intended for 500 miles of left turns around the next month's oval in Darlington, South Carolina. Withdrawing from Sunday's race wasn't an option – he needed the purse money – but there was only so much time to get his Chevrolet ready for the main event.

* * * *

Saturday also saw second-round qualifying, and with it, the completion of the forty-car field for the Budweiser at The Glen. Fastest in the session were, unsurprisingly, Rusty Wallace and Ricky Rudd, whose laps would have been fast enough for third and ninth, respectively, had they happened on Friday. As it stood, they would roll off twenty-first and twenty-second. Hut Stricklin could only manage thirtieth in his rebuilt Raybestos Buick.

Michael Waltrip, still mending from his wreck on Friday, didn't participate in the session. In practice that morning, his backup No. 30 Pontiac had a miss in the engine. So instead, Waltrip took a "provisional" spot, putting him in the fortieth and final starting spot. "I think I may be able to run the entire race," said Waltrip. "I'll see how I feel after forty or fifty laps."

Six "road ringers" filled out the field. Many had competed in the weekend's companion events, including Saturday's double-header between Trans-Am and the IMSA Firestone Firehawk Series. Most had decades of experience on tracks even tougher than the one they faced. Despite all this, NASCAR rules required each carry "rookie stripes" – strips of yellow tape across the rear bumper of their car – warning others of the driver's stock car racing inexperience.

Some, like Chaska, Minnesota's Jim Derhaag, struggled in qualifying. For more than a decade, Derhaag ran street courses and road courses across the country. Now, he was set to make his NASCAR debut in the No. 54 Hakes Equipment Oldsmobile. "They were a lot different," he said when comparing the two cars. "A race horse and a plow horse is what it amounts to."

Derhaag's "race horse" was his Trans-Am ride, his No. 40 Chevrolet Camaro from his 2,200-square-foot shop. That same Saturday, he set a series record by making his 118th Trans-Am start – impressive for an owner-driver with limited funding and just three full-time employees. The NASCAR Olds, his "plow horse," was a handful. Derhaag was second-slowest in qualifying, only good enough for thirty-eighth on the grid.

Derhaag's one-race deal to drive the Olds came about when a friend contacted the crew chief for car owner George Hakes. Hakes' team, based out of a shop just down the street from Watkins Glen, had been struggling to compete in NASCAR's top division for more than two seasons. In its six previous starts, Hakes-Welliver Racing had finished no better than twenty-sixth, when Tommy Riggins, another road course driver from the IMSA ranks, came home four laps down at Pocono. Coming into Watkins Glen, Riggins' finish marked the only time the Hakes entry had even finished under power. In the other five starts, five different problems ended their day: a blown engine, busted brakes, a broken transmission, a fractured oil pan, and a crash. Derhaag could hardly do worse.

Others, like thirteenth-place starter Irv Hoerr, impressed with fast laps. The Peoria, Illinois driver competed against Derhaag in Trans-Am, and would compete alongside him on Saturday in Team Rocketsports' black Oldsmobile. Unlike Derhaag, Hoerr also had a background in oval racing. His father Rudy fielded stock cars when USAC held its own stock car events at northern tracks like Pocono and

Michigan. Irv, his father's chief mechanic, then began a relationship with Oldsmobile, who hired him to compete both in Trans-Am and the "modified showroom division," a stock car division that raced production models. This extra experience allowed Hoerr to best understand how to finesse a stock car around a road course.

"You just basically had to understand, you couldn't hurry them the way you could a road race car," said Hoerr. "You couldn't be aggressive with them, because basically you had to wait on it. And you couldn't use the brakes near as hard as you wanted to because with the truck arms you get wheel hop, and even today as far as they've come in development that's still an issue for them."

Hoerr's first exposure to NASCAR came when Oldsmobile hired him to test for the manufacturer's other drivers. Among them was Buddy Baker, who like his predecessor Al Unser gave Hoerr the opportunity to race his No. 88 on a road course. Following a twenty-second-place finish for Baker in his series debut at Riverside in 1987, Hoerr began to work with Terry Labonte, who joined Richard Jackson's Oldsmobile effort in 1990. Labonte and Jackson arranged for Hoerr to drive a team car, No. 0, at Sonoma and Watkins Glen. Hoerr surprised both times, finishing eighth in the former and tenth in the latter. Each time he ranked higher than his teammate.

Labonte and Hoerr continued their alliance into 1991, which contributed to Labonte's win in June's Busch Series race at Watkins Glen, then his pole in August. Hoerr would drive as well, but this time in a "research and development" car owned by Labonte himself. Unlike most Winston Cup cars of the day, which were built in Mooresville, North

Carolina, Hoerr's 1991 ride was built in Lansing, Michigan by Bill Markel and designed by GM engineer Terry Satchel. Hoerr's blue-and-silver No. 44 ran well at Sonoma, but without a professional pit crew, the driver lost too much ground on pit road to earn another Top Ten. For the Budweiser at the Glen, however, Labonte loaned the Busch Series pit crew from his younger brother Bobby. With a good qualifying run in the books, he looked to return to form on Sunday.

Leading the "road ringers" from the eleventh spot was Skip Barber Racing School instructor Dorsey Schroeder, who edged Hoerr for the 1989 Trans-Am championship. Unlike Hoerr and Derhaag, the thirty-eight-year-old Schroeder's "double-duty" involved being both driver and announcer. He'd be the color commentator for the Firestone Firehawk and Trans-Am events, then race on Sunday. Though he'd previously relieved Dick Trickle during a Winston Cup race the year before and had attempted to make the 1991 Daytona 500 for Lucky Compton, The Glen would be Schroeder's official series debut. This time, he would drive for team owner Sam McMahon and Team III Racing.

As the economy struggled during the Gulf War, Team III found themselves without a sponsor for the season-opening Daytona 500. R.J. Reynolds of title sponsor Winston arranged a temporary fix for Team III and four other Winston Cup programs in the same situation: special paint schemes representing the five branches of the military. Team III finished second in class when Mickey Gibbs finished seventeenth, but the team remained without sponsorship for the rest of the year. It became Schroeder's task to turn heads in Team III's gray No. 24 Pontiac with their first top-ten finish of the year.

Though the remaining three "road ringers" at Watkins Glen started near the rear of the field, each had an impressive resume. Tyrone, Pennsylvania's Oma Kimbrough, a veteran of the IMSA GT, GTO, and GTU divisions, also favored his road racing Camaros. On Sunday, Kimbrough would be making his third Winston Cup start from the thirty-ninth spot. He drove for Jim Rosenblum's Linro Motorsports in the same No. 13 he raced to a thirty-seventh-place finish at The Glen the year before. Rosenblum tabbed Kimbrough to run The Glen following the serious injuries suffered by driver Jocko Maggiacomo, who suffered a catastrophic wreck with Bobby Allison at Pocono in 1988.

Texan commodities broker Kim Campbell arrived in NASCAR following seven years running in SCCA Can-Am and lower-division CART open-wheel cars. At dusk on Saturday, Campbell got his weekend started right when he and co-driver Bill Cooper won the two-hour Firestone Firehawk race from the pole, driving a Porsche 944 S2. In Winston Cup qualifying, he recovered from a spin on Friday's timed lap and was now set to make his NASCAR debut from the thirty-seventh spot. Like Rosenblum, team owner Dick Moroso was coping with tragedy, though of a much more personal nature. One year earlier, he'd fielded a Winston Cup ride for his son Rob, who at just twenty years old became the youngest NASCAR Busch Series Champion in series history. On September 30, 1990, in the closing stages of a turbulent rookie season, Rob and a young woman were killed in a traffic accident outside Mooresville, North Carolina. Campbell would be the seventh different driver to drive the No. 20 Oldsmobile since Rob's death.

Lawrenceville, Georgia's John Paul, Jr. had just made

his third Indianapolis 500 start in the summer of 1991, but an oil leak kept him twenty-fifth, well short of his then career-best fifteenth in 1985. Combined with multiple open-wheel road course starts at Road America, Cleveland, Mid-Ohio, and Laguna Seca to name a few – not to mention three starts in the 24 Hours of Le Mans, where his team's Porsche finished second in 1984 – Paul had one of the most impressive road course resumes in the field. However, in Winston Cup, this was only his second career start. His debut two months earlier at Pocono resulted in just a thirty-second-place finish after an engine failure well before the halfway point. Another engine let go in qualifying at Watkins Glen, and he had to time in during the second round. He ended up seventh-best among the cars not locked in on Friday. On Sunday, he rolled off twenty-seventh for Irishman Martin Birrane, the sponsor "Longhorn Steaks" stamped in bold white letters across the hood of his perfectly black No. 53 Chevrolet.

One "road ringer" was noticeably absent that August: Tommy Kendall. At Sears Point in June, the late-race incident between Ricky Rudd and Davey Allison was, in part, the result of an earlier battle for the lead between Kendall and Mark Martin. By then, Kendall was already one of the most accomplished road course drivers in the country. Just twenty years old when he won his first of two consecutive IMSA GTU championships in 1986, Kendall broke into Winston Cup in 1987 and three years later finished a career-best eighth at Watkins Glen. When Kyle Petty broke his leg, Kendall was tabbed to drive Petty's fleet No. 42 Mello Yello Pontiac at Sears Point. Kendall started fifth, led twelve of seventy-four laps, and was still out front with just two laps to go. Trying to keep Mark Martin behind him off Turn 7, the two made contact, sending Martin into a spin and cutting down Kendall's left-front tire. Kendall settled for eighteenth, but the team bucked him up in the garage area, saying "next time, we'll lap the field."

Three weeks later, Kendall was at The Glen running the 150-minute IMSA GTP Camel Continental VIII race. The expensive prototype cars pushed the limits more than ever. German driver Bernd Schneider wowed onlookers with his blazing pole lap, his Joest Racing Porsche peaking at 212mph down the long back straightaway. Near the midway point, Kendall was running fourth and following Geoff Brabham through Turn 5 in his Chevrolet Intrepid RM-1 IMSA GTP. A third of the way through the corner, the hub broke on Kendall's left-rear wheel. The car left the course at a point where the Armco barrier drew closer to the track surface, leaving just enough space for the car to complete one full 360-turn as it hurtled toward the tire barriers.

"I was dicing with Brabham," said Kendall in a later interview with Pat Patterson, "and the next thing I know I'm backwards and I saw the background was blurry and I realized how fast I was going, so I said 'Well, shoot, I'm gonna hit something.' And I was gonna hit it backwards, but I didn't, I hit it head-on. Came to rest, and the first thing I thought was I tried to call on the radio and I looked down and saw my legs were not pointed the right way. And I called the radio and said, 'I've broken my legs, send help as quick as you can.'"

Kendall smashed head-on into the tire barriers at over 180mph, shattering both his ankles and breaking his right leg in two places. It took nine hours of surgery, two weeks in the hospital, three months bed rest, and six months of re-habilitation to get him back on his feet. Even today, Kendall calls the wreck "a crossroads in my career."

Kendall's injuries kept him from competing in both the Budweiser at the Glen and its support events, including Saturday's fourth and final round of 1991's International Race of Champions (IROC). On the first lap of the eleven-car race, for which Kendall gave the command to start engines via telephone, Al Unser, Jr. ran high in Turn 5. Unser, Jr.'s yellow Dodge Daytona clipped the grass, quickly switched ends, and bounced off the tire barrier with the passenger side of the car. Uninjured in the wreck, Unser, Jr. returned to the race driving Kendall's car.

Saturday's two other support races were also slowed by accidents in Turn 5. Midway through the Trans-Am event, Jim Stevens' car lost control entering the corner, spun, and smacked the tires so hard with the passenger side of his Ford Mustang that the rear windscreen popped out. The Firestone Firehawk Series event saw Chip Hanower's Toyota lose its brakes entering the corner and spin backwards into the barrier. Both drivers avoided serious injury.

It had been a long couple of days by the time NASCAR's final practice session drew to a close. Frustrated by the sheer number of accidents in Turn 5, NASCAR's Dick Beaty said over the radio, "I'm going to be ill if someone crashes in that turn." He hardly finished the sentence when the No. 98 Banquet Frozen Foods Chevrolet nosed head-on into the tires. The driver, Jimmy Spencer, was uninjured, and the Travis Carter-led crew was able to attach a new nose to No. 98 – one side pop-riveted, the other glued with a strip of Bondo.

From Thursday through Saturday, fourteen drivers had crashed at Watkins Glen. Eight wrecked in the fifth turn.

CHAPTER 12
Green

McDuffie will have to run into a wall to
get any attention.

—*Larry Woody, The Tennessean, February 15, 1987*

Like Morgan Shepherd, J.D. McDuffie had a hard time getting to Watkins Glen. During his long ride north, "Old Blue's" brakes failed, the culprit this time a wheel cylinder on one of the rear wheels. Unable to find parts with just hours until he had to sign-in at the track, McDuffie improvised. He nailed a pop rivet into the brake line. It was risky, but by driving 35mph with limited brakes, he managed to arrive at the track on time. He parked "Old Blue" at the far end of the garage area, the truck completely dwarfed by rows of colorful tractor-trailers. If the weekend went well, it would stay there. He'd be able to afford to get the brakes fixed, or perhaps even repair the air conditioning, the lack of which had kept his wife from traveling with him.

This time, McDuffie had a lot of help waiting for him at the track. Mike Demers was there. Over the next few days, he would update his wife Lesley, who was on a beach trip back in New Jersey. Jerry Glenn brought his son, and both were accompanied by engineer Don Owens. Marty Burke, once a student in Owens' high school shop class, was there to discuss road course strategy for his ARCA debut that was still to be announced. "Colonel" Don Tyndall of Run-A-Bout Auto Sales followed McDuffie to the track in his own car. The Rumples often made it to Watkins Glen, but couldn't make it out that year. Donald Mangum couldn't make it either to hold the pit board. His wife was expecting their first child. To fill the gaps, McDuffie picked up a handful of volunteers at Watkins Glen to help pit the car. One of them was an employee of the L.C. Whitford Company, Inc., a construction firm based out of nearby Wellsville, New York.

* * * *

Sometime on Friday, August 9, a deal was struck where L.C. Whitford would sponsor the No. 70 for the weekend. McDuffie often arrived at the track with the quarter-panels blank just in case such local sponsorship was found. If none came, Burke's "Classic Trophies" logo would fill in the empty space. Today, L.C. Whitford president Brad Whitford still doesn't recall how the agreement came together or who the employee was. But by Saturday, the burgundy Pontiac had two large rectangular "LCW" decals on both sides of the rear end. L.C. Whitford also provided ringer t-shirts and trucker caps to the crew, each the same green-and-white colors as the company's logo.

Though McDuffie was pleased he acquired his first new sponsor in years, he was still reluctant to follow-through with the deal. For years, NASCAR racers believed green to be an unlucky color. Even today, some short track racers won't let their crews use green wire ties under the hood. McDuffie was no exception. During one race at Pocono, a thunderstorm hit, and the race was red-flagged. The crew couldn't find the car cover, so when No. 70 pulled in, someone threw a green blanket over the car. McDuffie made them take it off. "Make sure it didn't go in the pit area," he said. "Get it out of here." And so, No. 70 sat in the rain, unprotected, for more than two hours.

This wasn't McDuffie's only superstition. "No green, no peanuts, and no number thirteen," he said in a 1976 interview. Fifty-dollar bills were also strictly forbidden. "I don't want people around me at the race wearing green, no eating peanuts, and I won't stay in a room with the number thirteen or thirty-one. I started two races in thirteenth position and I wrecked both times."

While the green superstition may have originated in the Indianapolis 500, some NASCAR historians point to a crash that took place during a race at the Langhorne Speedway on September 14, 1952. Years after its demolition, the one-mile track remains one of the most dangerous in the sport's history. The track was a perfect circle, forcing drivers to race in a perpetual four-wheel drift. One of the forty-four set to challenge "The Big Left Turn" that day was rookie Larry Mann in his No. 43 "Green Hornet," a dark green 1951 Hudson Hornet. With less than forty laps to go, Mann's car caught a rut in the dirt surface and flipped several times. The accident left Mann with the dubious distinction as the first NASCAR driver to die in an on-track accident.

Forty years later, corporate sponsors made the color more commonplace on the track. In fact, coming into The Glen, Harry Gant, Ken Schrader, and Kyle Petty had already driven their green cars to victory in a combined four of the season's first seventeen races. It was nearly two years since a NASCAR driver had been killed in a crash, and the No. 22 Oldsmobile that claimed Grant Adcox at the Atlanta

Motor Speedway that day was bright orange. A NASCAR driver hadn't died on a road course since 1967, when Canadian USAC star Billy Foster crashed at the end of a long straightaway during practice at Riverside.

Still, McDuffie held fast to the superstition. Maybe he was mindful that Gant and Schrader had wrecked in practice that weekend, and that Kyle Petty was on his third relief driver. Maybe it was because at Riverside, he nearly crashed in the same place as Billy Foster when a piece of tape on the wiring harness snagged on the throttle cable. But he also knew there weren't any other sponsors waiting to sign on that weekend. McDuffie knew that L.C. Whitford brought some much-needed revenue at a time when he desperately needed it. So, with some reluctance, McDuffie's car carried L.C. Whitford's logos and his team wore the shirts and hats.

* * * *

Despite his concerns, McDuffie enjoyed an uneventful lead-up to the "Budweiser at The Glen." In fact, the car ran faster than it had in a long time. Jerry Glenn had put together a strong motor back at Medford Speed with a brand-new carburetor on it, replacing one McDuffie had been using for at least a decade. The transmission was also new. It originally belonged to Blue Max Racing, the 1989 NASCAR champions with driver Rusty Wallace, who also won Watkins Glen that year. When Blue Max closed its doors early in the 1991 season, Demers and Burke arrived at the shop's Charlotte auction to bid on it. Burke set a $1,000 limit – Demers got it for $950.

The team even figured out an answer to a persistent oiling problem that handed McDuffie two engine failures at The Glen. They discovered the oil pan and pickups were designed only for left-hand turns, which as in The Glen's past, starved the engine on most of the track's right-handers. When replaced with a setup that drew oil from the center, the car ran much faster. So fast, in fact, that on Thursday, he ran faster on a set of used tires than any of his previous races at Watkins Glen.

Most of the following details are paraphrased from Mike Demers' fan club newsletter written after the race:

McDuffie wanted to borrow another set of used tires to qualify with on Friday, but when rain shortened practice, the only way he could get tires was to spend $1,000 on a new set still outside his budget. Then, just before first-round qualifying, Melling Racing came through again, loaning McDuf fie a set of one-lap tires for qualifying. Only then did the team discover that the tires they ran on Thursday were the wrong compound, radials that were designed for ovals and not approved by Goodyear and NASCAR for Watkins Glen. Thus, without any time to change the setup, McDuffie's first laps on the proper radials would come on his qualifying lap. Out on the track, No. 70 pushed hard in The Esses and wasn't able to run twentieth or better, which would have locked them in during the first round. Still, the team felt good that their lap of 114.573mph would get them into the race. McDuffie's team returned Melling's tires and got another set of used rubber from another team. These tires would be used to set up the car in practice on Saturday. That evening, McDuffie and his crew went to the Guthrie Inn at Sayre, Pennsylvania for steak – the driver's favorite.

The team paid. On Saturday, the team woke at 5:30 A.M., had breakfast, and headed out to the track. Some of the crew was already there, cleaning the car which now bore the L.C. Whitford Co. logos. The Glen's garage, located on the inside of Turn 11 near the start/finish line, had entrances on either side such that two rows of cars faced each other. As McDuffie looked over his pre-race checklist, taped to the inside of the lid to his old red toolbox, his No. 70 was surrounded by the cars and crews of Winston Cup regulars Dale Earnhardt, Geoff Bodine, and Dave Marcis, as well as "road ringers" Irv Hoerr and Oma Kimbrough.

Whatever wasn't fixed during the two Pocono races, the crew took care of. They removed the shocks and brought them to the Bilstein company's trailer to be repaired. Then they continued to go over the rest of the car, using the Demers' parts from Son's Auto Supply. The front brake rotors were replaced along with the rear brake pads. The front and rear wheel bearings were inspected and greased. A new oil pump drive belt was added, and so was a new transmission oil pump. They changed the front sway bar, adjusted the chassis, and put the repaired shocks back on the car. The cooling hoses were reconfigured from their Pocono setup to better cool the brakes and the transmission on the road course.

After one practice lap in "Happy Hour," McDuffie was "very satisfied" with the changes and pulled in. The car had good straightaway speed and closed on Terry Labonte's pole winner as the two braked for Turn 5. The team then adjusted the valves and, as always, had the AC Spark Plug representative check the plugs while the engine was hot. The representative recommended leaning out the fuel-air mixture, which was also done. After another single-lap run, the car was still fast and wasn't leaking oil. "We were polishing the air cleaner on the engine because we didn't have nothing to do," recalled Mike Demers.

McDuffie was so pleased with Glenn's engine that he even considered swapping it out for his older one on race day. He told Glenn he wanted to set it aside and use it to qualify for the next few races. Glenn convinced him otherwise. "Don't worry about it," he said. "Put it in there and run it. If it blows, we'll build a better one." So, the Medford engine stayed under the hood of No. 70. McDuffie couldn't have been more excited for Sunday. Later, the team learned he called his wife during the weekend to tell her how well the car was running, something he never did when he was at the track. At least one official also came by to congratulate him on the improvement.

In qualifying, Jim Sauter looked to make his first Watkins Glen start since 1989, when he and road racing specialists Group 44 finished a strong ninth. Auburn, New York driver Jerry O'Neil tried to make his first start of the season in Alan Aroneck's sponsorless No. 65 Oldsmobile. And rising Busch Series star Ed Feree looked to make the first Winston Cup start of his career at his home track. All three drivers were too slow to make the race and left the track early.

But J.D. McDuffie wasn't going home. He wasn't scrambling to fix his car, either. He didn't even participate in second-round qualifying. His first-round lap was good enough to not only make the field for the first time in three weeks, but to start thirty-fifth in the field of forty. In a matter of hours, he'd be making his 653rd Winston Cup race and sixth in a row at Watkins Glen.

So, as night approached on Saturday, August 10, 1991, McDuffie and crew locked No. 70 in the garage area, climbed in their personal cars, and left the track to let off some steam.

CHAPTER 13
Winners Buy

*"I know I can't run up front with the equipment I've got,
but I like to try to get the most out of what I have to work
with. To me, that's the challenge. And who
knows…someday maybe I'll get lucky."*

—J.D. McDuffie, 1985

Today, outside Owego, New York, there's a gravel
mine. But on August 10, 1991, there was a half-mile asphalt
oval known as Shangri-La Speedway.

Since 1946, race fans from upstate New York came to
see everything from unsanctioned stock cars to NASCAR
Modified Series stars Richie Evans and Jerry Cook, now
NASCAR Hall of Fame inductees. Located some forty
miles outside Watkins Glen off Route 17C, Shangri-La had
a special slate of racing on hand this particular Saturday
night, known as the "Night Before The Bud." This time, the
Winston Cup stars were in attendance. Among them was
J.D. McDuffie.

At 3:30 P.M., McDuffie was invited to the track to
come by at six to sign autographs. The meet was arranged
by Scott Haight, a member of the J.D. McDuffie Fan Club.
Haight showed McDuffie the track, and the driver was
greeted warmly by the drivers and fans. "J.D. is in the pits
talking to racers and autographing hats, helmets, shirts, race
cars, tow trucks, and anything else presented to him," recalled Mike Demers in his fan newsletter. "J.D. is laughing
and talking, having a real good time."

The driver arrived that night with Mike Demers, Marty Burke, Jerry Glenn, Sr., Jerry Glenn, Jr., and eight other members of his crew. Demers set up a table at the track to sell fan club memberships and t-shirts. The shirts, produced by J.P. Tees in Philadelphia, carried No. 70 on the back and the "J.D. McDuffie Racing" logo the Demers made for the team's letterhead. The shirts, printed on white, black, blue, and red tees, were also worn by many members of the team, including McDuffie himself. There were plenty of takers among the short track faithful.

The team worked on producing more merchandise for their driver. One artist produced a graphic of McDuffie's No. 70 Pontiac from the front and the side, the driver's name in bold splashed proudly across the top and "Sanford, North Carolina" across the bottom. The design, set against a checkered-flag background, proved so popular that it was printed on seat cushions, caps, hat pins, and shirts made by RSS Motorsports' "Roll'n Shirt Shack" of Naples, North Carolina. To keep up with the many different looks of No. 70, the shirts were printed with the cars either dark blue or bright red.

At the table, McDuffie signed autographs for more than an hour and a half. "J.D. was one of the nicest people around," said Ron Miller, Shangri-La's track announcer. "He talked with kids; stayed late signing autographs. His fan club there received new members. While the crewmen took a helicopter, J.D. drove himself."

Among the fans in attendance was Brent Wentz, whose father Gary was a modified racer also running that night. Brent didn't know who McDuffie was at the time, but still remembers the smell of cigar smoke when he got his autograph. "Gained a fan and memory that night for sure," he said. Years later, Brent would become a crew chief for Penske Racing's Xfinity Series program.

"Since J.D. was not a super star the fans must have found him very approachable, and he never disappointed them," recalled Marty Burke. "We would be out to dinner [and] they would come up [and] ask for his autograph and he would always oblige. The fans always wanted to talk with him as I really believe they thought of him as a blue-collar racer, and many fans related to that. The kids really were more attracted to the stars of the day. J.D.'s fan base was much more of the true racer and race fan."

Joining McDuffie at the track were fellow NASCAR drivers Greg Sacks and Jimmy Spencer, who arrived by helicopter to participate in a Modified race. McDuffie told Mike Demers the open-wheeled cars of the Modified tour looked like fun and hoped to race them some day. Local driver Tim Connelly charged from fifteenth to win the feature. The night's other feature winners were second-year driver Gene Kotary in sports modifieds and Glen Lippolis in late models.

Dale Jarrett was paid to sign autographs by the Mirabito Fuel Group, the night's presenting sponsor, by way of his own sponsor Citgo. And drawing the biggest crowds was Dale Earnhardt, who the track managed to get for two hours. Like McDuffie, Earnhardt arrived with his pit crew, the notorious "Flying Aces," four-time winners of the Unocal 76 Pit Crew Challenge held in Rockingham, North Carolina. The track had something special planned for them.

* * * *

The promoters at Shangri-La arranged a twenty-lap "celebrity race" where members of the "Flying Aces" would compete against a few local drivers in a late model stock car race. Joining three local drivers were Earnhardt's tire changer Scott Cluka, assistant engine builder Danny Lawrence, gasman Danny "Chocolate" Myers, and crew chief Kirk Shelmerdine. As the field rolled around the track, however, none of them noticed that an eighth car had joined the field on the outside of the fourth and final row. Sliding into a blue No. 07 Monte Carlo late model was J.D. McDuffie.

The No. 07 was owned by late model point leader Tom Schwarz, another friend of Scott Haight who'd arranged the meet. Schwarz, who won his heat that night and finished third in the main, had never met McDuffie before then, but the two got along quickly in the garage. "He was a real quiet guy," Schwarz recalled. "Very friendly. He was a short-time friend, but it felt like I knew him better than I did."

For the first time in years, McDuffie had the advantage. He cut his teeth running trophy dashes on forgotten bullrings across the south and returned to his roots whenever he could. On June 17, 1972, the night before he was to run NASCAR's Golden State 400 at Riverside, McDuffie appeared at the Orange Show Speedway in San Bernardino to run a sportsman race. McDuffie finished a close second that night to local driver Jimmy Lee Phillips, but in so doing also finished ahead of two of his fellow NASCAR veterans: Benny Parsons and James Hylton. On May 24, 1982, he finished fifth in a forty-lap late model race at the Pender County Speedway in North Carolina, an event won by inaugural Talladega victor Richard Brickhouse. By that night, he'd earned at least eighty-two victories in racing's lower levels. The "Flying Aces" never stood a chance.

The green flag flew, and McDuffie took off. At the end of the first lap, he rocketed all the way to the lead, taking the top spot from Lawrence. When Cluka's car ran off-track, drawing the first caution, Lawrence pulled along the No. 07. "I pulled up alongside the car which had passed me to see who was driving it. There J.D. was, with a big smile on his face and that cigar in his mouth. I said to myself, 'What's he doing here?' We had no idea he was in the race. Then he checked out on us. He was gone."

McDuffie's car was the class of the field, but he didn't want to show it. Lap after lap, he braked early and throttled back, keeping the other cars close to put on a good race for the fans. "He was all about the fans, not just going out there and trying to show everybody up," recalled Jerry Glenn, Jr. "It was a pretty good race – let me put it this way, he made it *look* good anyway."

On the final lap of the race, McDuffie pulled out ahead of Myers by a couple car lengths and cruised under the checkered flag. In a career marred by so much frustration and adversity, of reduced expectations and of survival, McDuffie had finally won a race – and by all accounts, his first on a paved track. The veteran driver climbed out on the front stretch surrounded by his crew, photographers, and fans. The "Flying Aces" were there to congratulate the veteran as he was handed his Rumple Furniture hat. "He was happy as hell," recalled Myers. "We didn't even know he was racing against us. I remember him up in the truck after the race, that cigar stuck in his mouth and smiling."

"He feels good and looks good," wrote Demers in the newsletter. "Photographers are snapping a hundred pictures and J.D. is shaking a hundred hands. The promoter (Dale Campfield) presents J.D. with a winner's plaque and slides a $100 bill into his hand. It has been a good night for everyone." Just like that, McDuffie was standing in victory lane, the plaque in one hand, the checkered flag in the other. One can only imagine what he was thinking.

"He shined like a star," said Col. Don Tyndall. "In a dark place you could have seen him." "We didn't have a million-dollar car," said crew member Ed Peters. "We had a million-dollar man."

"We had a real good time," McDuffie said over Shangri-La's public address. "I hope I can repeat this tomorrow."

* * * *

Sunday, August 11, 1991 began for McDuffie Racing with a 5:30 A.M. wake-up call in McDuffie and Burke's room. The two met up with Mike Demers and two other crew members and went out to breakfast at the Huddle House restaurant down the street. McDuffie was still smiling. He talked about the night before and was visibly excited for the day's main event. After a big meal, the waiter brought the receipt. Burke and Demers grabbed for the slip of paper, but McDuffie snatched it away. He brought out the $100 bill from the night before.

"Winners buy," said McDuffie.

Burke and Demers always covered expenses – lodging, meals, anything the team needed. But they could tell how much it meant to their boss. So, they didn't protest. The group loaded up, stopped to fill up their coolers with sodas and ice, then headed back to Watkins Glen.

CHAPTER 14
The Race

"Racing is my passion. I just love it. I guess I'll keep doing it until I die."

—*J.D. McDuffie, July 1991*

The morning of August 11th was mild for a late-summer day, just seventy degrees at its warmest. A gentle breeze blew across the front stretch from east to west, fluttering flags atop the concrete stalls behind pit road. By noon, the dark, foreboding clouds that brought so much rain the day before were still there, blanketing the sky in a quilt of grays and whites. Even so, there was only a thirty percent chance of showers hitting the track, and they weren't expected until early evening. The green flag was scheduled for 1:10 P.M. and the race would be over by then.

In the Turn 11 infield, across a road from the garage, fans shopped for souvenirs at two rows of colorful trailers. In the middle of the bustling midway sat at least six show cars, including those of Dale Earnhardt, Rick Mast, Rusty Wallace, Morgan Shepherd, and Davey Allison. Allison, Shepherd, and Wallace's each had a passenger seat installed, allowing VIPs to be driven around the track. Dale Earnhardt's car sat roped-off behind checkered flag banners. Nose-to-nose with No. 3 was the bright yellow No. 33 Duracell Chevrolet Camaro, a backup car belonging to Trans-Am driver Scott Sharp, who cruised to a dominant win at The Glen the previous day. Long-time race fan Don Feeley snapped pictures of the cars, then worked his way down to the gathering crowds at the exit of Turn 1. Back in souvenir alley, sitting in front of the Kodak Film trailer, was a butterscotch-colored No. 4 Chevrolet. Its driver was Ernie Irvan.

Irvan looked forward to the start. With Kodak based in nearby Rochester, he hoped to end a challenging weekend with a win at his sponsor's home track. Irvan blew an engine on Thursday, rolled out last in first-round qualifying, and somehow still pulled out the third-fastest time. He managed to avoid any accidents that weekend and urged his fellow drivers to be cautious with Goodyear's new radial tires. "You just can't get these tires broken loose," he said in an interview Saturday with the *Democrat and Chronicle*. "That doesn't mean they're bad tires, but we've just got to learn their limits...You've got to make sure you don't go past the limit. That's when you wreck."

It raised eyebrows that Irvan was the one urging caution. With two career wins, including the season-opening Daytona 500, the hard-scrabble driver from Modesto, California had a number of fans in the stands, but not many in the garage. The previous year, his spin while trying to unlap himself from leader Ken Schrader at Darlington triggered an accident that critically injured veteran Neil Bonnett. At Talladega in May, Irvan's was one of twenty cars eliminated in another grinding pileup – the same one that fractured Kyle Petty's leg and infuriated team owner Felix Sabates. Two months later, near the halfway point at Pocono, Irvan spun Hut Stricklin during a race for second, starting a wreck that collected eight cars including point leaders Dale Earnhardt and Ricky Rudd. Rudd suggested that NASCAR intervene on behalf of the drivers. Darrell Waltrip said Irvan's

short-track aggression had no place in Winston Cup. Rusty
Wallace threatened to wreck Irvan if he so much as bumped
him.

One week after the Pocono crash, when NASCAR returned to Talladega for the DieHard 500, it all came to a
head. During the driver's meeting on July 28, Irvan walked
up to the podium and apologized to his fellow competitors.
"I want to earn everybody's respect back," he said. "I want
to be liked in the garage area, and I'd appreciate it if you
guys gave me a shot at it." Most in attendance clapped po-
litely. Most, that is, except Wallace.

To Irvan's certain relief, he wasn't the talk of the driver's meeting on August 11th. Instead, everyone was talking
about J.D. McDuffie and his win the night before at Shangri-La Speedway. A photograph taken at the meeting
showed McDuffie sitting next to Mike Demers and talking
with Jimmy Spencer. The outspoken Irvan couldn't help but
give the veteran a good-natured ribbing. "J.D., you smoked
'em last night, didn't you?" he said. "You've been holding
out on us all these years!" McDuffie, wearing his navy
Son's Auto Supply shirt, jeans, and his Rumple Furniture
cap, only laughed.

Irvan knew McDuffie's struggle too well. The aggression for which drivers criticized the Californian was a product of a difficult rise through the ranks. In 1982, Irvan was a
virtual unknown in NASCAR, a local racer who brought
what his trailer could carry to North Carolina to make his
name on the national circuit. He worked odd jobs for years
as a welder and fabricator, earning just enough to run late
models at the Concord Speedway. It wasn't until 1987 that
Irvan made his Winston Cup debut with car owner Marc

Reno, and for another three seasons, he ran near the back with limited sponsorship. The fast No. 4 had been his for barely over a year. Perhaps for this reason, his Morgan-McClure Motorsports team lent McDuffie the set of tires No. 70 practiced with on Saturday.

In the meeting itself, NASCAR's Dick Beaty addressed the issues with Turn 5. "If you go down there in Turn 5 and knock the wall down, we will red flag the race and fix the wall," he said. "And you will miss your flights. I want to go home. But if I've gotta stay, you will, too." The drivers laughed.

* * * *

There wasn't much left to do to the No. 70 that morning. So many parts and pieces had been replaced during the season's two Pocono races, and so many more were added and upgraded for Watkins Glen, that the team only had to look over the car one more time. By 9:30 A.M., the fluids had been checked, the brakes had been bled, and the wheel studs were lubricated. The crew also waxed the car, tightened the wheel nuts, and installed a new radio. Don Owens moved an air duct on the right side of the car. The steering was one of the few parts McDuffie always instructed the crew to leave alone. So, Mike Demers stepped back and took a picture of McDuffie himself using a long socket wrench to tighten the nut on the end of the outer tie rod. The driver also made a mount for the rearview mirror to keep it from vibrating during the race.

Six crew members wearing L.C. Whitford Co. trucker hats and t-shirts pushed No. 70 to the gas pumps and filled the twenty-two-gallon tank. Then they steered it to the inspection queue where NASCAR officials performed a visual check of the carburetor, manifold, fuel cell, and tires. Despite its older body and chassis, the car fit all NASCAR's templates for a 1991 Pontiac Grand Prix and weighed a proper 3,500 pounds.

At 10:00 A.M., the crew pushed No. 70 through the gate separating the garage area from the pits, a string of small checkered flags and Unocal 76 logos threaded through the chain-link. The crew turned the wheel and rolled it onto pit road – the first car out. As fans took pictures of the car, the crew set up their gear in pit stall No. 5. Behind them was the crew for the No. 24 Team III Racing Pontiac of "road ringer" Dorsey Schroeder. In front was Junior Johnson's No. 11 Budweiser Ford for local hero Geoff Bodine. In the past, McDuffie scuffed tires for Johnson. This time, the crew had tires mounted and ready to go. There would be no "rolling around" today.

After the driver's meeting, McDuffie saw his name on a banner on a beam twenty feet in the air and asked Demers who wrote it. McDuffie then stayed in the paddock, relaxing in "Old Blue" for a moment before he changed into his blue-and-white driver's uniform, the same one he wore the night before at Shangri-La. McDuffie acquired the uniform from George Sekanina, a crewman for Ken Schrader's team who got his start turning wrenches at McDuffie Racing. While other NASCAR drivers wore uniforms from American companies like Simpson or Bell, this uniform was leased from Leaf Safety Equipment, based in Sekanina's native Canada.

Marty Burke met McDuffie at the hauler and asked

once more about the green L.C. Whitford shirts and hats. "If you don't want us to wear this, we will not wear this," said Burke. The driver looked back at him, thought, then shook his head. "Nah," said McDuffie. "That's just kind of a silly thing anyway."

* * * *

Heading toward the fifth turn was Terry Letton and his ten-year-old son Jesse. Letton, a department store employee and long-time race fan from Massachusetts, was attending his first NASCAR race. The two scored tickets from Letton's sister, an employee of Olivetti Computer, the Italian technology firm which sponsored both Irv Hoerr's Winston Cup and IMSA Oldsmobiles that weekend. Letton was getting plenty of use out of his Canon T70 camera with a 500mm lens, including a shot of Hoerr's No. 44 as it roared down the backstretch.

Jimmy Means' No. 52, now lined up to McDuffie's left on the grid, also stood out to Letton. "The car looked like it was painted with house paint," he recalled. "You could tell it was not the big-bucks sponsorship." Driving the same Pontiac Bobby Hillin, Jr. ran at Sears Point, Means had also managed to avoid the weekend's accidents. Despite back-to-back transmission failures in the previous two runnings at The Glen, he also had a strong fourteenth-place run in 1988 and was looking for another good finish.

* * * *

Wearing a maroon J.D. McDuffie Fan Club shirt beneath his gray-and-black photographer's vest, Charlie Berch prepared for another day on assignment for *Instant Replay Sporting Photo News*. Two years earlier, Berch and three friends started the paper using a discarded typesetter that now sat in the middle of his mother's living room. With the support of the people of his native Dundee, New York, who paid for advertising space, and his father's news distribution business in Rochester, *Instant Replay* gained a statewide following and more than 200 retailers. Twin brothers on the staff followed Formula One and were credentialed at the Canadian Grand Prix. A college friend studying journalism wrote most of the articles. Berch was the staff photographer, and every August he looked forward to NASCAR's return to The Glen.

Berch first heard about J.D. McDuffie in 1988, when he witnessed firsthand the fire at Daytona. Right away, the aspiring photographer identified with the man from Sanford. "I raced at Dundee," he said. "I had a junk car and I related to the guy. He never caught a break and neither did I."

Like his predecessors, Berch wanted to help at McDuffie Racing and aspired to work his way up the ranks into the pit crew. He soon found out he could also help in other ways, such as producing press kits for the media center. Among the materials in the kits was an *Instant Replay* article by staff writer Paul Long:

Time marches on, but, in his fourth decade of racing, J.D. McDuffie still loves to race. The desire is still there, and, where an all-important sponsorship is concerned, "hope springs eternal." Given the proper financial backing, there is little doubt that John Delphus McDuffie, Jr. can return to the competitive ways he has clearly exhibited in the past. And who knows? J.D. McDuffie's trademark cigar may yet be replaced by a victory cigar.

"J.D. never had anything like that," said Berch. "I thought that was something we could offer to him, so I offered to do and make these press kits, so he could have something to give to the press and in exchange he'd put the name of my newspaper on the back of his car at Watkins Glen in 1990." Berch said he would've made the decals larger if he knew McDuffie's car didn't have any logos on the quarter-panels. Nevertheless, the small yellow print in front of the rear bumper carried McDuffie to his much-needed twenty-second-place finish.

In November 1990, Berch made a trip to Sanford, where the McDuffie family welcomed him to stay for the weekend. There wasn't much to do at the garage. The Childress car, awaiting its new Medford Speed engine for Atlanta, was in the paint shop, receiving another coat of fresh burgundy paint. On Sunday, Berch and McDuffie watched ESPN's broadcast of the NASCAR race in Phoenix, which the No. 70 team decided to skip. As they watched, the McDuffies noticed an advertisement for a contest where if you called in with the name of the leader of the halfway lap, you could win a brand-new Chevrolet. "I remember me and J.D. were joking and said if we got the car we were going to gut it out and throw a roll cage into it and turn it into a race car," said Berch, "and Jean said 'no you're not, that's gonna be my car!' (laughs)."

On the morning of August 11th, Berch was at the track

with his sister Sally. He met up with McDuffie in the paddock. When he noticed Richard Petty and Dave Marcis talking near Petty's trailer, he had an idea. "Hey, J.D., come here for a minute." Berch had McDuffie stand to the left, his right hand on the edge of an oil drum, with Marcis in the middle and Petty to the right. All three smiled as the shutter clicked. "I was gonna put it in a little plaque and say *Albany-Saratoga Speedway, August 1971, NASCAR Winston Cup Top Three Finishers*," said Berch, "I knew he'd never win a race, but I wanted to give him something to commemorate his best-ever finish." The photographer thanked them, told McDuffie "Go get 'em, champ."

Berch knew his way around Watkins Glen better than some of the drivers in the field. He always shot from the same corner, his "money corner," the place where he knew he had a good chance of selling his pictures to other publications. It was there in June that he caught Tom Kendall's crash, a picture which made the cover of an Elmira newspaper and the *National Speed Sport News*. Just twenty-four hours earlier, he sold a picture of Al Unser, Jr.'s wreck during the IROC race.

"I'm just like pumping my fist," Berch remembered, "just loving it – *cha-ching cha-ching* – I'm racking them up."

As with much of his work, the picture of McDuffie, Marcis, and Petty was shot on black-and-white film. But today, the photographer also had several high-quality color slides. With any luck, Berch thought, maybe this time Turn 5 could give him something spectacular enough for *Road & Track*.

* * * *

That same weekend, Berch was coordinating with his friend Janine Pestel, who was shooting for *Area Auto Racing News*. Another long-time supporter of No. 70, Pestel had already made a plaque of her own out of a picture she took of McDuffie at Pocono and that Saturday presented it to the driver. When a worker at the Ford souvenir stand took notice, he offered to help sell the plaques trackside as soon as she could make them. "We'll put it on the trailer," the man told her, "but when you do, bring it to me, don't bring it to my boss, because he won't allow it because he doesn't drive a Ford, he drives a Pontiac. But J.D.'s a good guy and all of that and I wanna help." When told of the plan, McDuffie only wanted ten percent, but she insisted he take twenty-five.

The Ford man also gave her another idea to turn her photographs into postcards to hand out to fans, much as teams do today. That morning, she worked out the design. On one side would be a short biography of McDuffie written by Berch, similar to the work he'd done on the press kit. Pestel would handle the graphics on the other side – a shot of No. 70 next to a picture of J.D. himself. She liked the picture she used in the plaque but wanted to try something different for the postcard. And so, minutes from the start of the race, she stood next to Row 18, waiting for McDuffie to arrive.

McDuffie and Mike Demers walked out to the grid, where the rest of the field was now lined up two-by-two. On the way, a fan named Gary Westfall handed Demers a hat

over the fence. Gary asked for McDuffie to sign it and make
it out to his wife Kathy, whose sister JoAnn also lived in
Sanford and introduced her to J.D. He obliged, signing it in
black pen. He handed it back to Demers, who gave it to
Gary. McDuffie accidentally spelled his wife's name
"Cathy." She didn't care. She clutched the hat tightly as she
and her husband took their position at their infield camper,
the one with the big "Go J.D., No. 70" sign on one side.
Demers said "Thanks, J.D., I'll talk to you later" and
grabbed his radio – it was his turn to be crew chief again.

Just as McDuffie prepared to climb into his car, Pestel
stepped in. "J.D., I need a picture of you," she said. "What
for?" asked the driver. "None of your business yet, just shut
up and smile." With that, she stooped down and aimed her
medium-format camera upward. J.D. smiled, staring across
pit road in the direction of Turn 5. She took two shots, finishing the roll of film. Then the crew stepped in.

Ed Peters served as the front tire changer. He helped
McDuffie climb into No. 70. "I told him to run 100 (miles
per hour) and win the race for us," he recalled. Once inside,
the driver put on his white open-faced helmet and bubble
goggles. Under his seat, he found his glasses which he lost
at Pocono three weeks earlier. Within view of No. 70, another McDuffie banner appeared from the stands on the
other side of the track. Chico Reyes, the jack man, stuck his
head in the window. McDuffie pulled his hair. The two
laughed. "He pulled my hair, every race," said Reyes, a
friend of McDuffie's son Jeff. "It was a tradition. It was
kind of like we'd put the window-net up and shove my head
in there and he'd pull my hair and off he'd go. He did it the
night we won at Shangri-La."

Ed and Chico were among the thirteen men and women on hand to pit No. 70. That day's full crew list, posted and re-printed by Mike Demers, was as follows:

front tires	Ed	New York
rear tires	Marty	Pennsylvania
jack	Chico	Pennsylvania
carry tires	Don	Pennsylvania
driver service	Bradley	Maryland
lap times and gas computation	Doug	Ontario, Can.
scorer	Lisa	New York
gas	Harold	Pennsylvania
catch	Kelley	Pennsylvania
second can	Jerry Jr	New Jersey
sign	Jerry	New Jersey
run gas	Cliff	Pennsylvania
chief	Mike	New Jersey

Marty Burke spoke to McDuffie one more time, going over their strategy for the race: take it easy for the first few laps, then in the final stages pick our way up to twentieth, maybe even fifteenth. This was no mere boasting. "It was the most prepared we'd ever been for a race," said Burke.

Mike Demers and McDuffie tested the team's radios. "Mike, can you hear me?" asked McDuffie. "Loud and clear, J.D."

Then came the command to fire engines.

* * * *

With James Taylor's "Traffic Jam" played over old racing footage, ESPN's television broadcast kicked-off just before 1:00 P.M. The forty starters idled on the grid, waiting for the signal from officials to enter the course.

Reporting for the network from pit road, Dr. Jerry Punch summed up a weekend of "injured stars and injured cars." He stood behind Dave Marcis' Darlington car as it warmed up in twentieth, then moved one row back to point to the repairs made on Ricky Rudd's Chevrolet. Behind pit wall, fellow reporter John Kernan discussed the road course debut of Goodyear's radial tires. Kernan said drivers still weren't sure how hard the radials could be pushed at Watkins Glen because rain had curtailed practice. During the segment, ESPN's camera man filmed Kernan through the center hole of a replacement wheel staged in McDuffie's pit.

For the road courses, ESPN's trackside reporting wasn't limited to pit road. Lead announcer Bob Jenkins stood by himself in the press box on the main straightaway. To help catch whatever action his cameras might miss, Jenkins' two color analysts came up with the idea of staging themselves at key passing zones. ESPN's producer Neil Goldberg agreed, and the feature became a signature of the network's road course coverage. During the pace laps, both analysts introduced themselves from high atop the track's forty-foot spotter's stands.

First to speak was Benny Parsons, the same driver who Bobby Hudson worked for in 1973. Parsons was cut from the same cloth as McDuffie, born in the small town of Ellerbe, less than fifty miles south-west of Sanford. A Detroit taxi driver as a youngster, Parsons worked his way up the racing ranks from local short tracks to ARCA and Winston Cup. He'd go on to claim the 1973 Winston Cup championship and the 1975 Daytona 500. Parsons continued to help McDuffie after he left the DeWitt team. In 1980, he put an engine in No. 70 that got McDuffie into a race at Talladega. After his racing career, Parsons eased smoothly into his new life as a color commentator for ESPN. His outgoing nature and excitable personality were a boon to ESPN, which organized pre-recorded segments to emphasize his playful side. The Watkins Glen broadcast would include new episodes of both "Buffet Benny" and "The Hat of the Week."

On this day, Parsons was stationed on the outside of Turn 1, just before the exit of pit road. "I'm in my favorite place on the race track, Turn 1," said Parsons as McDuffie rolled onto the track behind him. "Terry Labonte on the pole will be coming down through here up to 140mph, braking – slowest part of the race track – down to 65mph. A good place to pass if the fella on the outside knows you're there. If he doesn't, you're in big trouble."

Next was Ned Jarrett, another former NASCAR champion turned broadcaster. "Gentleman Ned" had retired at the peak of his career in 1966, and in the decades that followed became a fixture on television and radio. The eldest member of the ESPN group, his was the quieter, more studied voice in the booth, breaking down the intricacies of a sport he'd seen change over three decades. Like Parsons, Jarrett was also a McDuffie supporter. In fact, one of the first cars the Sanford man drove, a blue 1961 Ford, was given to him by Jarrett. The two struck up a friendship then, and no matter what network he worked for, Jarrett found time to meet and talk with McDuffie in the garage area.

McDuffie was also Jarrett's favorite guest on "Ned Jarrett's World of Racing," a radio program he put together on

MRN each Thursday. "He was just very straightforward and, you know, had a very dry wit about him," Jarrett recalled. "He was not the – how should I put this – not the most fluent interview that you have ever done, but he was so genuine...so I had him on my show fairly often just because I enjoyed talking to him and the fans told me they enjoyed the interviews we did with him."

On top of his live television and radio duties, Jarrett was also preparing segments for "Inside Winston Cup Racing," a television program that aired on TNN. At 10:30 A.M. on the morning of August 11, Jarrett recorded "Inside's" opening segment overlooking the front stretch. "There was a lot of excitement here this past weekend," said Jarrett, anticipating the race to come. "Some drivers had some trouble negotiating the turns here."

Jarrett's post for the race itself was Turn 5, standing atop another wooden tower. The tower stood behind the tire barriers, on the opposite side of the track from Berch, the Lettons, and the rest of the crowd in the infield. This time, Jarrett spoke more candidly about the weekend's accidents. "If you get in trouble here, it's big-time trouble," he said as the cars rumbled by behind him. "Most of that trouble that happened you fellas talked about happened right here in Turn 5. But, after that much trouble in the days leading up to a race, it seems like the guys calm down a little bit. Let's hope that'll be the case today."

As ESPN went to commercial, the field continued behind the Ford F-150 pickup that would serve as the race's "pace car." With Ford as one of The Glen's presenting sponsors that weekend, the truck featured Ford's black-on-black "Nite" appearance package, introduced the previous year. Carrying two photographers who sat in the bed facing the field, the truck led the cars slowly down pit road.

A pit road speed limit was one of the latest rule changes for 1991. The sanctioning body's hand was forced following a series of disastrous pit road accidents, culminating in the tragic death of Michael Rich. Rich was changing Bill Elliott's tires at Atlanta when he was struck by a spinning Ricky Rudd, pinning him between the two cars. NASCAR's first proposal for the season-opening Daytona 500 didn't involve a speed limit at first, but instead a ban on pit stops under caution. A blue or orange sticker with a white "1" or "2" was handed to each driver before the race. The sticker determined which of the first two green-flag laps after a caution their team could pit. Since the rule forced drivers to restart the race with worn tires, crashes and confusion ran rampant. It wasn't until the seventh race of the season that a pit road speed limit was introduced. The limit varied by track and the size of pit road. Watkins Glen's was one of the slowest – just 35mph.

That weekend at The Glen, NASCAR also debuted its own mascots. The "NASCUBS," a cadre of anthropomorphic animals in driver's uniforms, were each matched with a lesson for young fans. Towering over the billboards behind the entrance to Turn 2 was a giant inflatable "Rocky," a grinning teddy bear whose message was "safety must come first, both on and off the track."

Before the start, Davey Allison surrendered his ninth starting spot. On top of his injured hand and rebuilt car, the throttle linkage on his Ford was now freezing up. The issue arose immediately after the command to start engines, so the Robert Yates Racing crew had to lift Allison's hood and make repairs as the field drove around them on pit road. One lap and one pit stop later, Allison returned to the track as the field lined up two-by-two.

After a second pace lap and ESPN's run-through of the starting lineup, Terry Labonte and Mark Martin addressed the starter's stand for a rolling start. At that moment, Davey Allison was running last coming into Turn 9, trying to catch the field as it drew away from him. Flagman Doyle Ford waved the green, and the Budweiser at The Glen was underway.

* * * *

As the field accelerated across the starting line, the leaders spread out four and five wide from third on back. On the inside, closest to the pit road wall, Wally Dallenbach, Jr. looked to make a move on Ernie Irvan, and was himself throwing a block on Dorsey Schroeder. To the outside, Mark Martin had to contend with Geoff Bodine and Ken Schrader. All of them followed Terry Labonte into "The Ninety" at Turn 1. The leaders came off the corner two-abreast, then funneled down to single-file trailing Labonte on the uphill march through "The Esses" of Turns 2, 3, and 4. Already, Labonte and Martin began to gap themselves from the rest of the field.

Meanwhile, at the back, six cars had already started to lose touch with the rest of the field. The group was led by fortieth-place starter Michael Waltrip, who by the exit of Turn 1 had already drawn to the inside of McDuffie in a battle for thirty-fourth. Five car lengths behind McDuffie was Jim Derhaag's No. 54 with fellow "road ringer" Kim

Campbell behind him in the No. 20 NAPA Oldsmobile. Two car lengths behind thirty-seventh-place Campbell was the red No. 13 Buick of Oma Kimbrough. In the first five laps, the trailing Davey Allison would catch and pass them all, climbing all the way up to twenty-eighth position. The first car he caught trailed this six-car pack by over two seconds: the No. 71 of Dave Marcis.

Prior to the start, Marcis had voluntarily surrendered his twentieth-place starting spot and joined Allison at the rear of the field. By the end of Lap 1, Marcis' Darlington car had lost so much time to the rest of the field that he was completely by himself, his Chevrolet so slow in Turns 1 and 2 that it seemed to have lost an engine. In reality, Marcis' Darlington transmission wasn't designed for the frequent gear-shifting of road course racing. Trying to do so resulted in a terrible vibration. To avoid losing another car with eleven races still to go in 1991, Marcis planned to pull out in the early laps. Failing another on-track incident, the result would be Marcis' first last-place finish in more than two years.

On Lap 3, Irv Hoerr's experimental Oldsmobile was holding down fifteenth, but something was wrong. Heading through Turns 2 and 3, No. 44 Oldsmobile started trailing white smoke from behind the left-front wheel. Slight damage to the upper part of the front valence seemed to point to an overheating problem caused by contact, but Hoerr later reported it was oil "blowing out the breathers on the engine." The smoke worsened as Hoerr slowed on Lap 4, the back half of the field maneuvering around him down the backstretch. Pit road was still more than a mile away.

When Hoerr's car started smoking, J.D. McDuffie had just been passed by Allison, moving him back to thirty-seventh. Heading through the Esses, No. 70 trailed Allison's No. 28 by a full second, allowing Derhaag to close his No. 54 Oldsmobile to McDuffie's rear bumper. For the next two laps, Derhaag pondered what move he should take around the burgundy Pontiac. McDuffie, meanwhile, had caught the next car Allison had passed – thirty-sixth-place Jimmy Means.

"I couldn't shake him (J.D.)," said Means. "He was running really well, and I don't remember where we qualified in that deal, I just couldn't shake him, he was running pretty hard and I just couldn't get away from him, that's how well he was running. Not that I was, I don't know how well I was running but I just couldn't shake him. So, thought I could get away from him but I couldn't, he was dogging me. Like I said, we independents, we race each other hard."

As Means, McDuffie, and Derhaag sailed down the backstretch on Lap 5, the group had passed the ailing No. 44 of Irv Hoerr, moving them to thirty-fifth, thirty-sixth, and thirty-seventh. McDuffie made his move first, steering toward the middle of the track to fill Means' mirror. Derhaag saw an opening to pass on the inside. A risky move, but possible. Whoever braked last and caught traction first would get the spot. But right when Derhaag was about to turn right and make a pass, something stopped him.

"I don't mean to sound goofy," said Derhaag, "but it's always like I've had this little angel on my shoulder telling me what to do and what not to do. Something just didn't look right." So, he backed off.

Then he spotted smoke coming from the left side of McDuffie's car.

* * * *

That same lap, ESPN's broadcast held on the roof camera of Dale Jarrett's No. 21 Citgo Ford, which ran just outside the Top Ten. Bob Jenkins relayed the real-time data from the computerized telemetry box displayed on the lower-right of the screen. Jarrett's top speed came on the backstretch – 174mph – then slowed to 86mph at corner apex. Jarrett accelerated into Turn 9 and slipped at corner exit, losing a spot to Brett Bodine's No. 26 Quaker State Buick. Then his father Ned broke in.

"And there's trouble! *Big* trouble here in Turn 5!"

CHAPTER 15
Witness To Disaster

"He hit me in the side, like someone coming up to you and punching you in the arm."

—*Jimmy Means, on the collision*

One moment, Jimmy Means was slowing to enter Turn 5. The next, something struck the right-front of his car, and he was sliding downhill through the grass. He saw McDuffie's Pontiac in front of him, skidding sideways as it neared the tire barriers. There was no time for either of them to slow down. He saw McDuffie's car hit the tires broadside and begin to flip. Then he slammed head-on into the wall of black. There was a loud crash, then silence.

It took a moment for Means to get his bearings. He soon realized he could breathe, could move, and looked for a way out. In front of him, the upper-left corner of the glass windshield had shattered, and all he could see were loose tires from the barrier closed around the nose of his car. No. 52 had wedged itself beneath the tire barrier all the way to the firewall. Beyond his view, the nose of the car had hit so hard that a length of blue Armco barrier had broken away and now protruded rudely from behind the catchfence.

With more tires pressed against the driver's window, Means looked to his right, toward the open passenger window. He stuck his head out and saw there still wasn't much room. Right next to him, close enough to grab it as he climbed out, was the underside of McDuffie's No. 70. The car had landed upside-down facing the track, just inches away from his.

Once free, Means crouched down between the cars, and peered inside the passenger side window. "I tried to talk to him (McDuffie), but he was unconscious," said Means. "There wasn't a mark on him, no blood." But something was clearly wrong. He wasn't moving, and his helmet was halfway up his ears. Means sprung to his feet and called for help, waving his arms and pointing at the upturned No. 70. Two track workers were already climbing over the damaged fence. The workers looked inside. Then they signaled to the approaching trucks.

* * * *

Back in Sanford, Ima Jean McDuffie was horrified. She, along with ESPN's viewers, saw the wrecked No. 70 upside-down, smoking, motionless in Turn 5. "I saw him turn over and I knew it was bad," she said. "I saw the number and said, 'Oh, Lord, that's J.D.' I started screaming, and I screamed all day."

Ned Jarrett, whose broadcasting post was barely fifty feet from the crash site, struggled to piece together what had just happened. "Bob, there are two cars," he said on-air, "that they came in here so fast, and one of them did hit the other one and, uh, did get upside-down. Both of them hit very, very hard." When Jimmy Means climbed out to check on McDuffie, the camera pulled back. A replay followed, shot from Ned Jarrett's post behind the Turn 5 barriers.

As the camera moved right to catch it, McDuffie's car raced straight off the track at more than 160mph, the nose aimed directly at the tire barriers on the other side of the grassy run-off area. At the same time, a black object appeared several feet above the car, trailing its own wisp of smoke. "Where in the world did that wheel come from?" asked Benny Parsons. Somehow, before the cameras caught it, McDuffie's entire left-front wheel assembly had ripped itself away from the suspension. The wheel was now several feet above and in front of the car, plummeting toward the barrier. It got there first. The heavily damaged fender of No. 70 dug deep into the grass, steering the car hard to the left. When the car dug in a second time, the passenger side was nearly parallel to the tire barriers. McDuffie's right-front hit first, then the right-rear an instant later. The impact pushed the tires, then the Armco against the catchfence, knocking down at least one of its support posts. Unsecured, a length of fence flopped outward from the impact site. Tires from the barrier scattered in all directions.

Jimmy Means must have started braking before impact. By the time contact forced him off the track, McDuffie was already several feet in front of him. Once on the grass, Means' brakes were useless. His No. 52 was now locked in a high-speed four-wheel slide with the left-front of his Pontiac aimed directly at McDuffie's sideways machine. By the narrowest of margins, the two cars avoided a second collision – but only because No. 70 was in mid-air. The passenger-side impact caused McDuffie's car to roll to the right as it rose several feet through a cloud of smoke. The car pivoted on the rear decklid, still held up by the tires, and landed upside-down next to Means.

During commercial, ESPN replayed the wreck one time at full speed. From the moment McDuffie's car entered the frame to the moment it stopped, the slow-motion replay took fifteen seconds. In real-time, it took less than three.

* * * *

Also watching the race was Lesley Demers. Her mother had come by that morning to watch the race with her at their New Jersey home.

"I can remember being excited as the race began and then the accident came," said Lesley in her cover letter to the August 1991 Fan Club Newsletter. "How thankful I was that my mother was with me. Even as an adult, nothing seemed more comforting than being consoled by your mother. My telephone began ringing off the hook with everyone calling to see if I knew anything. Deep inside I suspected the accident was worse than they were reporting."

Later, when Marty Burke's wife Judy called, she knew.

* * * *

"J.D., there's a full-course yellow."

Mike Demers released the button on his radio. No answer. He looked to his left as Doyle Ford waved the yellow flag from his perch on the flag stand at the top of the hill, then watched the slowing cars as they passed under him. At first, Demers wasn't concerned. McDuffie hadn't said a word those first five laps. He only ever keyed the radio if something was wrong with the car – a flat tire, a blown engine, a bent fender, something the crew could fix by the time he came around. But No. 70 didn't come by. Demers tried the radio again. This time, he heard someone's voice, but there was so much interference that he wasn't sure if it was his driver.

Barry Dodson, the crew chief for Dorsey Schroeder's No. 24, was standing in the next pit stall to the crew's left. Moments after the caution, he relayed a radio message from Schroeder to a nearby Marty Burke: McDuffie had crashed and was on his roof. The wreck was serious, but none of McDuffie's crew had any way of knowing if their driver was hurt. Turn 5 was well out of view of pit road, and neither the crews nor most of the spectators had access to the television broadcast.

* * * *

As the field rolled slowly under caution, Jim Derhaag replayed the wreck in his mind. The moment he braked in Turn 5 and saw smoke from McDuffie's left-front wheel, No. 70 kept going at full speed, instantly closing his gap between he and Jimmy Means, who was also slowing for the corner. The two hit and slid off the track so quickly that the rest of the wreck disappeared from Derhaag's periphery as he made the corner. When Derhaag came by on Lap 6, he looked at the accident scene. "We came around the next time and I saw the corner workers and safety workers, and everyone was just standing there."

The sight brought back a terrible memory from Derhaag's Trans-Am days. On November 8, 1987, he was racing Jim Fitzgerald for position in the fifty-lapper on the street course in St. Petersburg, Florida. The sixty-five-year-old Fitzgerald was a popular veteran who that year teamed with actor-turned racer Paul Newman in Newman-Sharp

Racing's fleet Nissan 300ZX Turbos. Heading into Turn 1 on the third lap, Fitzgerald clipped the wall with his left-rear. The veteran's No. 38 spun, then smacked a concrete barrier flush with the passenger side. Fitzgerald was killed instantly. "I had no inkling with Fitz at all," Derhaag recalled. "Sometimes the most simple things can end up with huge tragic results."

Then a voice came over the radio. "They're gonna go red." It was Derhaag's crew chief on pit road. The driver keyed his microphone. "How do you know?" The crew chief answered him flatly. "They're gonna go red."

Derhaag heard the same thing in 1987.

* * * *

By the time Ned Jarrett caught sight of McDuffie's car, it was already speeding through the grass, the wheel sailing through the air. He knew McDuffie and Means, knew it was unlikely they had deliberately wrecked each other due to how much both needed to conserve their equipment. Something must have broken on one – or both – of the cars.

Once NASCAR officials stopped the remaining thirty-eight cars on the front stretch, Jarrett climbed down from his post overlooking the scene and spoke with a dazed Means. The driver had cut his chin in the accident, and there were large blotches of red blood on the chest of his white uniform.

"Yeah, Ned, I don't know what happened," said Means, scratching his head. "I've been looking – J.D.'s been in my mirror the whole time and I was kind of watching him. He was running really good, and I don't know he came in there, lost his brakes or what, but next thing I knew he hit me in the side. I hope he's all right, you know, he took a pretty bad lick there. So, I'm fine. But I don't know about J.D."

"Whether he (Means) knew at that time whether J.D. had lost his life, I don't know," said Jarrett later. "I didn't specifically ask him that question because we hadn't been told, I wasn't sure. I thought it, but I didn't...I handled it more on a friendship basis than a hard reporter style."

After the interview, Ned looked back over the crash scene. Countless bits of debris lay scattered in the wet grass. Ahead of him, eight other emergency and track vehicles had arrived on the scene. McDuffie was still in the car, and paramedics now peered through the driver's window. Moments later, several other corner workers in orange vests brought out large white sheets and stretched them at chest level, keeping the paramedics' work out of view of the fans on the other side of the track. Jarrett thought about checking on McDuffie. But the white sheets made him think better of it.

"I told our producer, Neil Goldberg, that I was going back up to my position because there was nothing else I could do," recalled Jarrett. "One of the workers on the scene overheard me and said, 'No, there's nothing else you can do here.' And that's when I had a feeling J.D. was dead."

* * * *

ESPN's Dr. Jerry Punch didn't have access to his network's video feed, either, but he could hear Jarrett's report from Turn 5, as well as traffic from NASCAR officials. He checked No. 70's radio frequency – nothing. Then his producer broke in.

"What have they heard? What have the crew heard? You better get that report."

Dr. Punch shared his producer's concern but didn't want to say there was no communication with McDuffie without some explanation. "I don't wanna make people afraid," he told him. "I don't want people to start thinking the worst."

"Well, just give the report and explain that sometimes radios don't work." Dr. Punch knew in-car radios did cut off frequently, particularly on a road course which tested the limits of their range. In that moment, he was also reminded of the accident that injured Kyle Petty that May, and that one of the hits disconnected the head-hugger plug on his radio.

While this was happening, one of McDuffie's crewmen pointed to the garage area. "We're gonna go back to the garage area and hang out until they bring the car back and we'll see what we gotta fix and load it up." But as Jarrett and NASCAR continued to talk about the accident, Dr. Punch intervened. "No, you need to get to the medical center. You need to go over there. And don't be hanging out in the garage area – you need to go to the medical center." The crewman looked at him. "Really?" Dr. Punch nodded. "Yeah." Among those headed to the infield care center were Marty Burke and Mike Demers.

Not long after they left, Dr. Punch came on camera from McDuffie's pit, where the gasman and four crew members in L.C. Whitford Co. gear stood by. One of the men had removed his hat. With little to no information coming in, Dr. Punch did his best to soothe concerns by focusing on the radio issue.

"Now, as you see, the crew members who work on J.D.'s crew week in and week out are not here, they've already left to go back to the garage area to check on J.D. McDuffie's condition," said Dr. Punch. "Now, they have radioed to J.D. a couple times after the accident and not heard back from him. That doesn't mean that J.D. is injured – it doesn't mean anything at all. In fact, if you remember back at Talladega, when they had the major pile-up in May, the crew for Kyle Petty couldn't talk to Kyle because Kyle's radio had come unconnected which is not uncommon with an impact back on the race track, and they thought he was more seriously injured than he was, and they were, of course, afraid. But the crew here unable to talk to J.D., so they have left the pit area and headed back to the garage area to try and get more information. We'll let you know when we hear more from down here."

* * * *

Back in the paddock, Jimmy Means' crew finished towing their pit cart to the garage, ready to repair No. 52. The car wasn't there yet. Neither was the driver. Quietly, Means had gathered his family, climbed in their van, and left the track.

CHAPTER 16
Holding Pattern

> *"I do remember going down through there before com-*
> *ing in the pits seeing J.D.'s car upside-down and think-*
> *ing it was pretty bad, but I was having so many issues I*
> *was just thinking of my issues."*

—*Irv Hoerr, 2016*

In the grandstands and campgrounds of Watkins Glen, time seemed to stop. Some fans were still drinking with friends, cans of Budweiser and Genesee Light stacking up in the grass. But even those fans were quieter than usual.

Not far from the finish line, seventeen-year-old Marc Cashman walked back from a concession stand, a Nestle Crunch bar in one hand and his race scanner in the other. He could tell something was wrong. Normally, his scanner would pick up a near-constant stream of communications between drivers and officials. But now they'd all but stopped. The few messages he heard seemed to be in code. "Bring those two trucks to Bravo," said a voice.

Marc rejoined his father Jim behind Turn 6, the spot they'd picked every year since 1987. The two arrived on Thursday, went to "Morgan Shepherd Day" in Montour Falls, and camped out through the rainy weekend. The Cashmans were Bill Elliott fans, but both also rooted for J.D. McDuffie. The two saw J.D. at Michigan the previous year, having sneaked into the garage area during a rain delay. They walked by Kyle Petty, idly throwing gum on the ceiling of the garage, and said "Hi" to Elliott, who was reading the paper. Then they saw "Old Blue," and McDuffie standing next to it, waiting to return to the track. Jim owned a t-shirt with McDuffie's blue Rumple Furniture car on the front, but during the red flag at Watkins Glen, he wasn't wearing it. He wasn't saying much, either.

"Unfortunately, you knew it was bad because when you heard they were using like a white tarp up right by the accident scene," Marc recalled. "We were both shocked, but I guess after a while in racing you kind of have to accept it. I mean, back in his (my father's) day Jimmy Clark was his favorite guy back then a long time ago. He was more accepting of it, you know, it was racing. It's just something back then at the time those cars were as safe as they could be. But I don't really recall what he thought about it."

The next day, the two drove past a hospital, wondering if that was where McDuffie had been taken. "It was a quiet ride home for a little while."

* * * *

After his report from McDuffie's pit, Dr. Jerry Punch went up to NASCAR's scoring tower. Back in 1991, the tower was a far cry from today's booths with live scoring, streaming video, and dozens of officials. Just two people stood sentinel with their radios, each with little to go on beyond Ned Jarrett's reports. But the reporter could tell something was wrong just by the looks on their faces. "You could see how visibly upset they were, and how much they cared," said Dr. Punch.

NASCAR's officials were also at a loss as to what to do, should the reports truly be as bad as they sounded.

"Fortunately, they weren't really good in that situation because it hadn't happened very often," said Dr. Punch. Unfortunately, this meant that even the officials weren't sure how to handle calling McDuffie's family, or how to tell the drivers and fans. "You've got these drivers – the race just started, it's like five or six laps – these drivers gotta get back in the car and try and go past that spot for the next two and a half hours knowing that one of their colleagues is gone because of a wreck there. And so how do they handle that?" Dr. Punch raised the issue of New York law, that when a fatal auto accident happens in the state, the county coroner is required to do a full investigation, which could require the track to shut down for two days.

"How do we get this information to the drivers without everyone else hearing?" an official asked Dr. Punch. "They need to know, because they're gonna be the ones interviewed."

The reporter had a solution. "Well, we're gonna be the ones talking to them."

* * * *

The silence was getting to Janine Pestel. "How bad is it?" she asked the person next to her, holding a scanner. "It's really bad," he answered. "NASCAR just went to their private channel."

Then another photographer walked up to her. "I think her name was Joanne, and I wanted – I swear to God I wanted to punch her in the face when she said this to me...but she looked right at me and goes, 'You like J.D., don't you?' and I said 'Yes,' and she said 'You realize he's probably dead, right?' And I just glared at her. I wanted to rip her throat out. But I realize what she was telling me was 'You're in the media. This happens. Get used to it.'"

* * * *

Out on the front stretch, the remaining drivers had climbed from their cars. Some talked with each other. Others talked with Dr. Jerry Punch and John Kernan, much as they did during rain delays. With so few laps complete, many drivers didn't have much to say about how their race was going or how their cars were performing. This must have been a challenge to Punch and Kernan, who, like the drivers themselves, were looking to distract from a crash whose reality was becoming clearer with each passing minute. Kernan was about to talk to Sterling Marlin when an ambulance sped by in the background. It passed again when Dr. Punch talked with Terry Labonte. Davey Allison and Dale Jarrett both verbally expressed concern for McDuffie and Means.

Seven interviews into the delay, during the next commercial break, Bob Jenkins in the booth checked with Ned Jarrett in Turn 5, wondering why the track workers hadn't turned McDuffie's car right-side up. Jarrett said he didn't have any new information from the scene – the car was still upside-down, the sheets were still up, and by all accounts, the driver was still inside. Eighteen vehicles now sat at the crash site, including a backhoe and a second ambulance. None were moving.

John Kernan's fourth and fifth interviews were with Michael Waltrip and Dave Marcis, both still smarting after their hard crashes on Saturday. Waltrip, who now planned to run the rest of the race, weighed in on the radial tires. "I hate to hang (my wreck) on that, because we'll come back here next year and beyond and say 'why did we ever have a problem with that' 'cause you get used to that. But, my situation a few people crashed, and I was tip-toeing into the corners and really being careful and never dreamed I'd wreck and when I was on the way off of one of the corners, I hit a curb and when the radials lose traction, they're more susceptible to spinning out than a bias-ply."

Dave Marcis was concerned about the safety of the barriers. "I'm not sure. There's a controversy on the tires – are they good or aren't they, but certainly they help cushion it. But I think everyone's concern is everyone that has hit the wall this week, even with the tires in front of it, the wall has given way behind it. So, our question is – is the *wall* really safe? I mean, even with the tires supporting it in front, it's still been extensive damage to the wall every time it's been hit this week." Kernan quickly moved on.

Between these interviews, many of the drivers were told the seriousness of the situation.

* * * *

Terry Letton didn't see the accident. He and his son Jesse were four rows deep behind the crowd standing at the entrance to Turn 5. When the red flag came out, the crowd in front of the Lettons began to move away quietly, and the two inched closer to the fence. Letton readied his camera, but when he got a clear shot, there still wasn't much to see. The wreck was downhill and to the right, and a number of track and emergency vehicles now blocked what little could be seen. He couldn't even tell who had crashed. But he knew something wasn't right.

"You knew it was bad, you knew it wasn't just bending up cars, which even in those days NASCAR was pretty damned safe, I mean, they would bend up a lot of sheet metal but, you know, guys would pop out and be fine," Letton recalled. "It was not safe by current standards, but it was pretty safe, you didn't expect people to get killed. It didn't happen that often."

Then he noticed a young man running up the track toward the scene.

"For some reason, I got the impression it was his son. I have no idea if that's true or not, but it was just a sad moment seeing him running up there, 'cause I gather he was if not his son somebody pretty closely involved with J.D., you know, that was a heart-wrenching moment. I was kind of wishing my son wasn't there at that point and time." Jeff McDuffie wasn't at the track. The man Letton saw was the L.C. Whitford employee on McDuffie's crew. Following him to the scene was *Instant Replay* photographer Charlie Berch.

In the opening laps, Berch caught a picture of McDuffie negotiating Turn 5, then felt the film roll retract in his camera. As the leaders came around again, he yanked out the roll, dropped in the slides, and aimed his lens back at Turn 5. To his excitement, the "money corner" paid off again. At the first sign of trouble, he clicked the shutter five times, capturing the wreck from start to finish. He then zoomed closer and took another two as Jimmy Means climbed from his car. When he did, he realized it was McDuffie who was upside-down. Berch's excitement passed, replaced by a gathering dread.

"I've seen a lot of guys wreck," said Berch, "and you're just waiting for him to get out, and Jimmy Means climbs out of his car and he starts waving his arms like panicking, like in a panicked state to get over there. I'm like 'man, I hope he isn't hurt that bad.'" More time passed, and no one climbed out of No. 70. Instead, another car showed up. A police car for the Schuyler County Sheriff. Berch knew what it meant. *Oh my god, that's the coroner.*

It was. At 1:20 P.M., Schuyler County Coroner Dr. Alaud Din was called at his Mountour Falls office to come to the track. According to Dr. Din's report, he was met by the sheriff's deputy at the county line, then driven to the accident scene. By the time he arrived some thirty minutes after the accident, Dr. Din reported that a preliminary investigation had already been completed. "He (McDuffie) was pronounced dead by medical officers at the race track at the scene," his report read. "But because of the tight schedule of the race, a few pictures were taken of the race car as well as the deceased."

Are you happy now?

The thought tormented Charlie Berch until he couldn't stand it anymore. He ran across the track to the scene, where track workers were then lifting the white sheets around McDuffie's car. "I went down, and I told one of the guys near the scene that I was part of the team and I needed to know right now what was going on. And I said, 'Is he gone?' And the guy kind of whispered to me and shook his head and said 'Yes, he's gone.' And I was a mess. I was an absolute mess."

The next few minutes passed in a blur. "John Saunders,

who was the track president, he was on the scene, and he drove me back in his car to the media center." By the time he arrived, Richard Petty had told others of the picture Berch took of McDuffie, Marcis, and himself. "Hardly anyone had any shots of J.D. back then because he wasn't a contender, one of the backmarkers, and they had no content on him, and the AP was always there, and they processed my black-and-white picture right on the spot and there it was." Before the red flag was finally lifted, Berch's podium photo was already on the AP wire, soon to be printed on papers across the country. The AP paid Berch $100. Petty himself would buy a copy for his racing museum in Level Cross. It was the notoriety he had always hoped for, but the cost gutted him.

"And then in the meantime, my sister was on this big scissor lift that a friend had, and she knew about me and J.D. and she came over to the corner and she came over looking for me in a panic and she says like 'Where's my brother? Where's my brother?' because she knew where I was, and they said, 'They took him to medical,' and then she lost it. So now you got two hysterical people, me and my sister, and they take her to the medical unit and I followed, and by the time I got to the pits, I was still crying, but the worst was done, and when I got into the media center, the press guy came up to me and told me 'your sister's in the medical center and she's looking for you, and it's not good.'"

* * * *

In Rockingham, North Carolina, Bobby Hudson was still working at "Body By B.H.," the race car body-hanging shop he founded in 1987. Sitting in his shop was McDuffie's blue Pontiac, destroyed at the end of the ARCA race at Talladega that May, its new body halfway done.

When McDuffie brought the car to Hudson, he offered to pay half the cost up front. "I'd rather you just make sure I get it finished," said Hudson. "I feel like I make more money, it just made me feel better, I feel like I do better if I just get all of it at one time." McDuffie insisted. "Bobby," he said, "let me tell you something. My daddy told me a long time ago, if a man's trying to give you some money, you take it." Hudson took the money.

That afternoon, Hudson had just come back from lunch when his mother told him the news.

* * * *

A few miles from the track in Wellsville, L.C. Whitford president Brad Whitford went to a local bar to see how the race was going. When he asked about McDuffie, someone answered, "I think he was just killed."

* * * *

Marty Burke was the first to reach the cinder-block building that served as Watkins Glen's infield care center. When he arrived, a priest met him at the entrance. His heart sank. A NASCAR official turned Burke away from where McDuffie was and towards another room where Mike Demers and another crewman sat. "This isn't good," Demers said.

At 1:40 P.M., Dr. Din arrived at the infield care center.

After a brief examination, he pronounced McDuffie dead, then contacted Ima Jean. She and her sisters didn't want an autopsy performed until they could discuss it with their family and clergymen. The next morning, Ima Jean agreed, and Dr. Din's autopsy was performed that day. Demers and Burke were told the news, and Berch and his sister joined the group in prayer.

"And you never expect that for sure," said Demers, his voice faint as he remembered that moment. "Never expected that for sure."

* * * *

Just after 1:50 P.M., ESPN had interviewed fifteen drivers with still no official updates from Turn 5. With McDuffie and Means' cars still sitting against the tire barrier, which also needed to be repaired, the decision was made to replay the broadcast of the previous day's Trans-Am race. MRN suspended its radio broadcast as well.

At 2:05 P.M., ESPN broke in with a brief update. McDuffie's car, covered by a dark green tarp, was now on the back of a flatbed hauler driving the wrong way up The Esses toward Turn 1. A picture taken by David Stephenson for the *Syracuse Herald-Journal* showed that the car was righted parallel to the Turn 5 fence, then loaded nose-first onto the back of the truck. Means' car, still uncovered, was now being loaded on another flatbed, the destroyed nose still facing the Turn 5 barrier. Minutes later, it would drive past the Cashmans. By then, ESPN had returned to the replay of the Trans-Am race.

Behind the scenes, the network, the track, and NASCAR

officials were trying to figure out what to do next. "We knew for probably twenty or thirty minutes that this was a tragedy," said Dr. Jerry Punch, "and they were just trying to figure out how to make the announcement and who to do it. And in this day and age of instant media and social media and texts and Facebook and Instagram, you know there's always a rush by someone to get it out there – 'He's been killed' – but back then, we had television partners, and we weren't trying to keep anything from our television viewers, but we were also trying to do what was right, because they hadn't specifically said he was gone, but we pretty much knew. And before we make any official announcement, we're gonna call and get a hold of the family, make sure everybody knows, get this right, so we know the right way to say it and how to say it."

NASCAR selected Chip Williams, the Winston Cup Media Coordinator, to make the announcement.

* * * *

In 1989, Marty Burke was pitting No. 70 at Daytona. His father John was in the grandstands cheering him on. Just a few weeks later, John was dead of a heart attack. Now, not even two years later, Marty found himself in the same position all over again, trying to pick up the pieces. "You kick into overdrive," he recalled. "You know, what do you gotta do? You've gotta do this, you've gotta do that, you've gotta do this. We knew Jean wasn't there, Jeff wasn't there, and they wouldn't let us go until we made sure we got in touch with Jean and confirmed it with Jean."

But McDuffie's team wasn't given time to grieve.

Right after they contacted Ima Jean, officials hustled them out of the infield care center and into the garage area. There, members of several pit crews were already loading the last of the team's equipment onto "Old Blue." Jack stands. An old jack. Two coolers. A pit sign. A gas generator. Electrical cords. A flash light. A pair of battered red fuel cans. Tires. McDuffie's uniform bag. One of the officials gestured at the truck and told Mike Demers "Okay, you drive." He climbed in and drove to the other end of the garage area. It was only then that Demers discovered "Old Blue" had no brakes. Even at a slow speed, he barely got it stopped.

There, sitting right-side up out of public view, was the destroyed No. 70. For some reason, the car was no longer covered, and the crew was confronted with the crash's true horror.

The contact which sent both McDuffie and Means off the course had left its mark on the damaged driver's side door. Faint streaks of light blue paint showed above and below the driver's side number. The slide through the grass pulled the left-rear tire from its rim, which was now dented along one-third of its circumference. The impact with the tires crushed every square inch of passenger side sheet metal against the roll cage such that the right-side tires and fuel stem now protruded out several inches. The right-rear of the car looked as though it had been struck by a wrecking ball, the whole of it pushed in and the rear decklid buckled upward. One-third of the plexiglass rear windscreen had broken away, as had the passenger side "opera window," the triangular window between the tattered "B-post" and "C-post." The flip shattered the windshield and hammered flat the rear spoiler. The roof was now warped, pushed toward the passenger side "A-post." The hood was mangled and torn away, the burgundy paint stripped on the impact side to reveal the gray primer beneath.

Most startling was how little of the car's left-front remained. Not only were the tire and wheel gone, but also the ball joint and much of the suspension. The fender was also gone, blown open as if by a bomb. What little remained inside was a single shock which held the damaged lower control arm. The bracket on the arm which held the ball joint, now covered in grass, had been ripped in half. Demers and Burke asked where the wheel was. The officials said they had placed it inside the car. It wasn't, and in fact couldn't – the car's windows were too small to fit a racing slick, much less a wheel and ball joint. Also missing was the car's front valence, still attached to the nose of the car at the time it was loaded on the flatbed, but somehow lost in the transfer.

Again, there was no time to protest. No time even to slow down. At least one official told the crew to hurry up their loading and leave so the race could be restarted. Now as then, NASCAR rules dictate that a race can be deemed complete if it is stopped after the halfway point. Otherwise, the race would have to be postponed to a later date, usually the next day. With nearly the entire race left to be run and no lights to allow running at night, NASCAR said they had a schedule to keep. But with hours of sunlight left on a mid-summer day, this may not have been the true reason. Even if it were, it was hardly justified – the officials' cold indifference only added to the misery of the emotionally drained crew.

Marty Burke had been given a black car cover by the

No. 42 SABCO Racing team. He covered what was left of McDuffie's car with it as it was loaded and chained onto "Old Blue" for the final time. Only then did he see the bottom half of the cover was green. Demers fired up "Old Blue" once again and crept toward the exit. His wife Lesley followed him in their car followed by Burke, Don Owens, "Colonel" Tyndall, Jerry Glenn and his son. It had all happened so quick that the magnitude of it all was still setting in as the small convoy began its long drive south.

* * * *

Back out on pit road, Joe Dan Bailey, the tire changer for Derrike Cope's No. 10 Purolator Chevrolet, was chatting with Michael Waltrip. Joe Dan's father Herring Bull "H.B." Bailey was another of the Winston Cup Series' few remaining owner-drivers, having run in the series since 1962. As the two talked, Bailey watched the helicopter carrying McDuffie take off from the infield, then fly overhead.

"It came, and it actually flew low down the front straightaway like it was going across the finish line again," recalled Bailey. "It went down into Turn 1, and instead of taking a right at the end, the helicopter hung a left and went off that way. It was the coolest thing to see, knowing he came down the front straightaway one more time."

* * * *

After a couple brief status updates on repairs to the wall, ESPN's live broadcast returned just after 3:00 P.M. with many of the drivers back in their cars. By the time the camera showed Turn 5, there was hardly any evidence the crash had occurred other than an uneven stacking of tires at the impact site. The five vehicles that remained at the crash site left the area to the mild applause from the crowd. Shortly after, the command to fire engines was given.

From beginning to end, the delay had taken one hour, forty-eight minutes, and six seconds. Through it all, there had been no official word on the condition of J.D. McDuffie. Most suspected the worst. A few knew it. But no one else was told until the moment the field started rolling again.

CHAPTER 17
A Pretty Sad Day Right Now

*"The night before he loses his life in a Cup race, he wins
and is celebrated as a winner and gets out, smiles, and
has the checkered flag at a race track just down the
street. Gives you chills just thinking about it."*

—Dr. Jerry Punch, 2017

Outside the media center behind pit road, Chip Williams looked physically ill as he spoke the words.

"I regret to inform you that J.D. McDuffie has passed away. He was fifty-three years old. Of course, our hearts right now are with his wife Ima Jean and his children Jeff and Linda and it's really a pretty sad day right now." Incidentally, Williams was incorrect about McDuffie's age – he would not have turned fifty-three until December.

"Right now, we don't know about the cause of death because the autopsy is scheduled for in the morning," he continued. "As far as what happened to the race car, it looks like the possibility of a wheel breaking loose. We're gonna look into that, we're gonna look at the race car and see what we can find out from there. Of course, we're not gonna be able to do that until after the race." By that point, however, the McDuffie Racing crew had already left with the car.

Some fans in the stands at Watkins Glen couldn't hear the announcement. The noise of the cars blocked the sound over the public address. But the mood was undeniably subdued. "I was at the race," said Julie Pfeil in a letter to the editor of the *Democrat and Chronicle*, "and I can guarantee that everyone there was suddenly reminded about the frailty of life and the risk drivers take each time they climb into their cars."

During the red flag, fans congregated around a camper belonging to Stan Dybka and his wife Jackie, trying to get a better view of the accident scene. "Everybody kept asking," said Stan. "When it was announced, there was a big lull in the crowd. I could feel my heart sink when we found out he was dead." The news hit Don Dombroski's friend hard. "The guy I was with was a member of his fan club," said Don. "I remember he said that if he could hook up his camper and pull it out, he would just pick up his trailer and leave, he was so upset. He didn't even want to watch the rest of the race."

* * * *

The harsh realities of racing were nothing new to Bob Jenkins. He cut his broadcasting teeth at the Indianapolis Motor Speedway, where speed and risk have always been at their greatest. He was in the booth for Grant Adcox's fatal wreck in the NASCAR race at Atlanta in 1989. Yet still, as he stood in the booth that day at The Glen, the emotions of the moment grabbed him – especially as footage played of McDuffie's win in the celebrity race just hours before. Prior to the event, ESPN had planned to air the footage during the race, building on the attention they gave to the driver the previous month at Pocono. Now, it was the centerpiece of an on-air eulogy.

"It is always difficult to report the death of any race driver," said Jenkins. "They know the dangers and the hazards, and they choose to race because they love it so very much. J.D. McDuffie was in his 653rd Winston Cup race. He had never won a Winston Cup event. But just last night, ironically enough, at Owego, New York at Shangri-La Speedway, J.D. McDuffie was involved in a celebrity race. And J.D. McDuffie driving the 07 car, believe it or not, took the checkered flag first and won that race, just down the road from Watkins Glen International where his career ended today. J.D. got out of the car with his son Jeff watching and received the applause and the congratulations of all of those in the grandstands. J.D. McDuffie leaves his wife Jean and his children Jeff and Linda and our sincere condolences to all the McDuffie family from all of us here at ESPN."

The tragedy cut close for Ned Jarrett and Benny Parsons, who'd both known McDuffie personally. Jarrett hardly spoke after his interview with Means. For a time, Parsons also seemed at a loss for words. Two months earlier, his wife Connie succumbed to a lengthy illness. Still grieving, Parsons offered an improvised message to Ima Jean McDuffie, and in so doing, transcended the moment:

"Jean – I know exactly what you're going through, sweetheart. And, you fans out there, you wonder how these guys can get in these cars can go back out and restart this race. Hey, it's their job. It's what they do and there's a hundred thousand people here this afternoon to watch them do that job. There's not a one of these drivers that wants to be in that race car right now – they want to be in the garage area hugging their wife, their girlfriend, their mom, their crew members, whoever. I don't want to be *here* now. I want to be over there looking at Ned and looking at Bob and just not saying anything. But we've got a job to do –

and that's report to you who wins, who loses, and what happens during the day. Jean, we all love you and we're sorry."

"This is the first time this has happened," said Bob Jenkins during the commercial break. Once again, Parsons found the right words to say. "Bob, I know you're having a tough time. Hang in [there], buddy."

Back on pit road, Dr. Jerry Punch returned to his post. For him, the feeling was sadly familiar. In 1975, as a medical student at Wake Forest University, he drove an hour out to Hickory Speedway, where NASCAR stars Bobby Allison and Tiny Lund were competing against local racers. After the race, Dr. Punch interviewed Lund as he signed autographs. He talked about the next day's race in Talladega, that he would driving for independent driver A.J. King for his first Winston Cup start in two years.

The next day, Dr. Punch was listening to his tape of the interview before he switched over to the radio. As he tuned-in to updates from Talladega, he heard of a multi-car accident on Lap 7. Lund, age forty-five, was killed in the crash. "And I think about 'holy cow, here I was the night before standing with this man. He was signing autographs and gave this interview, this tape-recorded interview, and now this happens." The reporter walked by the empty stall where McDuffie's crew had set up hours earlier. Then he adjusted his headphones, hearing the field rumble by in the distance, and prepared to go back to work.

* * * *

Back at the McDuffie household, the reality of it all had yet to hit his brother Glen. "Being a participant in the profession in the past years myself, I wasn't totally surprised," he said later that week. "I really don't know how to explain it...But I had prepared myself over the years for this to happen. I've had myself prepared in case it did."

* * * *

Tom Schwarz was devastated. Just hours after McDuffie drove his late model to victory at Shangri-La, he was mourning the loss of a newfound friend. "We cried about it Sunday," he said. "I was heartbroken. It was a grim day. I didn't feel like doing anything." In the days that followed, he soon did. The next time Schwarz raced at Shangri-La to defend his points lead, he'd carry a decal reading "In Memory of No. 70" on the side of his Chevrolet.

At the same time in Ohio, short tracker Darren Jones was working on his first race car, a red 1972 Torino. When he heard the news, he stopped, got some white paint, and drew on the passenger side C-post "Rest In Peace No. 70 J.D. McDuffie 1938-1991." His next time out at the Union County Speedway, Jones took his first checkered flag.

* * * *

On the other side of the Atlantic, Tom Clegg was in Germany. He enlisted in the Army in 1966, not long after his first trip to the Rockingham dirt track. In that time, he followed McDuffie's career as best he could, and like many others, helped out in the garage whenever he was stateside. He introduced his son to the driver in 1978, and ever since they cheered for No. 70 at Dover, at Pocono, and at Richmond.

On this day, Clegg had just walked into his new quarters when a friend told him the news.

* * * *

Sometime after 4:00 P.M., the race restarted. Nine laps were complete. Eighty-one remained.

High atop the media center, Charlie Berch sat with his sister in a daze, neither of them speaking a word to each other. "It was like getting a boot in my ass. I was just sick," said Charlie later. "I got a really hard dose of reality." He didn't take any more pictures that day, nor did he sell any. The seven slides of McDuffie's crash would remain in his camera for more than two months. They remained unpublished until they were printed in this book.

When the green flag fell, Terry Labonte's No. 94 Oldsmobile took off, leaving Mark Martin to deal with Ernie Irvan for second. Irvan was so anxious to get going that he bumped the rear of Martin's Ford, knocking a crush panel loose behind the rear bumper. On Lap 20, Irvan had dispensed with Martin and now passed Labonte for the lead entering Turn 1. Coming off the corner, Labonte's right-rear tire went down, sending him into a spin. The blue Oldsmobile limped around almost the entire track, shedding torn rubber and sheet metal that drew the second caution of the day. Labonte's engine failed just after the midway point, leaving him a disappointing thirty-fourth.

Irv Hoerr, whose Labonte-owned No. 44 was smoking before McDuffie's wreck, didn't restart the race and wound up thirty-eighth, citing engine trouble. Dave Marcis, unable to cure the vibration on his Darlington car, pulled his No.

71 off the track on Lap 11, making him the fourth retiree in thirty-seventh. Michael Waltrip, the last-place starter, didn't need Scott Pruett's relief. His car was so slow that Terry Letton got a clear shot of it passing by in Turn 5. Waltrip lost two laps on the track and was about to lose a third when the checkered flag waved, leaving him twenty-first.

Wally Dallenbach, Jr.'s new Roush Ford ran as high as third, then lost the spot to a charging Ken Schrader in his white No. 25 Chevrolet. Dallenbach's day only grew worse from there. A few laps later, he lost the brakes entering Turn 10 and ran off course. He missed the tire barriers but couldn't avoid a spinning Brett Bodine in Turn 1. The contact cut the right-front tire on Dallenbach's No. 90 down the backstretch but didn't bring out a caution since his debris landed off the racing surface. His day finally ended with steering issues, leaving him thirty-second.

Morgan Shepherd's wild week ended on Lap 35 when his Ford broke down in Turn 1. Under his caution, Dale Earnhardt stayed out to score five championship bonus points for leading a lap. It was the only lap he led. A spin with Earnhardt's long-time rival Geoff Bodine exiting Turn 5 knocked the toe end out on his No. 3 GM Goodwrench Chevrolet. He was then handed two consecutive pit road penalties for jumping the start and violating the 35mph pit speed limit, much to the anger of car owner Richard Childress. Earnhardt finished fifteenth. Bodine crashed by himself off the final corner on Lap 62, and he limped home twenty-second, a bungee cord holding down his Ford's buckled hood.

The lead changed fourteen times, but undoubtedly the best car belonged to Ernie Irvan. His No. 4 Kodak Chevrolet made three green-flag passes for the lead. The last of these came on Lap 68, when something broke on the top of Ken Schrader's engine, knocking him out of the race. Irvan also had the best luck. He saved his car from a spin through the Turn 7 grass. Then, heading into Turn 1 on the final lap, Mark Martin, who had yet to lead, made a move to the inside. Irvan threw the block. Martin backed off at the apex, then spun coming off. Davey Allison, closing fast on Martin, also spun from third to avoid him. Now up front and all alone, Irvan cruised to an easy seven-second victory, much to the joy of Kodak. Martin recovered to finish third while Allison wound up tenth. The spin allowed Irvan to take Allison's third spot in points.

Squeaking past Martin for second was Ricky Rudd, who not only led eleven laps in his bandaged Chevrolet but closed his points deficit from 160 to 108 markers behind Earnhardt. Rusty Wallace also rebounded from his poor qualifying run to come home fourth. Dale Jarrett held off Darrell Waltrip for fifth. Seventh and eighth went to Bill Elliott and Hut Stricklin, who spun together off Turn 7 just short of the finish line. Right behind them in ninth was Richard Petty and his iconic No. 43 STP Pontiac. It was Petty's first top-ten finish since Pocono in July of the previous year. It also turned out to be the 712th – and final – of his career.

Only two more drivers found trouble in Turn 5. One was Alan Kulwicki, who spun at the apex with seven laps to go but made only light contact with the right-front of his No. 7 Hooters Ford. Kim Campbell, however, hit much harder. Campbell was having a miserable time controlling his No. 20 NAPA Oldsmobile down the backstretch, resulting in three off-course excursions. On Lap 27, he spun at the entrance of Turn 5, looped his car twice, and stopped short of nosing into the spot where McDuffie and Means hit the barriers. On Lap 45, Campbell ran wide at the apex and nearly lost control again. Finally, on Lap 70, he spun into the corner much faster and backed hard into the tires. Unhurt, Campbell managed to drive his battered Olds back to the garage, leaving him thirty-first.

Among Campbell's fellow "road ringers," Dorsey Schroeder had the best overall performance, though his finish didn't show it. After running inside the Top 15 in the early stages, he took the lead during a brief rain delay on Lap 60. Schroeder paced the field for three laps, pitted under green, then looked to retake the top spot when Campbell's last wreck drew an ill-timed caution. Unfortunately, many of the leaders stayed out, dropping No. 24 back in the order, and he then lost a cylinder, leaving him seventeenth. The top "road ringer" of the day ended up one spot ahead of him: sixteenth-place John Paul, Jr., who turned in his best Winston Cup finish in his second – and final – series start.

Third among the "road ringers" was Jim Derhaag, whose car owner George Hakes was ecstatic with his twentieth-place finish. As the team loaded up, Derhaag was approached by Les Richter. Richter, the Hall of Fame linebacker for the Los Angeles Rams, was one of NASCAR's most accomplished and prolific officials, having risen to the sport's Senior Vice President of Operations. Richter asked Derhaag what he saw when McDuffie crashed. The driver replayed it once more – the puff of smoke, McDuffie not slowing and collecting Means, the crash.

"Well, what do you think?" asked Richter in his heavy Southern accent. "You gotta put a chicane on that back straightaway because everyone's going too fast," said Derhaag. The driver wasn't sure how Richter would react, but when the two continued their conversation, he was impressed. "The guy was so competent in the way he looked at things and his questions and the way he addressed it," he recalled, "the way he interacted with me being a rookie the first time."

When the two were done, Richter started to walk away when he stopped and turned around. "You did a right nice job with that piece o' shit car you had to drive," said Richter. "You come on back and race with us anytime you want. You leave that damned yellow tape at home."

"It really meant a lot is what I'm saying," said Derhaag. Unfortunately, neither he – nor car owner George Hakes – ever made another NASCAR start.

* * * *

Back in victory lane, Ernie Irvan climbed out of his Chevrolet, his wife Kim by his side. By then, both had heard the news. "We want to dedicate this race to J.D. McDuffie," said Ernie, "you know, we won the last race he was in. A great man. It was hard to drive by that corner every lap, but we just wanted to dedicate this race to him."

"Every time we went through the turn where he crashed, I thought about him," he continued in another interview that afternoon. "I've known what it is like to struggle in this sport without a sponsor just like he did, and I'll always remember him...J.D. has been great to our sport. He showed that an independent could keep on racing and be part of this. It's always going to hurt our sport for something like this to happen and we're all going to re-member J.D. McDuffie."

* * * *

Thirty-one miles north-west of Sanford in Siler City, Wayne Andrews finished up work at his garage, Wayne's Alignment Service. As he got to his car, he looked out at the stretch of US Highway 64 in front of him. Days earlier, "Old Blue" had driven down that road on its way to Watkins Glen. He didn't see the truck, but he heard the horn. McDuffie always honked on his way to the track, his way of saying "hi" to his friend from those dusty IRA days on the dirt tracks. As he left the shop, Andrews knew he'd hear the horn again a couple weeks later as McDuffie drove back home. That is, until he turned on the evening news.

* * * *

Back at a silent Watkins Glen International, fans camping at the track stayed overnight. Some did so to wait out the traffic and head home on Monday. Others made their way to Turn 5. "There were people here all night long (the night of the crash)," said Jackie Dybka. "A lot of people, they put flowers there. They put a sign up that said 'We love you, J.D.' Every time you come sit here at the corner you think about it."

* * * *

As night fell, McDuffie's convoy stopped at a coffee shop, and the crew tried to piece together what had happened. The group decided not to drive past Siler City to Sanford, but instead further north to Medford Speed Shop in New Jersey, where the Glenns would remove their engine and the Blue Max transmission from No. 70. When Mike Demers got back behind the wheel of "Old Blue," it wouldn't start. As he tried to diagnose the problem, his hand fell on a random toggle switch on the dash. The truck started right up.

Just four miles from the Medford shop, Mike Demers had somehow managed to avoid an accident. But now the brakes had gone completely. Suddenly, a car pulled in front of "Old Blue." Demers gripped the wheel and turned it hard. By the closest of margins, he missed. The work done, the group went their separate ways. Demers drove home and hugged his wife. Lesley could still smell cigar smoke on his clothes.

Back in "Old Blue," there was a bit of white paper stuck in the visor. It was the receipt for the breakfast the group shared that morning.

CHAPTER 18
Just A Lap Ahead Of Us

"If there was a race, J.D. was there, just like the air."

—Kirk Shelmerdine, Dale Earnhardt's crew chief, 1991

Ima Jean tried to take her mind off what had happened by going to the grocery store. "I cried all over Sanford," she said. "I went to the store, I set down and cried. I couldn't buy my groceries. I cried all over Sanford, and not one soul asked me what was wrong." As she went back home, her daughter Linda was almost there. She found out about the accident on the radio before NASCAR called. When they did, they offered to fly her from Florida to Sanford on their private plane. "I'm very grateful for that," she said later. "Probably in that one instance they probably did more for me than they ever did for my dad. That's what's so sad."

When Linda arrived at the house, her mother was bed-ridden. "I was really sick when J.D. died...when I woke up Linda was home and I was on the bed and the doctor sent a couple of nurses out here and he give me shots and I heard one of them say 'we better get them to the hospital,' I said 'if you drag me outta here that's all right.'"

On Monday, August 12, Lesley Demers tried to reach Ima Jean by phone. The line was busy until 9:00 P.M.

"I think she was reassured after speaking with Mike about how happy J.D. had been for the whole week-end," Lesley wrote later. "The evening at Shangri-La meant so much to J.D." Ima Jean's sister said there wasn't a need for the fan club to keep going. Lesley convinced her otherwise. Her husband Mike had secluded himself in his office all day, writing the fan club newsletter that would sum up McDuffie's final two starts at Pocono and Watkins Glen. Copies of it would be mailed with Lesley's cover letter, which included these and other details of McDuffie's services, set for Thursday, August 15.

Once again, the convoy headed south. Mike and Lesley loaded up their conversion van early Wednesday morning. In the back was the trophy McDuffie won in Shangri-La and a photo plaque the driver received from Janine Pestel at Watkins Glen. The two crossed paths with the Glenns in Baltimore, then Tom Rumple and his wife Pam at a hotel in Sanford. Marty Burke met the group at Ima Jean's home as she returned from the Bridges-Cameron Funeral Home in Jonesboro with the family minister. Pestel clipped the final negative from her roll of film from Watkins Glen and handed it to Ima Jean – the last picture ever taken of her husband. The previous shot was developed and first reprinted in Greg Fielden's "Forty Years of Stock Car Racing," then the cover of this book.

* * * *

On Wednesday, the streets around the funeral home were jammed with cars, and a line of mourners stretched more than two blocks. From 1:00 P.M. until just before midnight, between 2,500 and 3,000 people filed into Bridges-Cameron to pay their respects at the open-casket viewing. So many sent flowers that five trucks were needed to deliver them. Among those who contributed were Louise

Smith – one of NASCAR's first female drivers – Ricky Rudd, Darrell Waltrip, and Dale Earnhardt with his entire Richard Childress Racing crew. Tommy Bridges, the funeral director, conducted the wake. "J.D. was a humble man that everyone liked," he said.

The growing group at the Baker Street home stayed for the rest of the day, sharing stories well into the night. "It makes me feel very proud to know I had a brother that everyone loved," said Glen. "I haven't found anyone that said anything bad about him." "That's what made it okay," said Mike Demers of the Watkins Glen weekend. "'Cause he was on top of the world. He was like a little kid. We'd seen him struggle. We'd seen him really disappointed, you know, where he'd sit in the truck for an hour and a half after he didn't qualify, for whatever reasons. We'd seen, not all the bad times, but enough of them, and to see him in a good time really made us all happy."

Even more visitors arrived Thursday morning for the services in Sanford. "He gave me everything he had, even took me to Daytona and let me drive his race car," said George Sekanina, who lived with the McDuffies when he moved from Canada. "He was a special man in my life, and I'll never forget him." "You only had to meet him one time and you knew he was a super person," said Tom Glenn, a crewman for McDuffie's final two seasons. "You'd think he was an everyday guy." "He was a good fella. He just never got the lucky break," said crewman Earl "Bud" Sloan. "He could drive with any of them. It's a sport that it just takes a truckload of money to do it, and J.D. just never did get the lucky break." "You wouldn't find a better fella," said Tom Usry. "J.D. was like a brother."

Rick Hendrick, Richard Childress, and Junior Johnson – car owners who each helped McDuffie in his final years – were there, as were Hoss Ellington and Les Richter. Other Winston Cup drivers were there, too, a rare event due to another long-standing superstition. Among them were Lake Speed, James Hylton, Cecil Gordon, D.K. Ulrich, and Dave Marcis. "He was well liked everywhere by everyone," said Marcis. "When I first came down south from Wisconsin in 1967, I was one of the little guys. He gave me the rundown on all the tracks and helped me feel at home." Joining them was Jimmy Means, the stitches on his cut chin covered by a bandage. "I don't think he felt any less of a driver or any less of a competitor," said Means. "It showed that he had more intestinal fortitude than the rest of them to stick it out. There's been a lot of people come and gone and he was still trying to make it."

Grasping a crutch for a leg he injured in a crash at Sears Point, Richard Petty arrived to pay his respects. Petty declined to speak with the media – "You won't get no comment from Richard Petty at a funeral," he said. Instead, Petty had offered his thoughts earlier in the week. "I've run with J.D. more than anybody, I guess, about every race that J.D. ever ran. The guy was doing what he loved, because all the stuff he's been through he had to love what he was doing. Very few people going away from this earth can say that. He was enjoying it to the last minutes." Seven weeks later, Petty announced he would retire from NASCAR at the end of the 1992 season. In an interview years later, the driver said he had decided to retire before McDuffie's accident, and not because of it.

The fans were there, too, their mobile homes parked

alongside news vans just as they had at Watkins Glen. So many arrived that the Grace Chapel Christian Church – like Bridges-Cameron, constructed of Sanford bricks – was filled to overflowing. Mourners spilled from the pews into folding chairs. A mix of checkered flags and blue and yellow floral arrangements decorated the inside of the church, many bearing the No. 70. There was a collection of letters from the fan club, which sent an arrangement of its own. Over the speakers played Marty Robbins' "Twentieth Century Drifter," the same song that accompanied CBS' feature on McDuffie in 1985. On this day, the lyrics carried even more weight:

...You might even call me a twentieth century drifter
Thirty-two weekends I load up the car and I'm gone
And my woman cries with each goodbye kiss that I give
her
And she prays that come Monday morning and I'll be
driftin' home...

McDuffie's family was ushered in. A sobbing Ima Jean was joined by her children Jeff and Linda, as well as McDuffie's mother Ruby and brother Glen. The family took their seats, joined by the crew members and families of McDuffie Racing. "It's something in the very back of your mind, but you never dwell on it," Ima Jean told reporters earlier that week. "I don't know what I'm going to do without him. I really don't."

At the center of it all, J.D. McDuffie lay peacefully. A cigar was threaded between his fingers, and he wore his favorite turquoise ring on his right hand. He wore a brand-new blue-and-white Simpson race suit, similar to the one he wore at Watkins Glen, embroidered with his name and car number. At the time, the whereabouts of the original Leaf uniform were unknown. Unbelievably, it was stolen. Sometime after the accident, a man named Jeffery Tobias Bennett wrote a letter to officials in Schuyler County, saying he was McDuffie's brother and would like the uniform mailed to him. The delivery was made, and Bennett sold the uniform to a hobby shop for $150. Bennett wasn't caught until the following February. McDuffie's bubble goggles are still missing to this day.

At 11:00 A.M., services were conducted by the Rev. Dr. Leland Dittman, the Rev. Max Helton, and the Rev. Robert Yandle. In 1988, when McDuffie suffered his burns at Daytona, the Reverend Yandle took the driver aside. "Maybe the Lord is trying to tell you something," he said. "He looked at me like that was the most stupid thing that any preacher had ever said. 'What would I do? This ain't no weekend hobby I got.'" Now, just over three years later, the Rev. Yandle performed his friend's eulogy:

"(J.D.) knew the odds that were against him and yet God let him have a taste of the checkered flag at the winner's circle Saturday night," he said, referring to the win at Shangri-La. "He lived for racing. I always joked if you cut him, he'd bleed Havoline. I think people admired him because he did the most with the least and showed a determination to find out what he wanted to do, did it, and was happy doing it."

"When I see somebody, who can face all of that and pick it up and go with the next race...it challenges me, not

[to] be a race car driver, but to be the best that I can be."

After the services, the group formed a procession. Burke and the rest of the crew joined Mike and Leslie Demers in their van and followed McDuffie's hearse down the two-lane road to the Buffalo Presbyterian Church. There was no traffic. People stood on the sidewalk or in their yards. Eighteen-wheelers sat idle at intersections, held back by white-gloved deputies who saluted as the casket passed. Flags stood at half-staff at post offices in Sanford, Broadway, and Lemon Springs. "That funeral was the largest funeral ever in Sanford," said Ima Jean. "Biggest ever in Lee County."

Third in line, Tom Rumple and his son Don joined the procession in their burgundy conversion van they drove to the races, the one with their driver's name and number painted onto the rear tire cover. "It was sort of eerie going up the road," recalled Don, "they were lining up, it looked like a presidential motorcade or something going by. Everyone was just standing at the side of the road, watching the proceedings and I know that's, it's not the first funeral proceedings going through Sanford, but it was really eerie the way people were just standing around watching the car going up the road. That was one of their homegrown boys and they saw the tragic end there."

The procession ended down a small hill at the far end of the cemetery, where a small mausoleum of white stone overlooked a lake. There, six members of the McDuffie Racing crew stood as pallbearers. Tom Rumple, Col. Don Tyndall, Tom Glenn, Ed Peters, Marty Burke, and Mike Demers wore trucker caps representing their sponsors, including

Rumple Furniture, AC Spark Plugs, Classic Trophies, Run-A-Bout, and Son's Auto Supply. The group decided to wear each other's caps. Col. Tyndall held a cigar. The team carried the coffin into the breezeway of the mausoleum. There, a display of white flowers with a small model of car No. 70 stood sentinel. There were prayers, stories, tears. Then J.D. McDuffie was laid to rest.

"He's in heaven, racing with the boys," said Col. Tyndall.

"He's got a sponsor now," said Peters.

"I don't feel that he's gone," said Burke. "He's just a lap ahead of us."

* * * *

The next day, the Winston Cup Series teams unloaded at Brooklyn, Michigan for opening practice of the Champion Spark Plug 400. Jimmy Means drove straight to the track from Watkins Glen, the reality of the accident still sinking in. His No. 52, like many of the other cars entered, carried a small black decal reading "J.D. No. 70." A few banners fluttered against RVs in the infield:

#70 J.D. We Miss You!

J.D. McDuffie Fan Club!

Decatur, IN sends our wishes to the family and friends of J.D. McDuffie

Like Means, J.D. McDuffie had planned to drive straight from Watkins Glen to Michigan. The Baileys were expecting him to meet them in Jackson. There was a space for him at Bailey Excavating to switch over No. 70's setup to tackle the oval, and a bed for him to stay the night. "My dad was gonna put his name on the car to help him out, 'cause he was really struggling," recalled John Bailey. "But he never made it."

* * * *

Months earlier, Ima Jean McDuffie recalled a race at Bristol. After 500 grueling laps on the high-banked short track, her husband pulled No. 70 into the garage area. Nearby sat the No. 17 of Darrell Waltrip, a driver who would go on to win twelve times at Bristol alone. Waltrip's crew stood there, watching the No. 70 grind to a stop. "I could see them looking at us, thinking, 'You poor fool, why don't you just go home?'" she said. "But he can't go home for the same reason they can't. He loves it. If he didn't live another day, he'd be happy because he loves it, and he's done what he wants to do."

Ironically, by 1991, Waltrip faced the same questions. He was forty-four, just coming off a serious injury the previous year at Daytona and had just left Hendrick Motorsports to drive for his own team. Even with three championships and, at that point, eighty-one wins, there was skepticism over the outspoken driver fans called "Jaws." "There are people who say, 'Why don't you quit?'" he said before that fateful race at Watkins Glen. "It's a question often asked of athletes in all sports by people who equate success with money made and who have never participated at the highest level, if at all."

Perhaps this philosophy guided Waltrip's words on the morning of August 18, 1991. Before the start of the Michigan race, it was Waltrip, standing beside his wife Stevie, who offered an on-track eulogy to McDuffie: "Even though we raced together and competed against each other – and sometimes complained about each other – we are a family, we do love and we do care...J.D. passed away doing what he chose to do, what he loved to do, what meant so much to him...J.D. was a good man, a righteous man." "Father," he closed, "if all of us had a little J.D. McDuffie in us, this would be a better world."

Nearly ten years later, as a broadcaster for FOX Sports, Waltrip would do Dale Earnhardt the same honor.

* * * *

"People are wondering why J.D. went on at age fifty-two when he'd never won in so many starts." said Benny Parsons, back with ESPN for the 400-miler. "I think I know, because I've been in cars that weren't supposed to have a chance of winning, like his. In their minds, guys like J.D. believe that when someone says, 'Gentlemen, start your engines,' this is the day a bolt of lightning is going to sideline the whole field and they're going to win." These thoughts would take shape in a second video tribute produced by Parsons and Ken Martin, ESPN's associate producer, researcher, and booth statistician. The segment aired during an early caution period.

* * * *

The Watkins Glen episode of TNN's "Inside Winston Cup" program, which aired the same day as the Michigan race, featured a tribute by Randy Pemberton, who was reporting from the track that Sunday. In it, Pemberton revealed he was in the stands at the Albany-Saratoga Speedway the day McDuffie earned his career-best third-place finish in 1971.

* * * *

On July 14, 1966, not long after "J.D. McDuffie Day" in Sanford, the NASCAR Grand National division hosted a 200-lap race in Fonda, New York. Early that day, thirteen-year-old Andy Fusco was dropped off at the track by his father to save them some seats while he was at work. While he waited, Fusco talked with the drivers in the paddock, snapping pictures with his Polaroid camera. Along the way, he noticed the No. 70 Ford and the man working on it, so he struck up a conversation with J.D. McDuffie. The driver was surprised. "How do you know so much about me?" he asked.

Fusco told McDuffie that there had been a feature about him in the local paper. McDuffie was even more stunned and wanted to know if he could read it and add it to the scrapbook Ima Jean kept in Sanford. Fusco said that his parents probably still had the copy at home. Just like that, McDuffie was driving the kid back home in "Old Blue." Fusco introduced the driver to his mother, who welcomed them both in. Sure enough, the article was still there. And over turkey sandwiches and Pepsi, McDuffie poured over his name in print.

After the accident, when he was Senior Editor of *Stock Car Racing* magazine, Fusco would commit this story to paper.

* * * *

Almost everyone in the NASCAR community had a story to share. "He was a guy you wanted to do something for if you could," said Herman Hickman, the public relations director at (Rockingham) North Carolina Motor Speedway. "We here at the speedway did whatever we could to help him – anything – but he never asked for anything."

"I think if he had gotten the right breaks in the late '60s, he could've won a lot of races," said Humpy Wheeler, decades after he watched McDuffie race at Rockingham and Gastonia. "He didn't get those breaks and he had to settle for the life of a guy on the road trying to make a living driving a race car." "I can remember passing him on an interstate the day after a race at Nashville, Tennessee," said Eddie Gossage, who would become president of Texas Motor Speedway, "He was all by himself, towing the race car home and cruising down the road with that cigar in his mouth. It's really tragic that it had to end like this."

Those in print media also came out in support. *Stock Car Racing Magazine's* November 1991 issue featured four pieces alone, led off by Fusco's memory from 1966. *Instant Replay Sporting Photo News* ran a four-page segment in

their Fall 1991 issue, including newspaper clippings from
Ima Jean's private collection. Deb Williams and Steve
Waid penned their own memories. "As the late George
Cunningham, Tom Higgins, Bob Myers and I agreed several years ago," wrote Waid, "'He may be one of the best
people we have ever known.'" Charlie Vincent's piece in
the *Detroit Free Press* ended with "[H]e left an example of
perseverance I will always admire." In *The Dispatch*, Ben
White later wrote, "I will never forget J.D. McDuffie. He
touched my life with his genuineness and I will always miss
him deeply." Even Larry Woody, who poked fun at No. 70
years earlier, changed his tune: "Right up to the final lap of
his final race, J.D. never quit trying. For that, his won-lost
record deserves an asterisk."

But perhaps the most emotional piece was penned by
Maurice Leggett, who recalled his meeting with the driver
just days before Watkins Glen. "This is by far the hardest
column I have ever attempted to write, as not only has Winston Cup racing lost a true member of its history, but I have
lost a good friend."

To others who hadn't covered McDuffie, it was a challenge to find information with which to write about him. "I
dragged out a variety of press guides, but none had J.D.
McDuffie mentioned," wrote Ernie Saxton in his own tribute for the *Area Auto Racing News*. Without one of Charlie
Berch's hand-made press guides – much less the internet –
Saxton had to enlist the aid of a number of fax services to
receive transmissions about McDuffie's biography and statistics. Even then, only New Jersey-based ARA Fax, produced by Progressive Management, was of much help. "Just
before I left for Daytona, Marty Burke called to ask if I

would sit down with him and talk about putting together some material for J.D. McDuffie and his sponsorship efforts," Saxton wrote in his piece. "We were looking forward to the meeting. I don't know if we could have helped but it would have been nice to chat and offer some suggestions."

The suggestion Burke had was the proposed deal for McDuffie to drive for Junie Donlavey in 1992 with sponsorship from Motorola.

CHAPTER 19
Chicanes and Barriers

"J.D. McDuffie's life could have been spared. The warnings were there but no one saw them."

—John Riley, Letter to Stock Car Racing Magazine

In the lead-up to the 1991 Budweiser at the Glen, the many accidents on the course were blamed on Goodyear's new radial tires. With the exception of a feature in *Winston Cup Scene*, the matter disappeared the moment J.D. McDuffie died. The controversy ended so completely that, when interviewed for this book, not one person could remember tires being an issue at all that weekend. Instead, most everyone talked about Turn 5.

The shift began before the race even started. In an interview published on Saturday, August 10, 1991, Watkins Glen president John Saunders was already looking for a solution. "We're considering a series of evaluations on improving the barrier system at the end of the back straight." He added, "at the moment, the best possible solution appears to be relocating the guardrail farther back with an intermediate system in front of the rail." However, he said "potential modifications will have to be done at the end of the season. In the interim, we've added a second row of tires to provide more of a cushioning effect." This second row of tires, added after Tom Kendall's wreck in June, were in place on August 11th. Tragically, they weren't enough.

On August 13, two days after the accident, Washington

Redskins coach Joe Gibbs announced the formation of Joe Gibbs Racing, a new Winston Cup team for 1992. During the press conference, the accident came up. While expressing his awareness of the risks athletes face in both racing and football, Coach Gibbs defended NASCAR's safety record. "I think more drivers have been hurt away from the track than have at the track," said Gibbs. "NASCAR has an amount of danger in it, but they have an excellent track record for safety. A lot of things are more dangerous in life than driving a race car or playing football."

That same day, Dave Marcis said that the barriers in Turn 5 were unsafe. "I'm sad for J.D. and I'm hot and I'm going to say it. NASCAR should not compete on race tracks that have metal railings." In their place, Marcis proposed an energy-absorbing barrier, such as plastic containers filled with water, as on freeways. "A water barrier certainly would help. Probably better still would be the new foam blocks that are three feet thick, which some tracks are using. They burst on impact and absorb energy." Geoff Bodine, involved in his own Turn 5 wreck in 1989, also "made the suggestion that (the track) should use peaked gravel piles and move the fence back some if possible." Saunders rejected Bodine's proposal in the past, saying "cars have a tendency to flip" when they slide into gravel.

Jim Bockoven, representing International Speedway Corporation, wasn't sure. "The wire cable gave, and the car went in and came back out," he said of McDuffie's accident. "It looked to me like it was soft. I don't know if a wall there would be any better. I just don't know." Terry Letton was also surprised by the seriousness of the crash. "Looking at it before the accident, it looked like if you're gonna crash, that'd be the safest place to crash, you know, going eighteen feet deep into the tires, and I guess the tires weren't that deep there."

Jimmy Means and Tommy Kendall, both nursing injuries, said that the speeds going into Turn 5 were so high that the existing brake systems weren't strong enough to slow the heavy cars. "If you lose your brakes or have any kind of problem at all (going into Turn 5), you're running too fast," said Means. "It's all flat and you go with the momentum of the car, wherever it's going to take you." "The effort needs to be directed toward keeping the cars from hitting the barriers that hard," said Kendall. "The most drastic is reconfiguring the track, but most people consider that unfeasible." On August 16, NASCAR's Les Richter said such a reconfiguration was on the table. One option involved setting the Turn 5 barrier another 150 feet back while turning the downhill slope of the runoff into an uphill grade, thus scrubbing speeds.

On September 4, the Associated Press reported that, despite the accident, Watkins Glen would still wait until that month's end of the racing season to make any changes to Turn 5. In the meantime, track spokesman J.J. O'Malley said that additional rows of tires would be added to the barrier. O'Malley had previously been asked about adding foam blocks in front of the barrier, much as they had on a short track in Lancaster, New York. "We considered it, but we didn't do it," he said. One factor was that the foam block manufacturer wouldn't assume any liability. "When they would assume no liability, we decided not to do it." Track president John Saunders, meanwhile, was talking with the sanctioning bodies and insurance companies about a proper solution. "They are the true experts," he said. "Those are the people we're talking to."

Among these experts was Irv Hoerr, whose engine let go during the early laps of the Budweiser at the Glen. A panel convened at the race track where drivers and other members from various sanctioning bodies considered solutions to make Turn 5 safer. Hoerr, a friend of O'Malley's, was there to represent sports car racing. During the meeting, various options were proposed. Letting the grass in the run-off area grow taller to catch cars. Installing a system of wires like those used to catch jets on aircraft carriers. But soon, the idea was suggested that a chicane – a rapid series of left and right-hand turns – could be added to slow cars before they reached the corner. The same thing had been done at Daytona, and for the same reason. In the 24 Hours of Daytona, the infield road course at the superspeedway once used an unbroken length of the track's 3,000-foot back straightaway. A series of accidents led the sanctioning body to adopt a chicane that was once reserved for motorcycles.

This turned out to be the winning proposal.

* * * *

The announcement came on October 8, 1991. A new chicane would be added near the end of Watkins Glen's long back straight. Called "The Inner Loop," the four-turn complex would start 1,839 feet down the 2,300-foot back straightaway. Drivers would have to slow much earlier to make a hard-right-hand turn, a left, then another left and right. Just 320 feet later, the cars would then enter Turn 5 – now Turn 9 or "The Outer Loop" – and would do so up to

50mph slower than before. In all, the project cost just over $1 million. The official word from The Glen was that the change had nothing to do with the accident but was "on the drawing board for a long time now...to create more room for spectator seating, parking, and recreational vehicle placement."

Curiously, Watkins Glen's Turn 5 already *had* a chicane installed when the track was first built, both to slow cars and to provide spectator seating. Track maps from 1959 through 1969, most notably the drawing by John B. Wait, show a chicane that avoided the entrance to Turn 5 altogether. Instead, it diverted traffic into the infield before rejoining the corner at its one-third mark. According to the Argetsinger family's own book on NASCAR at Watkins Glen, the narrow right-left-right was intended to be used by amateur racers, forcing them to brake much earlier for the corner. Professional drivers, including those in Formula One and NASCAR, were allowed to skip it altogether. In time, the corner was deemed too tight for even amateur racers to negotiate, and in 1985 its pavement was pulled up and replaced with gravel.

Footage of the track prior to 1992 showed the chicane was not part of NASCAR's "short course," but was still accessible to cars on the track. The entrance of the chicane was used to allow cars with mechanical issues to pull off the track, as Brett Bodine did that day in 1991. The chicane brought Bodine's No. 26 Quaker State Buick so far into the infield that Terry Letton's son Jesse was able to walk up to the driver's window and get an autograph. Today, a stretch of steel-and-foam "SAFER Barrier" has since blocked off the chicane's entrance, but the road is still used for emergency vehicles to enter the track under caution. Tow trucks and ambulances drive out from the exit, located across the spot where McDuffie's car left the track.

* * * *

In June 1992, Ima Jean McDuffie filed a $4.25 million wrongful death lawsuit against NASCAR, Watkins Glen, ISC, and the SCCA. She claimed that both the track and sanctioning bodies were negligent for allowing Turn 5 and its barriers to be arranged in a dangerous manner, that they failed to warn drivers of that danger, and that these failures caused her husband's death.

After owner-driver Raymond Williams declined to testify, McDuffie brought on former SCCA driver John Fitch as an expert to describe the risks of Turn 5. Linda McDuffie conducted her own research, pulling news articles from before and after the accident. Among the family's concerns was the manner in which the tires were arranged at the barrier – horizontally instead of a more traditional vertical stacking. She also picked up her father's helmet from Les Richter and was surprised to see there was no blood inside, only a small bit of red on the back of it. This indicated to her that the helmet had come off in the collision, perhaps struck by an object.

NASCAR was adamant in its defense, and on August 23 said that McDuffie's negligence, not negligence on the part of the sanctioning body, caused his death. The statement infuriated the family, who had been told a "mechanical failure," though not what kind, caused the accident. "Mechanical failure is their polite way of saying my Daddy was driving junk," said Linda. "When people talk about him, the one thing I get so upset with is people are like 'Oh, he had junk in his car,' you know 'Junk in his car, that's what killed him.' That upsets me so bad because it's like, you know, he didn't put something that was worn out in his car...My dad would never put junk in his car and know he could die from it."

Marty Burke had doubts about the case. "If he (McDuffie) felt it was that dangerous," he said of Watkins Glen, "he could have taken the green flag and parked the car. I mean, that's not usually what he does, but if it's my life I'll park the car and say it was oil pressure or a vibration. So, I don't know it wasn't, obviously in retrospect it wasn't the best designed turn."

In the end, the court used McDuffie's experience against him. On September 3, 1993, The Honorable Judge Michael Telesca threw out the case. In his rather conclusory decision, the judge said that McDuffie was aware of Turn 5's dangers and, by obtaining a NASCAR license, assumed the risk of competing on the circuit in its existing configuration. He also opined that Turn 5 was not exceptionally dangerous, and that a mechanical failure on No. 70 was responsible for McDuffie's death. An appeals court upheld the decision.

Thus, Ima Jean could only recover the insurance benefits provided by NASCAR as part of her husband's membership – just $30,000. The original payout was only half that amount, and Linda had to fight for the remaining $15,000 they were entitled to since J.D. was both owner *and* driver.

* * * *

In August 1992, the NASCAR Winston Cup Series returned to New York for the next Budweiser at the Glen. Rain stopped the event after Lap 51 of 90, giving Kyle Petty the win. During the weekend, a fan made it onto the track and placed a lit candle on the wall in The Outer Loop at the spot where McDuffie crashed.

"Nobody removed it," said Doug Seebach, a fan at the scene. "The cops didn't even remove it. I was impressed."

CHAPTER 20
Searching For Answers

"It's not the speed that kills you. It's the sudden stop."

—Terry Shaw, Automotive Legal Service, 2017

J.D. McDuffie died instantly. The autopsy, completed by Dr. Alaud Din at the Schuyler Hospital Morgue on August 12, concluded McDuffie's cause of death was "extensive laceration of brain and brain stem secondary to skull fracture both basilar and thru and thru." In short, the impact caused part of his jawbone to pierce his brain and skull. Contrary to rumor, other than a broken bone in his right humerus (upper arm), McDuffie sustained no other injuries.

False conclusions about McDuffie's accident are commonplace today because so little information about it has been made public. There is no record that NASCAR performed an investigation into the accident, neither at the scene nor in the months following. Efforts to obtain a fatal accident report from both the New York State Police and Schuyler County Police Department have yielded no results. However, a private analysis of McDuffie's Pontiac *was* completed in anticipation of a lawsuit.

In September 1991, the No. 70 had been sitting on the back of "Old Blue" outside Medford Speed for more than a month. In addition to removing the engine and transmission, the Glenns had washed the inside of the car. Otherwise, the car remained in exactly the same condition as it had after the crash. The left-front wheel and assembly that came off that Sunday was still missing – no one had come forward to return it.

On September 13, accident investigators Phil Moser of Advanced Driver Training Services, Inc. and Terry Shaw of Automotive Legal Service came to Medford Speed, where they met with Don Owens. Shaw and Owens knew each other from their own time operating several machine shops in Delaware. Concerned about the possibility of a counter-suit by NASCAR or the race track, Owens hired Shaw and Moser to search for evidence of what caused McDuffie's fatal injury. What they found clears up several mysteries.

One rumor proposed by some was that the roof came down on McDuffie when the car landed upside-down. However, the investigators found the roll cage had survived the impact. "The passenger compartment was fully intact," read the report. "The framework did not bend, or buckle in the least. If one was to sit in the driver's seat of this vehicle without the view of the exterior of the vehicle, it would be virtually impossible to determine that the vehicle had been in a collision." In fact, one of the investigators did just that. When he sat in the seat, the halo bar – the uppermost portion of the roll cage – was still inches above his head. The man was six-foot-two. McDuffie was five-foot-ten.

Another rumor was an object pierced the roof of the car during its flip, such as one of the posts holding up the high-tension wire fence behind the tire and Armco barriers in Turn 5. This was resolved through Shaw's photos. The roof of No. 70 was bent on the passenger side around the "A-post," but wasn't pierced.

However, the investigators did notice something

strange. The impact with the tires threw McDuffie to the right, jerking the steering column more than a foot that direction. This movement pushed the right side of McDuffie's open-faced helmet against a vinyl wrap-around extension which protruded from the right side of the headrest. According to Burke, this extension, used to support the driver's head when the car made turns, was brand-new. But at the time of the investigation, there was a small cut on its lower front corner, near the location of McDuffie's chin. What could have caused that damage? And how could this account for McDuffie's fatal injury?

This led to another theory about the crash, expressed earlier by Linda McDuffie: an object entering the car. While NASCAR stock cars are closed-cockpit vehicles, this does not necessarily mean all the windows are sealed. On the driver's side, the window is replaced by a fabric "window net" latched onto the roll cage to prevent the driver's head from exiting the car during a crash. On the passenger side, a plexiglass window is used – but only on the circuit's fast superspeedways. On all other tracks, including the road courses, the passenger side window is left unprotected.

This fact drew the investigator's attention to a pair of black marks on the white-painted border of the passenger side window – one on the B-post, and another on the horizontal strip above the number on the passenger side door. The opening for the passenger-side window was itself heavily damaged, the top edge of the door rolled over so much that it had been torn from the bottom of the B-post.

"What this indicates," said the report, "is that it is probable that a foreign object entered the McDuffie vehicle through the passenger side window during the crash. If this is the case it is reasonable to assume that this foreign object struck Mr. McDuffie, causing his fatal injury to(sic)."

But what was this object? Linda McDuffie believes a post from the catchfence found its way through the open window, causing both her father's broken arm and the fatal injury to his head. "There's no way his arm could've been broken, but it was," she said. "The steel post went inside that car and killed him...he had a broken arm because that post hit him in the arm." Donald Mangum recalled a similar account from Jeff McDuffie. "The guardrail hit his neck right at the brain stem and broke his neck. The guardrail got in the car."

But Terry Shaw disagreed. During his investigation, Shaw also examined McDuffie's helmet. When looking over the foam inside, he noticed the foam covering the right side of the driver's head was crushed flat and had not expanded back to its original shape. Also, the tab holding the microphone attachment to the radio, fixed to that same side of the helmet, was bent at a forty-five-degree angle. To Shaw, the damage to the microphone tab and the foam – but not to the helmet's outer shell – ruled out the possibility of the guardrail or a post caused the injury. "If a pole had entered there, he probably wouldn't have had a head to look at because the window opening was very parallel to his head in the seat."

Instead, Shaw took note of the marks on the car's passenger side window, as well as a "black tar-like substance" on the window opening which he identified as rubber. Taken together, Shaw concluded that a tire from the barrier had entered the car through the passenger side window, leaving rubber residue on the window as it entered, and struck the right side of McDuffie's head near his jaw, inflicting the fatal injury:

"And the thing was earlier in that race, they used barriers made of upright phone poles with old tires on them, and earlier in that race that very same pole that the tire came from had been re-erected by some of the grounds crew at the race track, they just stood it up in the ground, threw the tires on it. They never reinforced it or solidified the base so it would deflect some of the pieces of cars or things that would come flying into it."

"So that was the whole issue that the phone pole wasn't securely up righted and when he came around the corner, it seemed to be a primary corner for getting hits, when he hit, the pole went right over, the tires went right over the top of it, one of them went right in the passenger side window of his car."

"...That's what led me to believe because you know the outer part of the helmet rebounded itself, when you looked inside and dissected that, you could see the compression and all the foam they used as absorption material was just crushed because that holds a fingerprint and that was I'd say a glancing blow, 'cause I could imagine the tire hitting the roll bar around his head and hitting the tab which would've been right next to his helmet then hitting the helmet probably going forward, maybe out of the windshield then into the dash."

Shaw was also certain that the tire was a passenger car tire off the barrier and not the much larger missing left-front wheel from No. 70. "I know something, it had to be flexible to bounce around like that and I can't believe if it was mounted on the rim and with any of the suspension pieces being dragged along with it would've made a mess out of him...It (the wheel off the car) would've ripped up the relatively thin sheet metal of the body of the car." While the specific tire was not found inside of McDuffie's car, Shaw says the circumstantial evidence is overwhelming. "I would say it would be considered a freak occurrence that it happened, but it did happen," he said. "I don't think he knew what hit him."

* * * *

The September 1991 investigation made no conclusions about any other phase of the accident, including what caused the left-front wheel to come off. NASCAR's Dick Beaty reportedly examined the car an hour after the crash. He told the *Star-Gazette*, "A piece of a gear broke on the automobile. It caused his left front wheel to come off," then offered no further comment. The subject remains the center of controversy.

Without the wheel itself, all that remains of it are photos and video. ESPN's replay of the accident appeared to show the wheel hit the tire barrier before No. 70 crashed. When both McDuffie and Means stopped, it then reappeared behind the wrecked No. 52 of Jimmy Means. The satellite feed doesn't show the wheel after that moment, nor does it reveal where it was taken during the nearly two-hour red flag.

One of the only photographs of the wheel once it left No. 70 was taken by photographer Tom Bernhardt. Bernhardt, who was standing near Charlie Berch in Turn 5 at the time of the accident, took a series of four photos of the accident. The first, taken the moment McDuffie left the track, shows the left-front wheel several feet above the nose of the Pontiac. The inside of the wheel that was attached to the suspension faces the camera. From a distance, it's clear that the rim was still inside the tire, and that some of the suspension appears to be attached. Not much more can be determined from the photo, nor from a brief video shot from the same position for TNN.

Without the left-front wheel, attention turns to the left-front of the car itself. The photos taken by investigators Moser and Shaw of the left-front suspension show that all that remained forward of the shocks and springs was the lower control arm. The attached lower ball joint is missing along the wheel, leaving a half-circular opening at the end of the arm. Although NASCAR didn't complete its own investigation into the crash, a failure of the ball joint – the part which attaches the upper and lower control arms to the back of the wheel and brake assembly – has become the most popular explanation for the accident. Since McDuffie was known for using used parts, many have concluded that the suspension parts were too old to be used, that they finally gave way in Turn 5 and caused the accident.

But Burke and the other members of McDuffie Racing disagree. While the car that ran that day at Watkins Glen was a six-year-old chassis, the parts were brand-new: Jerry Glenn's fresh engine, Goodyear's new radial tires, the parts Mike Demers installed, and the rebuilt Bilstein shocks. Since McDuffie wasn't involved in any of the weekend's previous accidents, there was no need for anything to be rebuilt – the car was ready to go with time to spare. No. 70

also passed each round of NASCAR's technical inspection and made it through the queue so quickly on Sunday that it was the first car to be pushed onto the grid. If No. 70 had a fatal flaw, it went unnoticed by several people.

Demers is adamant that the nuts on the upper and lower ball joints were properly secured – it was something the crew checked on a regular basis. His concern, however, revolves around a separate suspension component: the nut on the tie rod, the part Demers photographed McDuffie adjusting the day of the race.

The tie rod has two critical purposes: to ensure the steering wheel turns both front wheels, and to make sure both wheels turn the same direction. The tie rod is held by a nut at both ends. NASCAR stock cars of the period secured each tie rod nut with either a metal cotter pin, as on production vehicles, or a length of safety wire, as used on the hubs and brake rotors. The purpose of using a pin or wire on the tie rod nut wasn't to hold the tie rod together, but rather to keep the nut from coming loose. This is important because if one tie rod nut comes loose and falls out, the tie rod falls to the ground. A disconnected tie rod severs the connection between the steering wheel and the wheels, making it impossible to steer the car. At high speeds, the unsecured wheel would jam itself under the fender, putting further strain on the suspension.

During the investigation, Demers stated that the tie rod nut was no longer on the outer tie rod, indicating it either split or came loose. But, if this happened, what caused it to fail?

Video of the accident and accounts of both Jimmy Means and Jim Derhaag indicate that, when McDuffie's car lost control, the driver's side of No. 70 made contact with the passenger side of Jimmy Means' No. 52, forcing both cars off the track. Tom Bernhardt's photo from Turn 5 shows extensive damage to the driver's side of McDuffie's car at the moment the passenger side impacted the tires. Moser and Shaw's photos also reveal small streaks of light blue paint on the driver's side door number of No. 70. Taken together, this indicated damage suffered when McDuffie caught and collided with Means as the pair entered Turn 5.

But Burke and Demers believe that the two cars made contact one other time before the accident, and that this contact – though not intentional by either driver – damaged or dislodged the tie rod nut behind McDuffie's left-front wheel.

Demers summarized the sequence of events. "What happened is he (McDuffie) and the 52 car Jimmy Means got together on the back straight and the nut came off the tie rod end – or broke off the tie rod, fatigued, or what have you – and when that tie rod end dropped to the race track, then the left wheel – was nothing to keep it straight or what have you – it basically ripped itself off."

Jimmy Means, Jim Derhaag, and Ned Jarrett could not recall any contact between the two Pontiacs prior to the moment McDuffie bumped Means off the track. Even if such contact *had* occurred, it's unlikely it was solely responsible for the failure. Stock cars are durable machines, capable of bumping and bouncing off each other without inflicting serious damage to their inner workings. "Rubbin's racin'," a line made famous in "Days of Thunder" a year earlier, distinguishes NASCAR from open-wheel IndyCar and Formula One competition. On those circuits, suspension components are so exposed that even slight contact can damage the entire car beyond repair.

So, the question remains: what triggered the accident? Unfortunately, we may never know. As Shaw stated, not much more could be concluded from analyzing McDuffie's car and helmet. His 1991 report is silent as to any other phase of the accident, including the meaning of the damage to the end of the left-front lower control arm. And so, some mysteries still endure. What caused McDuffie's wheel to come off? When did it come off in relation to the contact that sent McDuffie and Means off the track? And why did the wheel take such a peculiar trajectory – high in the air, ahead of No. 70?

This much seems to be known. On Lap 5, as McDuffie entered the fifth turn at over 160mph, the tie rod behind the left-front wheel dropped. The unsecured wheel sheared off, taking with it much of the suspension, and severing the brake lines. Since NASCAR stock cars at the time had just one master cylinder, a severed brake line resulted in an in- stant loss of brake pressure. With both the steering wheel and brake pedals disabled, McDuffie was out of control. His No. 70 closed the gap on a slowing Jimmy Means and side- swiped the No. 52, sending both cars off the track. Once on the grass, the nose of No. 70 dug in, steering the car left un- til it was pulled parallel with the tire barrier. Upon impact, a passenger tire from the barrier entered the No. 70 through his open passenger window. The roll cage held as the car flipped and landed upside-down, but by then, McDuffie had already suffered the injury.

CHAPTER 21
Aftermath

*"J.D. was more like a brother to me than anything else.
We were in and out of each other's homes all the time.
And my brother passed away about the same time that
J.D. was killed at Watkins Glen, and I didn't miss my
brother any more than J.D. That might be bad to say, but
we were that close."*

—*James Oldham, 2017*

August 11, 1991 has never left Ima Jean McDuffie. Despite extensive counseling, she was hospitalized for high blood pressure eight times over the following seven years. When she watched a tape of the wreck twenty-five years later, the sight alone gave her a heart attack. "I couldn't believe it," she said. "It was horrible. Horrible. Oh, Lord—"

As the McDuffie family struggled to make ends meet, fans once again tried to help. This time, they donated to the "J.D. McDuffie Memorial Fund," sending funds both to Ima Jean's home and Rumple Furniture. Mike and Lesley Demers kept the J.D. McDuffie Fan Club going as more fans joined. Membership and t-shirt sales went into the fund. Artists helped as well, donating proceeds from colored prints of J.D. sold for $100 apiece. More funds came from a September 1991 celebrity softball game in Fort Mill, South Carolina which matched NHRA drag racers and NASCAR stars, including Watkins Glen winner Ernie Irvan. Maxx Race Cards invited Ima Jean to their yearly autograph session. The first time out on October 4, she stayed the entire day, not leaving until just before 11:00 P.M.

Today, Ima Jean lives with Jeff and her grandson Jeffrey in Sanford. "I still get cards and stuff sometimes, calls," she said. In addition to her scrapbook from her husband's racing days and his trophies, she keeps a journal that she updates daily, recording memories of her husband.

* * * *

In 1992, some of McDuffie's fans and supporters looked into helping another NASCAR team. Most went to James Hylton, the owner-driver who fell short of bumping J.D. McDuffie from his 652nd start at Pocono. In true independent fashion, Hylton had just acquired an old car from a big team, buying one of SABCO Racing's No. 42 Pontiacs that Kyle Petty drove the previous year. The car wasn't ready for the Daytona 500, so Hylton leased a trailer and a brand-new Chevrolet Lumina from car owner Dick Bahre.

Joining the Hylton effort were Mike and Lesley Demers, Marty Burke, Tom Rumple, and Jerry Glenn and his son. Thus, Hylton's white-and-yellow Chevrolet had their company's logos in familiar places: Son's Auto Supply and Medford Speed on the hood, Classic Trophies on the rear deck lid, and Rumple Furniture on the "TV Panel." With his crew on hand, Hylton looked to carry the torch for McDuffie. He wore Rumple Furniture's trucker caps, and at Daytona participated in a benefit bowling tournament at LaPaloma Lanes. "J.D. always participated in this," said Hylton. "I'm just kind of taking his place."

Additional funding came from Tennessee's National Sports Card Association, which formed Resco Racing.

Perhaps inspired by the Demers, Resco printed pamphlets to
be distributed at area hotels for fans to sign on as "Associate Sponsors." $100 by mail earned fans the benefits of a
fan club, including a t-shirt and hat, and their name on the
side of Hylton's No. 48. "Share the excitement of racing
from an inside perspective," the pamphlets read. "While
you root for your favorite driver you can point to Hylton's
number 48 and say, 'That's my car.'" At Daytona, at least
ten fans had their names printed in black around the rear
wheels. Though Hylton hadn't run a full season since 1980,
his newly crowned "HARD Racing Team" now had enough
money to attempt the entire 1992 season.

For SpeedWeeks '92, the Glenns provided Hylton with
two Medford engines as well as the very same Blue Max
Racing transmission pulled from No. 70 after Watkins Glen.
Hylton first took to the track using the engine that came
with the car, but when it was clearly not fast enough, they
swapped in the first of Medford's power plants. Unfortunately, someone on the team hooked up the hoses wrong,
pumping water into the fuel cell. The mistake forced a
complete tear-down, another run through inspection, and
just one more lap of practice before a big wreck stopped the
session. While the McDuffie crew wanted to give Glenn's
engine another try, Hylton's sponsor leaned on the driver to
use the leased engine, paying him an extra bonus to do so.
The decision didn't help. Hylton finished twenty-fifth of
twenty-nine drivers in his Twin 125-mile qualifying race,
missing a spot in the Daytona 500.

The following week, the lease was up on Bahre's
equipment, so Hylton towed the SABCO Pontiac to Richmond on the back of an open trailer. The car didn't fare

much better, failing inspection multiple times before withdrawing from the event. Ken and Nancy Settmeier, whose names were on McDuffie's No. 70 car at Dover the previous year, joined HARD Racing's list of Associate Sponsors. Still, the rest of the season didn't go much better. Hylton attempted just nineteen of the season's twenty-nine races. Of the eight he actually made, he finished under power only twice, and each time came home more than ten laps down. The other times, he either parked the car, lost the motor, or was flagged off the track for failing to maintain NASCAR's minimum required speed. Hylton made just two more Winston Cup points races in 1993 before finishing out his career in ARCA. One of Hylton's last NASCAR attempts was 1994's inaugural Brickyard 400 at Indianapolis, in a Pontiac sponsored by Rumple Furniture.

* * * *

Jimmy Means never again raced at Watkins Glen. The car he drove that day sat unused in the back of his shop until he sold it years later. Were it not for a change in management, Alka-Seltzer would have stayed with Means beyond 1991. "Alka-Seltzer said that was the best investment that they had ever done and the best return they'd ever done," said Means. As it was, Alka-Seltzer left at season's end. Means Racing scaled back in 1992, and the driver continued to hand over the wheel more frequently.

On February 11, 1994, Means was in Florida, preparing his No. 52 Ford for another run at the Daytona 500. In between runs, he watched Neil Bonnett on the track, his stopwatch running. Suddenly, in Turn 4, Bonnett's No. 51

Country Time Chevrolet lost control and slammed head-on into the outside wall. Bonnett was killed instantly. Three days later, another NASCAR driver, rookie Rodney Orr, lost his life in a similar single-car crash.

"I decided I didn't want to do it anymore – my heart wasn't in it," said Means. "That's all I wanted to do for like twenty-five years and my heart was out of it. I said don't need to be in it, my heart's not in it, so I quit." Means handed the wheel over to Brad Teague and stepped out of the seat for good, winless in 455 starts. In 1995, after missing the first seven races of the season as a car owner, Jimmy Means Racing suspended operations, and the driver became a crew chief for Bud Moore Engineering.

But this wasn't the end for Jimmy Means Racing. The Forest City shop re-opened in 2001 when Means saw an opportunity to help fill fields in NASCAR's second-tier division, known today as the Xfinity Series. As he once again began building up his single-car program, Means crossed paths with young Iowa driver Joey Gase, who actively supports the "Donate Life" program for organ donation. When Gase lost his ride at Go Green Racing in 2012, Means picked him up.

Three years later, on May 2, 2015, the partnership paid off. During the hotly contested Winn-Dixie 300 at Talladega, Gase recovered from multiple accidents to muscle his overheating No. 52 Chevrolet to a fifth-place finish – the first time a Means car had finished inside the Top Five. As of this writing, Means still fields No. 52 Chevrolets in the Xfinity Series.

Means and Dale Earnhardt, Jr. are still close friends. In December 2016, Earnhardt invited him to his wedding.

"And still today he acknowledges that," he said. "That just means everything in the world to me that, even though I didn't know it at the time we were molding a friendship that's lasted thirty years or so. Just honored that he recognizes me like that. And he told me at the wedding, he said 'Man, I love you.' And I said 'Well, I do to you, too.' It just – you don't forget where we all came from and how we got here. He's just a special man."

* * * *

Another driver Means hired was Tommy Kendall, who in 1992 returned to action for the first time since his Turn 5 wreck at Watkins Glen. He teamed up with Means for NASCAR's return to Sears Point in 1992, a combined effort with car owners Rick Hendrick and Felix Sabates. Kendall finished thirteenth that day after a last-lap, last-corner pass.

Today, both Kendall and Dorsey Schroeder remain active in television. Among their fellow "road ringers," Jim Derhaag still fields Chevrolets in Trans-Am and Irv Hoerr sells performance parts through his company Hoerr Racing Products. The No. 54 car Derhaag drove on August 11, 1991 currently sits in a private collection. A layer of dust covers the windshield through which the driver witnessed McDuffie's accident.

As of this writing, Mark Donohue remains the last "road ringer" to win in NASCAR's elite series.

* * * *

Not long after the paper's tribute to McDuffie, the old typesetter finally broke down at *Instant Replay Sporting Photo News*. With the ads for the next issue paid for, Charlie Berch and his team assembled the last issue with a typewriter, a razor blade, and a glue stick, and managed to get it distributed on time. While this spelled the end for *Instant Replay*, Berch continued to have a successful career in photography. He joined *Winston Cup Scene* and would cover between seven and fourteen races a year for the next fifteen years. In 2011, Berch realized a lifelong dream when he stood in victory lane at The Glen as a crew member for the victorious TRG Porsche team. With *Scene* now gone, Berch remains an active photographer, particularly at his home track.

After the crash, Berch's friend Janine Pestel helped Stanley Smith, still another owner-driver on the NASCAR tour. "What made me become a fan of Stanley's was we were at, I think it was Darlington and he and I don't think he crashed, something was wrong with the car, but I remember they pulled him behind the wall. He didn't go to the garage, but he went behind the wall there, and there was this kid, you know, by the fence, and he had something in his hand and he was trying to get Stanley's attention. He wanted Stanley to sign it. Now, here's Stanley having trouble in the race, and I remember Stanley sticking his hand out and he pointed to the kid. One of the crew members stops what he's doing, walks over, got the paper from the kid, handed it to Stanley, Stanley signed it, gave it back and gave it back to the kid...He was awesome. Probably still is." Pestel left *Area Auto Racing News* in 1994, not long after Smith suffered a near-fatal accident at Talladega. She and her husband now live in Arizona, where both still photograph the racing action at the Phoenix Raceway.

* * * *

McDuffie's friend Bobby Hudson went on to have a tumultuous career in racing. On two occasions, he worked as a crew chief for Bobby Allison, who in 1984 served as the best man at his wedding. "Body by B.H." stayed in business through 1995. During one race at Darlington, eleven of the forty cars in the field had been assembled in his Rockingham shop. In 1993, Hudson started to work for Roush Racing, spotting for Greg Biffle, Paul Menard, Mark Martin, and Carl Edwards. In 1996, he became the shop foreman for the new No. 99 Exide Batteries team with driver Jeff Burton. "I always told (crew chief) Buddy Parrott, I did all the work, he got all the credit," he said.

In 2007, after surviving a near-fatal heart attack, Hudson spotted for Edwards during a blazing-hot September day in Dover. When Edwards took the win, Hudson was awarded the team's prestigious "Jack Award" by team owner Jack Roush for going above and beyond the call of duty. He rounded out his racing career in 2011 as Ty Dillon's spotter the year he claimed the ARCA championship.

In 2016, Hudson went to the Darlington Raceway, where the No. 72 Chevrolet he worked on in 1973 took ceremonial pace laps with Dale Jarrett behind the wheel. He still plays cards with his friends, though away from the track.

* * * *

NAPA purchased Son's Auto Supply in 2011, and the New Jersey shop is still in business today. There, Mike Demers programmed automotive computers as the "NAPA Flash" until his death in 2019. His wife Lesley has taught water aerobics at two local chapters of the YMCA. Not far away, Medford Speed & Machine is also still open, where Jerry Glenn, Jr. clocks in at dawn to craft performance parts. His father Jerry Sr. passed away in October 2016. Jerry Jr.'s son-in-law Bob Lineman, Jr. continues the family's racing tradition, having driven Medford engines to two Sportsman Series championships at the New Egypt Speedway.

Also still in operation is the L.C. Whitford Co., Inc., which in 2016 marked their 100th anniversary. After the crash, company president Brad Whitford received many offers to sponsor other race teams, but every time he refused. The sight of his logo upside-down at The Glen was too much.

Terry Shaw still works as an accident investigator and has operated at Automotive Legal Service, Inc.'s Dresher, Pennsylvania headquarters since 1985. In his office, there's a model of No. 70 on his shelf.

Both Terry Letton and Marc Cashman still go to races in the northeast. Cashman works track side for a petroleum company at speedways across the north-east, including Pocono and Dover. Just across the border in Canada, former McDuffie Racing crewman George Sekanina has a successful career in television. Leland Moore would remain in NASCAR for years to come, including a job on D.K. Ulrich's team in 1995. He would go on to write his story for a local magazine, entitled "J.D. McDuffie Changed My Life."

After the accident, crew member Donald Mangum continued to handle 911 calls in Raleigh until he retired after twenty-seven years. Today, he works the family farm with his brother. As of April 2017, Mangum hadn't been to a NASCAR race since May 1991, when he watched McDuffie attempt to qualify for the Coca-Cola 600. He returned to the track at Martinsville, where his friend Todd Parrott then worked as crew chief for NASCAR single-car team Leavine Family Racing.

James Oldham lives near Charlotte with his wife. Once a month, he meets with his classmates, known as "The Rowdy Bunch." He's kept the same long white beard from his days at the *Herald* and can be found each holiday season playing Santa Claus at local functions. Still carrying his J.D. McDuffie Fan Club card signed by Oldham is Tom Clegg, who retired from the Army in 1993. Both he and Wayne Andrews still live near Sanford. Andrews still works at his shop, Wayne's Alignment Service, off US Highway 64 in Siler City, where "Old Blue" once passed by before each race.

Six miles down the road from David Slezak, now an avid historian in addition to a race fan, Classic Trophies is still in business today at the original Hatford, Pennsylvania shop. Marty Burke sold Classic in 1997 and moved to Leonard, Texas, where he lives today. Though he never got to compete in ARCA or in NASCAR, he started his own drag racing team. From 2000 to 2004, Marty Burke Motorsports held NHRA National records for elapsed time and speed. His race-modified Mustangs are painted burgundy. He doesn't allow anything green near them. Pictures of J.D. and No. 70 ring his office.

After the accident, Burke contacted Steve Jones of Advantage Management, then the agent for driver Sterling Marlin, and arranged with die-cast manufacturers Racing Champions and White Rose Collectibles to sell scale models of No. 70. In time, these and other companies would issue nine different McDuffie cars. Search the driver's name on eBay, and the burgundy Childress car shows up more than any other. The next year, Advantage featured McDuffie's final three cars on a new shirt produced by Motorsports Traditions. Above a black-and-white photo of McDuffie, a cigar pinched between his teeth, read the words "A True Competitor."

In 1994, Roger Lankford, McDuffie Racing's chassis set-up man who worked alongside Burke during the 1989 Daytona 500, started his own race team, Lankford Brothers Racing. He began racing four-cylinder cars at the Friendship Speedway, a half-mile dirt oval not far from Rumple Furniture in Elkin. Four years later, on September 7, 1998, Lankford took the checkered flag in a Limited Late Model event at Friendship. Like his other cars, his ride that night bore McDuffie's iconic No. 70. Today, Lankford works for Jimmy Means Racing.

* * * *

Watkins Glen's original 1948 course named two turns after drivers involved in spectacular accidents. The Formula One circuit briefly included the "Scheckter Chicane." But despite the suggestions of many, including Rusty Wallace, the track has never renamed the "Inner Loop" in McDuffie's honor. Instead, in 1994, the track sold title sponsorship to the complex, which was briefly known as the "McDonald's Loop." Today, it's known colloquially as "the chicane" or "the bus stop." The Glen's only memorial to McDuffie remains the fact that there has been just one fatality at the track since – SCCA competitor Ken Buchel on July 9, 2011.

* * * *

After the crash, the McDuffie family struggled to figure out what to do with J.D.'s shop. Jeff wanted to keep the race team going, but without funding, the plan wasn't workable. Nor was an unsolicited plan from a man in Florida, who tried to talk the family into giving them the equipment so he could start his own team. In the end, the family kept the Sanford shop shuttered and idle for more than four years. Finally, after a series of break-ins and vandalism, Ima Jean had enough. "I just can't hold on to it forever," she said. So, on October 23, 1995, following a two-day inspection, the last remnants of McDuffie Racing went up for auction.

Just after 10 A.M., Tom McInnis of Iron Horse Auctions opened the bidding. Richard Pugh, a collector from Alabama, bought the two Hutcherson-Pagan-built Pontiacs. Hudson finished the blue car, though his heart wasn't in it, and was paid by the McDuffie family. The red car still bore the scars from the wreck at Dover. The land and the shop went for $72,500 to Ellis Ragan, who at the time was fielding cars for Tom Usry in the NASCAR Goody's Dash Series. Years after J.D. sold him cars to race in ARCA, Usry's own cars would be built in the same shop.

Mike Demers made it to the auction, where he purchased

the team's pit road banner, a container of used lug nuts, and a Hollywood-style director's chair McDuffie received for his start in the Busch Clash of '79. Jimmy Byrd was there as well, where he bought McDuffie's wire welder for $675 and thirty-seven boxes of wire for thirteen dollars a box. The welder still works today, kept in the Broadway-area home where he cares for his wife. In his free time, Byrd makes lamps from glass bottles.

Before the auction, there was a movement to put "Old Blue" into a museum. Ima Jean had re-acquired it from New Jersey, albeit with some difficulty due to the faulty brakes, then left it sitting inside the Sanford shop for several years. Instead, it went to John Parsons, who bid $7,750 on behalf of Ken Schrader, one of the drivers who also found the barriers that weekend at Watkins Glen.

By sunset, the building stood empty.

* * * *

McDuffie Racing's shop on 923 Willett Road still stands today, protected by a chain-link fence and surrounded by old cars. One of the later owners added an awning over the front of the building and a rear sliding door. Since 2008, the building has served as storage space for Sanford Transmission & Automotive, which operates out of another shop across town. Despite the 1995 auction, there are still signs of McDuffie Racing inside, including the team's decals for Pontiac Motorsports and AC Spark Plugs on the original white wood paneling.

Not far away, McDuffie's previous shop still stands as well. After the team moved to Willett Road, it became a passenger car garage called "The Tune Up Shop," which is now leased by a tenant. Next door, Jimmy Thomas still tends to the family farm. In 2019, Wilbur Thomas died after a short illness at age 84. Wilbur's name, as well as J.D.'s, are on a brick near the entrance to the NASCAR Hall of Fame in Charlotte, North Carolina. The engraving reads "WILBUR "BADEYE" THOMAS ORIGINAL CREW CHIEF J.D. McDUFFIE RACING TEAM." It's the only mention of McDuffie at the Hall.

* * * *

Linda McDuffie finally did move out of Sanford, where her mother and brother still live today. Linda and her wife Wendy now live in Colorado. In college, Linda discovered a passion for cartography and now designs aeronautical charts for the military. "If there's one thing my dad taught me," she said, "do what you love, and I'm doing exactly what I love." She remains protective of her father's legacy. "He was my hero, my role model, my everything."

A couple years after the accident, Linda was invited to the Shangri-La Speedway, where track officials greeted her warmly. Among them was Tom Schwarz, who once again had a special surprise: he invited Linda to take some laps in his No. 07, the very same car her father raced to victory on the night of August 10, 1991. "I will admit this – I spun the car out," she said with a laugh. "It was a lot of fun, and I was honored that he would let me even do that and take it around the track because it was like when I was in that race car, it was like my dad had his hand on my shoulder."

Such memories became part of a speech Linda gave in

January 1997, when the Eastern Motorsport Press Association Hall of Fame inducted her father along with Nick Fornoro and Sonny Kleinfeld. She still remembers the moment she took the stage in front of a crowd of 400, including Tom Rumple. "I got up there and you could frickin' hear a pin drop, and that's probably one of the best memories I have as far as people acknowledging my dad and speaking about him, so yeah it was pretty cool."

* * * *

When Mike and Lesley Demers were unsuccessful in persuading the Atlanta Motor Speedway to name its new grandstands after J.D. McDuffie, Charlie Berch of *Instant Replay* joined them in petitioning NASCAR to retire the No. 70. A letter-writing campaign unfolded, calling on fans to write to media coordinator Chip Williams. Though NASCAR turned them down, the number did disappear from the sport's elite division for nearly two decades. A handful of drivers and teams, including West Coast racer Rick Bogart, tried to put the number into the occasional Winston Cup race, but for one reason or another, it always failed to qualify.

It wasn't until May 28, 2006 that No. 70 took another green flag in NASCAR's top series, this time with Johnny Sauter and the HAAS-CNC team. The pair finished twenty-fourth that day in the Coca-Cola 600. The next year, Sauter and HAAS brought the No. 70 to Watkins Glen for the first time since 1991. During the SPEED Channel's pre-race segment "RaceDay," the network aired a brief tribute to McDuffie. Sauter finished twenty-third.

As of this writing, the No. 70 is again missing from Sunday's lineups, unused on the Cup circuit since Mike Skinner finished last at Texas on November 8, 2009.

In 761 tries, it has yet to win a race.

CHAPTER 22
Darlington

While we won't see him take another green flag, his spir-
it will always be present wherever the roar of the engines
is heard.

—*a J.D. McDuffie memorial trading card, 1991*

When John Bailey's son Jacob texted me the picture on
April 13, 2016, I could hardly believe what I was seeing.
There was "Old Blue," parked in a garage among tool boxes, engine parts, and dangling chains, its blue paint faded by
a gathering patina of dust. It was then I understood why Jacob's voice went quiet when I said McDuffie's name, why
he closed the door to his office before he answered my next
question.

The Baileys acquired "Old Blue" from Ken Schrader
and brought it back to their Jackson, Michigan facility.
With the truck's brakes mended, John put the hauler into
service, fielding his own race cars on the weekends. When
the ordeal of racing became too much, the Baileys hired
other Michigan drivers to run in their place, fielding ARCA
cars for Dan Ford, Jr. and NASCAR Camping World Truck
Series rides for Andy Ponstein. The last pavement late
model John drove, painted the same shade of blue with a
big No. 70 on each door, still sat on the back of "Old Blue."
Bill Bailey passed away in 2010. John and Jacob now run
the family business.

During our call, the Baileys told me they were thinking about fixing the truck. The engine McDuffie got from that Chevrolet dealer in 1977 had been a good one. They were just now replacing it.

A few months after we spoke, the Baileys received another phone call.

* * * *

On September 17, 1978, fifteen-year-old Jerry Freeze was in the grandstands at Dover Downs International Speedway for NASCAR's Delaware 500. As the thirty-seven cars were pushed onto the grid, Freeze was surprised to see the No. 70 Bailey Excavating Chevrolet sitting in the first row. "Oh my god," he said to his family. "J.D. McDuffie's on the pole position! How did that happen?" Nearly four decades after that moment, that boy from Washington, D.C. was still very much a race fan. In fact, he became the General Manager of a NASCAR Cup Series team: Front Row Motorsports.

Front Row was founded by Tennessee businessman Robert "Bob" Jenkins (not to be confused with the ESPN broadcaster). Jenkins' involvement in NASCAR began in 2004, when he began sponsoring cars with the money from his investments in several businesses, including the Morristown Driver's Services logistics company. The first team Jenkins sponsored was none other than Jimmy Means' No. 52 in the Busch Series, which at the time still had Brad Teague behind the wheel. Jenkins and Means formed a partnership, Means-Jenkins Motorsports, with eyes on moving to NASCAR's top division. In 2005, Jenkins took full control of the program, changing its name to Front Row and making its first Cup start with second-generation driver Stanton Barrett.

Front Row didn't run the full NASCAR schedule until 2009. That year, the team's two cars carried logos – but not sponsorship – from Taco Bell and Long John Silver's, as both were among the 150 franchises that Jenkins owned. The team supplemented its income by making their No. 37 Long John Silver's car a "start-and-park" entry, collecting last-place money to help fund John Andretti's No. 34 Taco Bell car. The investment paid off, and in 2010, the team suddenly had three full-time teams, including Rookie of the Year winner Kevin Conway. David Gilliland earned the team's first top-five finish in the 2011 Daytona 500, and at Talladega in 2013, David Ragan took their first checkered flag. By the summer of 2016, Front Row had two rising stars in its stable. Chris Buescher, the defending NASCAR Xfinity Series champion, pulled an upset victory in the No. 34 at Pocono when fog cut short the Pennsylvania 500. The team's second car, No. 38, was piloted by fan favorite Landon Cassill.

In 2007, the Iowa-born Cassill began his NASCAR career as a seventeen-year-old development driver for Hendrick Motorsports, eventually earning five top-ten finishes. When the deal fell through in 2009, however, he moved from team to team, looking for a full-time ride. In 2010, Cassill made his Cup debut in his first attempt at Michigan, and from there earned a reputation as an exceptional qualifier. He made races for start-up teams like TRG Motorsports, Gunselman Motorsports, BK Racing, and Circle Sport, and away from the track held qualifying challenges against online sim racers. In 2016, his efforts were rewarded with a full-time effort for Front Row. Cassill impressed with strong runs at Bristol and Talladega, but Front Row's sponsorship issues remained. The team didn't have a backer for September's Southern 500 at Darlington.

When the Southern 500 returned to its traditional Labor Day weekend in 2015, many drivers and teams celebrated by running "throwback" paint schemes, many of which honored other drivers from the sport's past. The spontaneous effort began with series champion Brad Keselowski, whose sponsor Miller Lite had already scheduled a tribute to Bobby Allison's 1983 championship as part of the brand's twenty-fifth anniversary in NASCAR. More than half the field joined in. Darlington 2016 would focus on NASCAR's "Golden Era" from 1975 to 1984, and all but a handful of teams had announced their "throwbacks" already. Front Row, who missed out in 2015, was determined not to miss it again. Love's Travel Stops, the sponsor for Chris Buescher's No. 34, elected to run an older version of the company's logo. But without sponsorship, Cassill's had yet to be decided.

In early August 2016, less than a month before the 500, Jerry Freeze was in Bob Jenkins' office, thinking about what paint scheme to run on the No. 38. "Everybody was announcing their commemorative schemes for Darrell Waltrip, Cale Yarborough, Bobby Allison, everybody," recalled Freeze, "and we were like, you know, we're one of the little guys taking on the big guys in the sport, let's commemorate one of the little guys from that era...We should be honoring everybody that was competing, not just the top five or six guys." The two started tossing out some names. Jimmy

Means. H.B. Bailey. Elmo Langley. "Well, how about J.D. McDuffie?" asked Jenkins. Suddenly, Freeze's memory from 1978 came rushing back.

The two agreed, but both wanted to make sure they went about it the right way. Tony Stewart unveiled his own Bobby Allison car with the man himself. Matt Kenseth's "Tide Ride" had past race winners Darrell Waltrip, Ricky Rudd, and Ricky Craven alongside. But with so little information on McDuffie compared to other drivers, Freeze wasn't sure where to look. He knew of McDuffie's children, Jeff and Linda, but couldn't find their contact information. Then, when searching Facebook for Linda, Freeze came across a picture of a young woman. "[I] saw she had a tattoo of J.D. on her shoulder, I said, I think I got the right Linda McDuffie right here. So, I friended her on Facebook really quick and she accepted and then reached out to her and she was so excited, so it kind of got the ball started. But if I hadn't come across that picture with J.D. on her shoulder, the cigar sticking out of his mouth, I don't think I'd gotten any further."

Linda McDuffie helped Freeze get in touch with the Rumple family. Sure enough, Rumple Furniture was still in operation from the same Elkin, North Carolina showroom built in 1978. The No. 70 "show car" Tom Rumple painted had stayed out in front of the store for several years, but when the paint faded, and the decals began to peel, it was moved into the back of the warehouse. Tom passed away in 2003. His son Don now ran the shop. When Front Row Motorsports called, Don agreed on the spot.

Then Freeze called John Bailey.

* * * *

"They contacted us," said John. "And I got a little emotional on that one."

Freeze and Jenkins decided that J.D. McDuffie would be the subject of Landon Cassill's "throwback" paint job at Darlington. As part of the tribute, the car would carry logos for both Bailey Excavating and Rumple Furniture. While the team was unable to change the car number to No. 70, the No. 38 team had a guaranteed starting spot in the Southern 500. The race, set for September 4, 2016, would mark the first time a Bailey-backed car competed in a NASCAR race since September 4, 2003, and the first for Rumple since May 20, 1995.

As Front Row put the finishing touches on Cassill's paint scheme, their two teams arrived at the Michigan International Speedway to compete in NASCAR's Pure Michigan 400. At the time, Jerry Freeze wasn't sure if the Baileys would be able to come down to Darlington, so he invited them to come to the track instead. During the conversation, John had an idea. "We need to get 'Old Blue' running again and bring it to the track one day," he said. "It needs an engine and maybe next year we can bring it out there." Freeze thought about having Cassill come by Bailey Excavating to look at the truck, but two days later, John called back. After a couple all-nighters, John and Jacob had dropped a new motor into "Old Blue" and got it running. "And we're gonna drive it to the track on Sunday," he said. Freeze didn't know how to arrange it. John told him not to worry. After working some of his connections at the track, Bailey got it done.

Twenty-five years after McDuffie's accident, "Old Blue" finally made it to the paddock at Michigan.

Landon Cassill was there to meet him, and Bailey showed him around the truck. Phone in hand, Cassill recorded the tour for fans on his Snapchat page. There were still cigar wrappers in the ash tray, a cassette in the eight-track player, and road flares under the seat. The vehicle was a time capsule, all the way down to its distinctive horn that blared from two steel trumpets. Among those who also came by was Richard Childress, who had three cars of his own in the race. The veteran car owner recognized it immediately. Someone at the viewing said "You've gotta have this thing at Darlington." Again, John Bailey grabbed the opportunity. "We're gonna bring it," he said. Again, Front Row wasn't sure if they could make it happen, but again the track was overjoyed. Bailey and his son would drive "Old Blue" to Darlington. On the way, they stopped in Sanford and met with Ima Jean McDuffie.

At first, Ima Jean wasn't sure if she wanted to come to the track. But the Baileys proved persuasive. "I just told John, I don't have any money left after I pay my bills, I'm broke," she said. "He said 'Don't worry about that, we're going.' So, when I got down there, John told me he left his credit card there for me, and that was nice."

* * * *

On August 23, 2016, two days after the Michigan race, it came time to unveil the new look for No. 38 at Front Row's Statesville, North Carolina shop. The final paint scheme was kept hidden for days – even Cassill didn't know what it would look like. That morning, he posted a picture of himself on Twitter wearing one of Rumple Furniture's old trucker caps. Fans tuned in to watch the reveal live. Don Rumple was in attendance to help lift the black car cover from the machine. When it was done, the two stood back as photographers snapped their pictures.

The scheme came out beautifully. Dark blue with a gold roof and mirrored gold numbers, resembling the Bailey Excavating cars from the 1970s and early 1980s. Bailey Excavating's logo was over the left-rear wheels and across the roof in bold white letters. Over the right-rear wheels, as well as its traditional spot on the "TV Panel," were the bold yellow letters of Rumple Furniture. The gold hood was blank, just like McDuffie's was so often in his career, a struggle matched by Front Row's own battle to become competitive in NASCAR. On the C-post, just as in the 1970s, were the words "With 'GOD' You're Always A Winner." And, like all Front Row's cars, it was a Ford – the same model Marty Burke always joked with McDuffie about driving.

Later that day in Forest Hills, Jimmy Means Racing announced that they, too, would be running a "throwback" scheme for Joey Gase in Darlington's Xfinity Series race. For the first time in twenty-five years, the powder blue Alka-Seltzer colors would return to No. 52.

* * * *

When Darlington weekend finally came, "Old Blue" stirred up memories for all who saw her. On Saturday evening, the Baileys – John, Jacob, and Jacob's son Jordan –

drove it in the annual Southern 500 Parade. The truck then parked in the track's midway for the first time in a quarter-century.

Ima Jean was pleased with the tribute car – mostly. "Those guys put yellow and gold, gold and blue on their car but they wouldn't let them put 70 on it. They wouldn't let 'em do it," said Ima Jean. But the team made one more change. Someone added a "70" behind the front wheel.

Several of the veteran drivers and owners gave her a warm welcome. Richard Petty talked with her, as did son Kyle. Leonard Wood, patriarch of the Wood Brothers, was there. So was veteran MRN pit reporter Winston Kelley. Finally, wearing a Rumple Furniture cap and matching velvet jacket, Landon Cassill personally came by to share stories.

The pinnacle of the weekend came on race day that Sunday, when Bailey drove "Old Blue" on the track during the pace laps, following a fleet of vintage race cars. Though she struggled with knee pain and a hot summer weekend, nothing could keep Ima Jean from climbing in the passenger seat and waving to the crowd.

In the race itself, the tough Darlington track showed Cassill no mercy. Starting twenty-ninth in the field after rains from Hurricane Hermine washed-out qualifying, Cassill fought handling problems for much of the night, losing a lap to leader Kevin Harvick on Lap 25. Flat tires and ill-timed cautions put Cassill down two more laps – despite a protest with timing and scoring – and on Lap 96, the No. 38 was running last in the field.

But, like McDuffie himself, driver and team never gave up. The team clawed their way to thirty-ninth on Lap 141, then gained nine more spots by the end of the race. Cassill took the checkered flag in thirtieth, five laps down, with the car intact. A McDuffie car has still never finished on the lead lap.

Despite the challenges, Freeze enjoyed the experience and looked forward to the next "throwback" race. "For us at Front Row," he said, "if we have some flexibility on who to honor, we're gonna just continue this tradition. I think that's our niche, that's what we need to do. We need to honor the guys who worked harder, or just as hard as everyone to scratch out a living and so we've gotta put our thinking caps on for next year and figure out who we're gonna run as next year, too."

"We had fun up there," said Ima Jean. "That's the most fun I've had in a long time."

Epilogue

In an article published August 22, 1991, Hank School-field of *Southern Motor Racing* criticized those who de-scribed J.D. McDuffie as "a holdover, a man from another era:"

"I don't think those people really knew J.D. McDuffie," he wrote. "He was one of a kind, but not the last one, and I think he's sitting up there chuckling about the rhetoric. He was like a lot of hardy men who lived by the sweat of their brows and the brawn of their bodies and the pursuit of their enjoyments. Different from a lot of rac-ing drivers now, because his first priority was the enjoy-ment and not the money."

"They're rare on the major league tour, where the taste for lifestyle has become such an obsession that it obscures the taste for life. But there are plenty of them in the sport's lower echelons, where J.D. McDuffie started three decades ago with greasy fingers and a few wrenches and a penchant for dirt tracks. I don't think you really would have known J.D. McDuffie without being one of them."

Indeed, there was a time after McDuffie's accident where owner-drivers were still a part of the NASCAR's elite series, and virtual unknowns could still make Winston Cup fields with just a few crew guys and one good qualify-ing lap. The pinnacle of this was Alan Kulwicki, a college graduate from Wisconsin, who the very next year after the crash won the Winston Cup. Like McDuffie, Kulwicki had turned down an opportunity to work with Junior Johnson to grow his own team, a decision rewarded when he edged

Johnson's driver Bill Elliott in the final standings. Kulwicki's success caused many series veterans to start their
own teams, including Elliott and Ricky Rudd. But another
tragic crash claimed Kulwicki's life in 1993, and by 2002,
most owner-drivers in Winston Cup had either signed with
other teams or retired altogether.

Today, a franchise system has eliminated independents
from Cup competition altogether. And as multi-car teams
and technical alliances continue to move the sport further
from its past, memories of men like McDuffie have also
faded. "Now I tell people that," said Mike Demers, "and
they just look at me. 'Are you sure? How many races? 653?
Nah. Come on...He's sort of got forgotten. You ask people
about the 70 car and they look at you – 'what 70 car?'"

Dr. Jerry Punch got a similar reaction when he mentioned McDuffie to a student from Sanford. "He looked at
me like I had two heads. I said 'you don't know that name
probably, but there's a guy from Sanford who raced and
was one of the best. So if you're from Sanford, I bet somebody in your family knows that name. You go home and
ask them.'"

But for those who knew him, J.D. McDuffie must never be forgotten – as a man, a competitor, and as a link between NASCAR's past and future.

"He struggled," said Wayne Andrews, "but I think he
was one of the best and the last independents that was
around. I mean, he stuck with it, and I think my hat's off to
him for the involvement he had in NASCAR. I don't think
they appreciated him, the ones that was struggling, but he
stayed in there a long time, that's for sure."

"I know he had a following because he was like Robin

Hood," said Terry Shaw. "He kept competing against overwhelming odds and was consistently in the middle of traffic, he wasn't 'Tail End Charlie,' it was great that he could do with what he had."

"He's the kind of guy that made NASCAR, brought it to the next level," said Jimmy Means. "He's a guy who didn't do it for the money – naturally, we all needed the money to survive – but he just did it because he loved racing. And you couldn't knock him down, you couldn't keep him down, because he was doing what he loved. And that's basically the only reason NASCAR went to the next level is because of people like him."

"There are guys who stay on today that say we don't have the money to go. J.D. somehow made it there. Maybe he shouldn't have been, didn't need to be, but he had to be. Just like all the independents – back then we survived off the plan money. You got on the plan you could make it. But he's a guy who truly *truly* did it for the love of being in a race car and he was just really a hell of a guy, great guy, a heart as big as the world. Racing survived because of people like him."

"There's a lot of talent in this series," said FOX Sports announcer Mike Joy, "and maybe the greatness didn't show because they weren't quite as great as some of the superstars of their day. And that's where I would rate J.D. He was dedicated, he and his family were all in. They were 100% into this sport right to the end."

"He deserves to be remembered in the aspect he should be – as a pioneer of the sport," said Linda McDuffie. "He was the kind of guy I mean NASCAR was built on those independents because nobody was going to go to a race and see five cars run."

"He was very down to earth, very humble. I couldn't have had a better role model."

Afterword

On the afternoon of Thursday, August 2, 2018, I was riding in a black SUV as it drove slowly through the infield at Watkins Glen International. Charlie Berch parked it just before the entrance to The Inner Loop. The moment we stopped, Linda McDuffie got out, a Rumple Furniture cap clutched in her right hand. In front of her, a row of motor homes gave way to a narrow path, the remnants of the track's first chicane from 1956. Down the hill in the distance, she saw the spotter's stand. The catch fence. The barriers. "That's where it happened," said Charlie. "Right there."

As Linda stood against the chain-link, tears gave way to anger – anger that such a tragedy had to happen for the track to change. "I'm just pissed off," she said. We stood there, the three of us. It was some time before it felt right to leave.

Up until that moment, Linda had never been to the track where her father died. The very idea of doing so didn't come up until well after I'd arranged to stay with Charlie for the NASCAR weekend. And when it did, it came from her wife Wendy. "You need to do this," she told her. I was on board, but I made clear to Linda that I didn't expect her to come. I didn't think she would until the day my brother and I flew out from California. Linda drove all the way from Denver to upstate New York. She still beat us to Charlie's place.

But for a specific series of events, Linda would never have made it to Turn 5 that day. The credential office was closed by the time we arrived at the track, so Linda couldn't pick up her hot pass. Fortunately, I had already bought a ticket, as had my brother. Those two tickets, combined with Charlie's photographer's pass, were what got us in.

Such obstacles met and overcome came to define the weekend of the 2018 Go Bowling at the Glen. A month earlier, I had been in final negotiations to do a book signing for this book at the track, but someone at the speedway stepped in and forced our contact to cancel. My credentials had been declined for not coming from an "accredited website" despite years of coverage at Sonoma and Darlington, barring us access to much of the media at the track. Someone even prevented Linda, Charlie, and myself from being interviewed by NBC affiliate WETM-18. The live segment was to take place at Watkins Glen's victory lane, an irony not lost on Linda. "Welcome to J.D.'s world," she said.

But Andy Malnoske, WETM's sports editor, brought us into his studio for a pre-recorded segment late Thursday night. It aired on WETM's pre-race show on Friday night, and I was amazed by how much work they put into it. I only expected our interviews to be aired. Instead, Andy and a skeleton crew stayed up into the early hours to produce a four-minute fully-produced segment, complete with archival footage and photographs.

At the end of the segment, Andy promoted our new book signing at Smalley's Garage, the original technical inspection location on the old Watkins Glen course. There, Karl and Karla, the current owners, stepped up big time and treated our group just like family. Among our visitors that night was an older couple in classic J.D. McDuffie gear. They told us they were camping at the track when the accident happened, and for each year after brought with them a sign they hung on the catch fence. The black plastic sign bore a wooden cross, a laminated McDuffie trading card, and the words "70 J.D.: Not Forgot'n." For years, the couple hung the sign by their camper every year at Watkins Glen. When camping prices became too high, they kept the sign in storage in a blue bag. On that night, they gave the sign to Linda.

An equally big surprise awaited us at Smalley's. On the sidewalk in front of the shop is a Walk of Fame honoring drivers who have raced at Watkins Glen. Charlie told me about it days before, and we prepared to get one made for J.D. But the very next day, Charlie took me aside and told me "It's already done." "What?" I asked. "It's done." Apparently, the International Motor Racing Research Center (IMRRC) at Watkins Glen had already had it made. Bill Green from the IMRRC presented it to Linda at the signing.

Now, when you're in downtown Watkins Glen, walk past the starting line of the original road course Cameron Argetsinger envisioned in 1948. On the sidewalk, engraved in stone, J.D. McDuffie can be found among the track's greats. A man no longer forgotten.

Three years after we returned home, there was another NASCAR race at Watkins Glen. Ima Jean McDuffie was in Sanford with her family at her bedside. During the race's early laps, she was finally reunited with her husband.

Acknowledgments and Special Thanks

First of all, thank you to the McDuffie family. To Ima Jean, Linda, and Jeff, this book is for you. As this edition is being published, Linda is preparing to unveil a mural in J.D.'s honor. Painted on the side of a brick building in downtown Sanford, the mural is scheduled for completion on Labor Day, 2022.

Thank you to Ernie Irvan, Richard Petty, Rick Ware, and Richard Childress for speaking to me during weekends at the Toyota / Save Mart 350, as well as Mike Joy and Larry McReynolds during the speedway's annual media luncheon. Each had their own unique contribution to telling the story of the way the sport once was, and how J.D. and other owner-drivers fit into it. Thank you also to the staff of the Sonoma Raceway for making these encounters possible and making this writer feel at home.

This project has allowed me to talk with these and other significant figures in the NASCAR community, people I'd only seen on television as a child. It was a thrill when Ned Jarrett called from his home after broadcasting alongside his son on NBC, to hear from Jimmy Means right after he went to Dale Earnhardt, Jr.'s wedding, and to speak with ESPN's Dr. Jerry Punch and NASCAR historian Ken Martin, who both worked at the track that day in 1991.

Thank you to Jerry Freeze and the staff of Front Row Motorsports for their tribute to J.D. at Darlington in 2016. I was fortunate to also speak with both Don Rumple of Rumple Furniture and John and Jacob Bailey of Bailey Excavating, both of whom sponsored both McDuffie Racing and

Front Row's "throwback" with Landon Cassill aboard.

More of this book came together through the throwback features at my website, LASTCAR.info. Joe Dan Bailey, son of the late H.B. Bailey, and fellow owner-drivers Philip Duffie and Frank Warren shared their memories of J.D. with me, all of which appear in this book as well as on the site. Thank you also to Rob at AC Spark Plugs for talking with me after that eBay auction back in 2011, which ultimately got this project rolling.

Thank you to Mike and Lesley Demers, who entrusted me with a treasure trove of photographs, video, t-shirts, and newsletters produced during their years of operating the J.D. McDuffie Fan Club. To Marty Burke, for sharing his stories with me and his hospitality during my first business trip. And Jerry Glenn, for taking the time to speak with me those early mornings before opening his shop. Thank you to Bobby Hudson and Donald Mangum, for sharing their extraordinary lives in racing, and to Tom Clegg for making the sport's past come alive. Special thanks to "Winding" Wayne Andrews, Jimmy Byrd, James Oldham, Wilbur Thomas and his son Jimmy Thomas, and the staff of Ted's Flower Basket in Sanford for speaking to me during my trip to Darlington. In telling the story of an underdog, no detail is too small.

My research brought me to Wellsville, New York and Brad Whitford at L.C. Whitford, Co., then to Sanford Transmissions & Automotive in North Carolina. Terry Letton and Marc Cashman, both spectators that tragic day at The Glen, gave the view from the other side of the catch fence, as did David Slezak, whose passion for history is matched by his love for racing.

Thank you also to Doug Schneider and Darren Jones for sharing your stories of J.D. To photographers Charlie Berch, Sally Berch Daggett, and Janine Pestel for sharing your own collection of photos, and to Charlie and Janine for your accounts of both Watkins Glen and McDuffie's final race. And thanks to Bill Green and the staff of the International Motor Racing Research Center, who shared their deep knowledge on the history of Watkins Glen International. Green treasures a Maxx trading card of McDuffie the driver signed at the track in 1990.

Thank you to Jim Derhaag, one of the first people I spoke to when I started putting words to paper. Thank you also to my fellow independent journalists, including Tom McCoart, whose historical features on Racing-Reference. info have always been something to look forward to, and Rob Dostie, for the pictures he's contributed to my website. Thank you, Rob Taylor for your continued friendship and your amazing motorsports artwork, particularly your work on J.D. And thank you to Dennis Michelson and Lori Munro at RaceTalkRadio.com for being there every step of the way in my own career. Thank you to Terry Shaw for providing valuable insight to his company's investigation of the accident. Also, a big thanks to Rick Houston, Steve Waid, Deb Williams, and the rest of the staff from *NASCAR Winston Cup Scene*.

There were also others I didn't get the chance to speak to, but their online sources were invaluable. StockCarRacersReunion, particularly Dennis Andrews and his collection of vintage local racing articles. The photo collections at The Historical Stock Car Racing Forum and Rubbin's Racin', photos by Brian Cleary, Scott Baker, Todd Crane, Bryant

McMurray, David Chobat, Travis Joyner, John Walczak, Rudy Roberts, and Roger Lankford, plus Don Feeley's online photo album from the paddock at Watkins Glen that weekend in 1991. To the others who weren't mentioned, my apologies and my thanks to you as well.

Big thanks to Waldorf Publishing for taking a chance on a first-time author and his passion when no one else would.

Thank you to my readers, my viewers, and listeners. Whether following "Karaoke for NASCAR Fans," "Barney and Me," "Brock's Starting Grid Network," "43 Stories," "LASTCAR.info," "LASTCAR Films," or just talking on Twitter, your support has meant the world to me. Let this project be an expression of thanks to you as well.

And last, but not least, thank you to my family. To Mom, Dad, and Miles, thank you for your patience, love, and support.

Bibliography

<u>ARTICLES</u>

Bailey, Greg. "Fans to decide drivers for Atlanta Invitational." *Gadsden Times*, January 28, 1986.

Berch, Charles. "In Memory Of: John Delphus (J.D.) McDuffie." *Instant Replay Sorting Photo News*, Fall 1991.

Berch, Charles. "Photographer's Bittersweet Break Turns Tragedy Into Triumph," *Today's Photographer International*, Summer 1993.

Berch, Charles. "Area pit crew member fulfills 28-year-old dream with a win at Watkins Glen International," *The Chronicle-Express*, August 23, 2011.

Berggren, Dick. "Would soft walls have saved a life?" *Stock Car Racing Magazine*, November 1991.

Berry, Steve and Charean Williams. "Strong Outing Turned Deadly." *Orlando Sentinel*,
June 27, 1994.

Biddle, Joe. "J.D. Landed Where He Didn't Want to Be." *Daytona Beach Morning Journal*, February 9, 1979.

Blain, Eddy, "Indoor races offer trip down memory lane." *The Intelligencer*, January 19, 1989.

Blain, Eddy. "McDuffie-Burke connection link to Winston Cup." *The Intelligencer*, January 10, 1991.

Brown, Clifton. "Bill Elliott stays true to form: Runs fast practice lap at MIS." *Detroit Free Press,* August 16, 1986.

Bruce, Kenny. "How the 'tire war' was won – at North Wilkesboro." NASCAR.com, September 29, 2016.

Caldwell, Dave. "A loser, but not a quitter." The Philadelphia Enquirer, July 22, 1990.

Campbell, Julie. "Racing writer cites track perils," *Sanford Herald*, 1991.

Catanzareti, Zach. "Jimmy Means' Lasting Impact on NASCAR Past and Present," Fronstretch.com, June 21, 2016.

Chevalier, Jack. "McDuffie left indelible mark on NASCAR scene." *The News Journal*, August 15, 1991.

Coble, Don. "McDuffie's clings to hard-work ethic." *Florida Today*, January 11, 1987.

Coon, Charlie. "Candle lighting rekindles McDuffie spirit," Star-Gazette, August 8, 1992.

Cooper, Kay. "Area bowlers square off against drivers." *The News-Journal*, February 21, 1989.

Crissman, Bob. "McDuffie Relief Fund Gets Tremndous Response." *The Enterprise*, 1988.

Crowe, Steve. "McDuffie's death hits home, brings call for safer track." *Detroit Free Press*, August 15, 1991.

Crowe, Steve. "Waltrip delivers moving tribute." *Detroit Free Press*, August 19, 1991.

Davidson, Eric. "REVS, Cunningham, the Glen and Me." VeloceToday.com, July 29, 2014.

Elliott, Walter. "Rusty Wallace Wins IROC Race & Title At Watkins Glen." *Area Auto Racing News,* August 13, 1991.

Elliott, Walter. "Scott Sharp Cuts Thru Trans Am Field." *Area Auto Racing News*, August 13, 1991.

Elliott, Walter. "Irvan Scores A Watkins Glen, J.D. McDuffie Dies In Crash." *Area Auto Racing News*, August 13, 1991.

Elliott, Walter. "J.D. McDuffie." *Area Auto Racing News*, August 13, 1991.

Esposito, Michael D., "McDuffie fans flood Sanford," *Sanford Herald*, August 15, 1991.

E-RazorHead (username). "My First NASCAR Race – 1991 Watkins Glen – And J.D. McDuffie Was Killed." *E-RazorHead*, https://carlupq.wordpress.com/2008/07/02/my-first-nascar-race-1991-watkins-glen-and-jd-mcduffie-was-killed/, July 2, 2008.

Esposito, Michael D. "Family, friends say goodbye to McDuffie." *The Sanford Herald*, August 16, 1991.

Fallesen, Gary. "J.D. McDuffie signs his last autograph." *Democrat and Chronicle*, August 12, 1991.

Finney, Mike. "Newark's Green eyes date at Dover." *The News Journal*, September 16, 1994.

Finney, Mike. "McKean senior eyes road to NASCAR." *The News Journal*, September 15, 2002.

Foreman, Jr., Tom. "Independent Means keeping car on track." *Rome News-Tribune*, April 21, 1988.

Foreman, Jr., Tom. "His Way: Challenging 'Big Boys' Inspired J.D. McDuffie," August 1991.

Fusco, Andy. *"J.D." Stock Car Racing Magazine*, November 1991.

Gaillard, Luther. "Sprint Racing: Daytona Pole, Clash Race, ARCA 200 to Provide Plenty Of Action." *Herald-Journal*, February 11, 1979.

Garrett, Mike. "Cale, Bonnett race favorites." *Arizona Republic*, November 26, 1977.

Gillispie, Tom. "Bodine's desire to get a victory." *Star-News*, September 30, 1987.

Girard, Eric. "One Accident at the 500—But What a Pileup It Was." *Florida Today*, February 17, 1975.

Granger, Gene. "McDuffie: 'Doing What I Want," *Grand National Scene*, 1976.

Granger, Gene. "J.D. McDuffie – 'I Race to The Best Of My Means,'" *Grand National Scene*, February 1, 1979.

Granger, Gene. "J.D. McDuffie And The 'Clash of '79' – 'With A Little Bit Of Luck…!'" *Grand National Scene*, February 1, 1979.

Green, David. "Drivers still anxious about new pit rules." *Herald-Journal*, February 14, 1991.

Green, David. "Terry Labonte claims his first pole of year." *The Dispatch*, August 10, 1991.

Green, David. "Watkins Glen has a storied past." *Herald-Journal*, August 11, 1991.

Green, David. "Busy trek for Shepherd." *Herald-Journal*, August 11, 1991.

Green, David. "Top qualifiers change face of favorites at Watkins Glen." *Herald-Journal*, August 11, 1991.

Green, David. "Usual favorites starting near the back of the pack." *The Times-News*, August 11, 1991.

Green, David. "Longtime race driver McDuffie dies in crash." *Herald-Journal*, August 12, 1991.

Green, David. "NASCAR fraternity held McDuffie in high esteem." *Gadsden Times*, August 12, 1991.

Green, David. "Drivers to compete in softball exhibition." *Herald-Journal*, September 17, 1991.

Green, David. "Hylton to lease Chevrolet." *Herald-Journal*, January 25, 1992.

Green, David. "NASCAR cracks down on inspections." *Herald-Journal*, February 9, 1992.

Green, David. "Hylton, 56, refuses to slow down." *Herald-Journal*, February 13, 1992.

Green, John. "'The thrill keeps getting bigger.'" *Times Daily*, May 2, 1991.

Green, Ron. "Stock-car racing was all McDuffie wanted." *Star-News*, August 13, 1991.

Hager, Anthony W. "Old Number 70: The Racing Life of J.D. McDuffie." *Carolina Country*, December 2009.

Hager, Anthony W. "Remembering NASCAR's J.D. McDuffie." AutoRacing1.com, August 1, 2011.

Harris, Mike. "Earnhardt Wins, Outduels Waltrip." *Schenectady Gazette*, September 14, 1987.

Harris, Mike. "Road race kind Wallace set to defend title at
    Glen." *Daily News*, August 10, 1990.

Harris, Mike. "McDuffie killed in Watkins Glen," *The News-
    Journal*, August 12, 1991.

Harris, Mike. "'Nothing would have helped.': McDuffie's death
    NASCAR's first since 1989." *Beaver County Times*, August
    12, 1991.

Harris, Mike. "Waltrip Invocation Is Tearful Tribute To J.D.
    McDuffie." *St. Louis Post Dispatch*, August 25, 1991.

Harris, Mike. "Waltrip, NASCAR drivers bid sad farewell to
    crash victim McDuffie," (Fort Myers) News-Press, August 25,
    1991.

Harris, Mike. "Earnhardt finishes race season on top." *Spring
    Hope Enterprise*, November 17, 1994.

Higgins, Tom. "Petty's Team Battered With Trouble." *Aiken
    Standard*, April 3, 1988.

Higgins, Tom. "Veteran McDuffie loses life in crash." *Sun Jour-
    nal*, August 12, 1991.

Higgins, Tom. "Higgins' Scuffs: NASCAR and poker." *The
    State*, June 26, 2013.

Hight, R.V. "J.D. McDuffie: Local racer gets rare tribute," *San-
    ford Herald*, March 1, 1980.

Hinton, Ed. "'When Is It Going To Be Enough?'" *Orlando Senti-
    nel*, July 6, 2001.

Hornack, Ken. "Jimmy Means business in the Firecracker 400."
    The News-Journal, July 2, 1988.

Houck, Mark. "Spindle suspect in crash," Star-Gazette, August
    12, 1991.

Ireland, Jack. "J.D. McDuffie tops big names to win pole in Del-
    aware 500." *The Morning News*, September 16, 1978.

Ireland, Jack. "Petty too speedy off track." *The Morning News*,
    September 16, 1978.

Kelly, Goodwin. "Driving J.D.'s top therapy." *The News-Journal*, June 30, 1988.

Kelly, Goodwin. "For Wawak, 30 years of race driving ends in a heartbeat." *The News-Journal*, June 30, 1988.

Kelly, Paul. "JC Man's racer will carry a memorial to McDuffie." *Press & Sun Bulletin*, August 1991.

Ketcham, Uadajane. "Connolly Gets Shangri-La 5th, McDuffie Wins Match Race." *Area Auto Racing News*, August 13, 1991.

Knight-Ridder News Services. "McDuffie clan wants answers." *Southern Illinoisan*, July 3, 1994.

Kramer, Roy. "Remembering J.D. McDuffie (editorial)." *AutoWeek*, September 9, 1991.

Kubissa, David and George Hawke. "Peers saw McDuffie as self-made racer," Star-Gazette, August 12, 1991.

Lankford, Roger. "Roger Lankford: #K70," LuvRacin.com, 2001.

Leef, Ralph. "Wallace says stay on the track," *Herald-Journal*, June 10, 1989.

Leggett, Maurice. "Dream of racing is now reality for J.D. McDuffie," *The Robesonian*, December 23, 1990.

Leggett, Maurice. "McDuffie's loss will be remembered." *The Robesonian*, August 12, 1991.

Levanduski, Ron. "Death brings talk of safety," Star-Gazette, August 12, 1991.

Long, Paul. "J.D. McDuffie: Determined Veteran Seeks His Due." *Instant Replay Sporting Photo News*, Spring 1991.

Long, Paul. "Watkins Glen International announces new parking, camping, traffic policies." *Instant Replay Sporting Photo News*, Summer 1991.

Marshall, Elbert. "J.D. McDuffie: Racing Is A Way Of Life," Durham Morning Herald, April 6, 1969.

Marshall, Elbert. "Butlers Inc." *The Daily Times News*, June 15, 1975.

Martin, Matt. "Friends and fans of McDuffie rally to support veteran driver," Sanford Herald, April 8, 1988.

Martin, Matt. "J.D. McDuffie killed in crash: Auto racing was his life," Sanford Herald, August 12, 1991.

Martin, Matt. "Editorials: Remembering a local hero." *The Sanford Herald*, August 16, 1991.

McCoart, Tom. "The Legend of JD McDuffie (Part 1)" Racing-reference.info, August 6, 2015.

McCoart, Tom. "The Legend of JD McDuffie (Part 2)" Racing-reference.info, August 11, 2015.

McCoart, Tom. "JD McDuffie's Final Darlington Race." Racing-reference.info, September 2, 2016.

McGee, Ryan. "You can still drive old Watkins Glen." ESPN, August 11, 2012.

McLaughlin, Matt. "50 Years of NASCAR Racing," reprinted at "Close But No Cigar" on Race Fans Forever, 1998.

Migdail-Smith, "Local race car driver dies a month after crashing." *Reading Eagle*, August 18, 2011.

Minter, Rick. "Earnhardt says Jimmy Means meant a lot to him." RacinToday.com, April 12, 2009.

Mitchell, Charlie. "Sharp captures first at fast Watkins Glen." *The Hour*, August 12, 1991.

Moore, Leland. "J.D. McDuffie Changed My Life," *Guideposts*, August 1995.

Morrison, Bob. "McDuffie Kept Trying Despite Low-Budget Operation." *Sarasota Herald-Tribune*, August 12, 1991.

Moyer, Don. "Winston Cup Notebook." *Area Auto Racing News*, February 26, 1991.

Myers, Bob. "Racing's One Man Operation: Sanford's McDuffie Does All Except Win," *The Charlotte News*, March 7, 1969.

Nascarman (username). "The L-R Series: NASCAR's Road Racing Experiment," Racing-reference.info, August 3, 2017.

O'Brien, Dick. "McDuffie's last victory came Saturday in Owego." *Syracuse Herald-Journal*, August 12, 1991.

Oldham, James. "Will it be Waltrip or Petty?" *Sanford Herald*, 1979.

Oldham, James. "Waltrip will be 'roastee' on Friday evening," *Sanford Herald*, February 26, 1981.

Oldham, James. "Rockingham getting a bad weather rep," *Sanford Herald*, October 27, 1982.

Oldham, James. "Why decide title on west coast?" *Sanford Herald*, November 10, 1982.

Oldham, James. "McDuffie to drive Dew machine," *Sanford Herald*, November 17, 1982.

Oldham, James. "Fourth annual Roast is scheduled," *Sanford Herald*, February 16, 1983.

Oldham, James. "Things are all set for the big 'roast," *Sanford Herald*, March 2, 1983.

Oldham, James. "Local man wins pace car," *Sanford Herald*, October 5, 1983.

Oldham, James. "Riverside to host final race of season," *Sanford Herald*, November 1983.

Oldham, James. "McDuffie getting set for Nationwise 500," *Sanford Herald*, October 16, 1985.

Oldham, James. "TranSouth field not close to Earnhardt," *Sanford Herald*, 1986.

Oldham, James. "McDuffie on Atlanta ballot," *Sanford Herald*, 1986.

Oldham, James. "Atlanta Invitational voting nears deadline; Hill shines at Winternationals," *Sanford Herald*, March 26, 1986.

Oldham, James. "McDuffie will not hold back in Atlanta," *Sanford Herald*, 1986.

Oldham, James. "McDuffie race team coming together," *Sanford Herald*, October 17, 1986.

Outlar, Jesse. "503 Setbacks Don't Stop J.D. McDuffie," The Atlanta Constitution, March 20, 1982.

Paschal, Charles. "Day for a Driver: Friends and neighbors turn out to boost a racer's career." *Stock Car Racing Magazine*, 1966.

PattyKay (username). "J.D. McDuffie lived and died for racing." Stock Car Racers Reunion, August 9, 2012.

Paulk, Ralph. "Aging drivers can't let go of their passion." *The Akron Beacon Journal*, September 7, 1991.

Pearce, Al. "NASCAR Studying Dangerous Corner." *Daily Press*, August 13, 1991.

Pearce, Al. "Point of Focus: For some, it was Irvan's victory, but for others, it was McDuffie's death." *AutoWeek*, August 19, 1991.

Pearce, Al. "The family gathers: Racing community reacts to McDuffie's death." *AutoWeek*, August 19, 1991.

Pheil, Jule L. "Article was insensitive (editorial)." *Democrat and Chronicle*, August 22, 1991.

Phillips, Benny. "Racing's Sharecropper." *Stock Car Racing Magazine*, November 1991.

Phillips, Greg. "The life of an independent driver is a tough one," *Sanford Herald*, December 4, 1976.

PMCDaniel (username). "Tributes / Memorials To Legends: J.D. McDuffie." STRL Road Runner, 2007.

Pope, Thomas. "But He Loves It," unknown, 1988.

Pope, Thomas. "...At The Beach," unknown, 1989.

Pope, Thomas. "McDuffie, 52, Dies In Wreck," *Herald-Journal*, August 12, 1991.

Pope, Thomas. Fractured Skull Killed McDuffie, Doctor Reports," *Herald-Journal*, 1991.

Pope, Thomas. "Last Of A Breed...," *Herald-Journal*, August 16, 1991.

Pope, Thomas. "McDuffie Sale Leaves Tears and Memories." *Fayette Observer*, October 26, 1995.

Read, Dennis. "Swervin' Irvan drives steady at the Glen." *The Ithaca Journal*, August 12, 1991.

Rhetts, JoAnn. "A Working Man's Hero," *Charlotte Observer*, October 11, 1987.

Robinson, Bill. "A Racing 'Cropper," The Atlanta Journal, August 13, 1991.

Saxton, Ernie. "My Two Cents Worth." *Area Auto Racing News*, August 13, 1991.

Schaefer, Paul. "A Look Back; Bowman Gray." *NASCAR Home Tracks*, http://hometracks.nascar.com/Feature/30_Years_Running/Bowman_Gray, March 15, 2011.

Schmitz, Brian. "He's 0 for 542 but still likes to race," The Orlando Sentinel, July 3, 1983.

Schoolfield, Hank. "Comments from the Publisher." *Southern Motoracing*, August 22, 1991.

Schoolfield, Hank (publisher). "McDuffie, 52, Is 24th Driver Killed In NASCAR Series." *Southern Motoracing*, August 22, 1991.

Sentinel Wire Services. "Veteran McDuffie dies in NASCAR wreck." *The Milwaukee Sentinel*, August 12, 1991.

Shearer, Ed. "Waltrip Claims Winston Pole." *Aiken Standard*, May 11, 1986.

Sherman, Doug. "Wallace uses race-day motor to win IROC." *Democrat and Chronicle*, August 11, 1991.

Sherman, Doug. "Loss of front tire leads to McDuffie crash." *Democrat and Chronicle*, August 12, 1991.

Sherman, Doug. "Kodak car wins Budweiser at Glen." *Democrat and Chronicle*, August 12, 1991.

Smith, Wayne. "By all Means: NASCAR veteran keeps finding way to go racing." *Times Daily*, July 25, 1992.

Strohl, Daniel. "Watkins Glen, a history told in course maps." *Hemmings Daily*, November 4, 2014.

Taft, Larry. "Elliott feeling tragedy's pain." *The Tennessean*, February 14, 1991.

Tarlach, Al. "Fangio Sweeps to Win at the Glen." *Instant Replay Sporting Photo News*, Summer 1991.

Teater, Robin P. "Friends remember McDuffie." *Herald-Journal*, August 16, 1991.

Toomuchcountry (username). "May 7, 1972: Pearson Begins His Talladega Triad," Bench

Racing From The Volunteer State, May 7, 2014.

Toomuchcountry (username). "June 3, 1978: My first Cup race." Bench Racing From The Volunteer State June 3, 2014.

Via, Roland et al. "J.D. McDuffie." *Legends of NASCAR*, 2003

Vincent, Charlie. "Racer's career uncheckered—but proud." *Detroit Free Press*, August 17, 1986.

Vincent, Charlie. "Remembering J.D. McDuffie." *Detroit Free Press*, August 21, 1991.

Vincent, Charlie. "Darrell's only fear is not finishing first." *Detroit Free Press*, June 22, 1991.

Waid, Steve. "Labonte Returns To Old Form; Speeds To No. 1 Spot." *Winston Cup Scene*, August 15, 1991.

Waid, Steve. "Radials Make Road Course Debut At The Glen." *Winston Cup Scene*, August 15, 1991.

Waid, Steve. "McDuffie's Death Saddens Fellow Competitors." *Winston Cup Scene*, August 15, 1991.

Waterman, Andrew. "Cigar-Puffing J.D. McDuffie is the Working Man's Stock Car Driver." *Era Motorsports*, 1990.

Waterman, Andrew. "Because I love to do it." *Stock Car Racing Magazine*, November 1991.

Wheeler, Rick. "McDuffie's memorial: The new Inner Loop at

Watkins Glen." *Democrat and Chronicle*, August 7, 1992.

White, Ben and Ernie Masche. "Leland Moore." *Winston Cup Illustrated*, June 1990.

White, Ben. "McDuffie's death still hurts a year later." *The Dispatch*, August 11, 1992.

Wilborn, Theo. "J.D. McDuffie's racing sponsorship falls through," *Sanford Herald*, 1984.

Wilkie, Jim. "McDuffie on comeback trail," *Sanford Herald*, May 1988.

Wilkie, Jim. "McDuffie pays return visit to Daytona," *Sanford Herald*, January 12, 1989.

Williams, Deb. "As A Person, McDuffie Ws A Winner." *Winston Cup Scene*, August 15, 1991.

Williams, Deb. "Reduced Speeds One Benefit of New 'Loop' At Watkins Glen." *Winston Cup Scene*, October 17, 1991.

Winderman, Ira. "No-Win Situation," Fort Lauderdale News, February 11, 1987.

Woody, Larry. "Times Hard for Means, But He Means To Hang On." *The Tennessean*, 1978.

Woody, Larry. "McDuffie Too Slow For Talladega 500." *The Tennessean*, August 1, 1981.

Woody, Larry. "McDuffie Still Tracking Elusive Victory." *The Tennessean,* March 21, 1982.

Woody, Larry. "McDuffie's Motto: Try, Try, Try Again." *The Tennessean*, February 14, 1985.

Woody, Larry. "McDuffie's streak won't end today." *The Tennessean*, February 15, 1987.

Woody, Larry. "McDuffie raced hard all the way." *The Tennessean*, August 13, 1991.

Woolford, Dave. "Racing world mourns loss of McDuffie." *Toledo Blade*, August 16, 1991.

Zeller, Bob. "Somber faces told a sad tale; Autopsy shows driver died instantly in crash," News & Record, August 12, 1991.

Zeller, Bob. "The Quitting Game: Another Bad Case of Vibration," *Car And Driver*, February 2009.

UNCREDITED ARTICLES
FROM THE ASSOCIATED PRESS

"Watkins Glen Race Is Fatal." *Gettysburg Times*, September 24, 1962.

"Drivers, fans killed in car racing." *Ottawa Citizen*, October 18, 1965.

"Racer Escapes Death In Crash." *The Tuscaloosa News*, October 4, 1968.

"Sanford's McDuffie is racing's 'little man,'" September 1969.

"Petty Triumphs in NASCAR 250." *Wellsville Daily Reporter*, July 15, 1971.

"Sanford Driver Is Hurt." *The Robesonian*, February 18, 1973.

"'Tiny' Lund Crushed." *The Evening News*, August 18, 1975.

"McDuffie feels he can race." *Star-News*, December 13, 1976.

"McDuffie fastest qualifier Friday." *Gadsden Times*, May 3, 1980.

"NASCAR Returns." *Gadsden Times*, October 18, 1985.

"Safety features, not luck, saved Petty's life." *The Times-News*, February 17, 1988.

"With backing Means seeks first victory." *Star-News*, April 8, 1988.

"Means hopes to end drought on race circuit." *Star-News*, April 8, 1988.

"Crash Course: Schrader Wins Wreck-Wracked Daytona Qualifier." *St. Louis Post Dispatch*, February 17, 1989.

"Hillin finds new ride at Pocono." *Times-Daily*, June 14, 1991.

"Top drivers crash in Glen practice." *The Robesonian*, August 9, 1991.

"'Road Warriors' square off again." *The Times-News*, August 10, 1991.

"Labonte sets mark, wins pole." *The Times-News*, August 10, 1991.

"Rudd recovers in qualifying," *Lima News*, August 11, 1991.

"'Road Warriors' set for charge at Glen," *Rome News-Tribune*, August 11, 1991.

"Independence earned McDuffie respect from fans and competitors." *The Item*, August 11, 1991.

"Irvan holds off Martin on final lap." *The Robesonian*, August 12, 1991.

"Veteran McDuffie killed in wreck." *The Robesonian*, August 12, 1991.

"Driver killed in crash at Glen." *Syracuse Herald-Journal*, August 12, 1991.

"Veteran Driver McDuffie Killed." *Sarasota Herald-Tribune*, August 12, 1991.

"Brain injuries killed McDuffie quickly." *Star-News*, August 13, 1991.

"McDuffie's death angers drivers." *The Dispatch*, August 13, 1991.

"Track officials were considering changes." *The Index-Journal*, August 13, 1991.

"J.D. McDuffie raced for the love of sport, nor money, says his brother." *The Index-Journal*, August 13, 1991.

"NASCAR drivers alarmed by conditions at Watkins Glen." *Ludington Daily News*, August 13, 1991.

"Veteran racer did the best he could." *Times Daily*, August 14, 1991.

"McDuffie's death may bring changes to Glen." *Hazleton Standard-Speaker*, August 14, 1991.

"Friends mourn loss of McDuffie." The Index-Journal, August 16, 1991.

"Friends remember McDuffie." *Reno Gazette-Journal*, August 16, 1991.

"McDuffie Eulogized By Racing Peers." *Aiken Standard*, August 16, 1991.

"Colleagues pay tribute to driver killed at Glen." *Spokane Chronicle*, August 16, 1991.

"Watkins Glen will wait to renovate Turn 5, where driver was killed." *Democrat and Chronicle*, September 4, 1991.

"Glen's Turn 5 to be revamped into 'inner loop.'" *Democrat and Chronicle*, October 9, 1991.

"Watkins Glen's Turn 5 will be eliminated." *The Times-News*, October 9, 1991.

"McDuffie's uniform recovered." *Gadsden Times*, February 3, 1992.

"Watkins Glen sued over driver McDuffie's death." *Democrat and Chronicle*, July 24, 1992.

"McDuffie isn't forgotten by rival drivers." *Sunday Star-News*, August 9, 1992.

"McDuffie memories rekindled." *Daily News*, August 9, 1992.

"NASCAR: McDuffie's negligence to blame." *Gadsden Times*, August 23, 1992.

"NASCAR Suit Thrown Out." *Titusville Herald*, September 4, 1993.

"Car failure led to driver's death." *The Bulletin*, September 5, 1993.

"Notebook." *Daytona Beach Sunday News-Journal*, April 23, 1995.

UNCREDITED ARTICLES

"J.D. McDuffie Wins First Race," source and date unknown, circa 1962.

"Top Drivers Here Sat. Night." *Richmond County Journal*, May 9, 1962.

"Sanford Driver Is Leading Money Maker At Speedway." *Richmond County Journal*, May 14, 1962.

"Brown, Tilley Capture Races." *Kannapolis Daily Independent*,
    May 14, 1962.

"McDuffie Is Driver To Beat At Speedway." *Richmond County
    Journal*, July 27, 1962.

"McDuffie Wins At Speedway." *Richmond County Journal*, Sep-
    tember 22, 1962.

"Race Death." *The Sydney Morning Herald*, September 24, 1962.

"McDuffie Day Set At Sanford." 1966.

"McDuffie Drives Chevy To Victory," *Richmond County Jour-
    nal*, 1967.

"Yarborough Ford Wins at Daytona." *Democrat and Chronicle*,
    February 24, 1969.

"Roberts Claims Main Event Win." 1972.

"Faster Car, Experience Are Mean's Two Big Needs." *The Ten-
    nessean*, July 9, 1974.

"Guard Rails A Problem For Watkins Glen." *Lakeland Ledger*
    (from New York Times), June 8, 1975.

"Nascar Driver Sanford's Pride," Carolina Bank flyer, circa
    1975.

"France Meets With Group." *Danville Bee*, April 29, 1976.

"In Southeastern 500, McDuffie Eyes 1st Win." *Kingsport News*,
    April 8, 1977.

"Dale Earnhardt Faces Big Weekend." *Kannapolis Daily Inde-
    pendent*, October 7, 1977.

"Practice at AIMS unlucky for Means." *Gadsden Times*, August
    1, 1978.

"McDuffie in Dover's pole." *Rome News-Tribune,* September 17,
    1978.

"Duffie finishes fifth." *Star-News*, May 24, 1982.

"Richmond on pole at Watkins Glen." *The Sumter Daily Item*,
    August 9, 1986.

"McDuffie second in race voting." *Kannapolis Daily Independ-
    ent*, March 30, 1986.

"Talladega 500 lineup." *The Anniston Star*, July 27, 1987.

"Twins stocks crash at Daytona." *The Palm Beach Post*, February 12, 1988.

"Means adds sponsor." *The Pantagraph*, June 16, 1988.

"Daytona 500 Field." *The Palm Beach Post*, February 19, 1989.

"Pit Passes." *Winston Cup Scene*, April 18, 1991.

"New Team For Rusty Wallace?" *Reading Eagle*, August 10, 1990.

"Trickle, Martin in crash." *The Milwaukee Journal*, August 10, 1990.

"Announced 1991 NASCAR Winston Cup Teams," *The Tennessean*, February 14, 1991.

"NASCAR (20 Fastest Laps on Thursday)," *Lakeland Ledger*, August 9, 1991.

"Labonte on pole at Watkins Glen," *Times-Daily*, August 9, 1991.

"NASCAR Glen Qualifiers," *Herald and Review*, August 10, 1991.

"Starting Lineup," *The Tuscaloosa News*, August 11, 1991.

"Peers: Saw McDuffie as self-made." *Elmira Star-Gazette*, August 12, 1991.

"Head injuries killed McDuffie," *The Journal News*, August 13, 1991.

"Fan remembers McDuffie," *Herald-Journal*, August 17, 1991.

"Pit Passes," *Winston Cup Scene*, October 31, 1991.

"McDuffie's uniform helps police catch man." *Times-Daily*, February 1, 1992.

"We will remember." *Times-Daily*, February 22, 2001.

BOOKS

Argetsinger, Michael and Bill Green. *NASCAR Watkins Glen International.* Arcadia Publishing, 2013.

Dutton, Monte. *Taking Stock: Life in NASCAR's Fast Lane*, Potomac Books, Inc., 2002.

Falk, Duane. *Legends of The Track: Great Moments In Stock Car Racing*, Metro Books, 2001.

Fielden, Greg. *Forty Years of Stock Car Racing: Vol. 1: The Beginning, 1949-1958*. Galfield Press, 1987.

Fielden, Greg. *Forty Years of Stock Car Racing: Vol. 2 The Superspeedway Boom, 1959-1964*. Galfield Press, 1988.

Fielden, Greg. *Forty Years of Stock Car Racing: Vol. 3: Big Bucks and Boycotts, 1965-1971*. Galfield Press, 1989.

Fielden, Greg. *Forty Years of Stock Car Racing: Vol. 4: The Modern Era, 1972-1989*. Galfield Press, 1994.

Fielden, Greg. *Forty Years of Stock Car Racing: Vol. 5: Forty Plus Four, 1990-1993*. Galfield Press, 1994.

Fielden, Greg. *NASCAR Chronicle*, First Edition, Publications International, Ltd., 2006.

House, Kirk W. and Charles R. Mitchell. *Watkins Glen Racing: Images of Sports.* Arcadia Publishing, 2008.

Wood, Perry Allen. *Declarations of Stock Car Independents: Interviews with Twelve Racers of the 1950s, 1960s and 1970s*. McFarland & Company, Inc., Publishers, 2010.

FILMS

1985 Daytona 500 at Daytona, CBS
1986 Budweiser at the Glen, ESPN
1987 Budweiser at the Glen, ESPN
1988 Twin 125s at Daytona, CBS
1988 TranSouth 500 at Darlington, ESPN
1988 Budweiser at the Glen, ESPN
1989 Twin 125s at Daytona, CBS
1989 Budweiser at the Glen, ESPN
1990 Budweiser at the Glen, ESPN

1990 ESPN Racing Highlights: "Thunder and Thrills" by Alka-Seltzer, ESPN Video

1991 Budweiser 500 at Dover, TNN

1991 IMSA GTP Camel Continental VII at Watkins Glen, ESPN

1991 Miller Genuine Draft 500 at Pocono, ESPN

1991 Firestone Firehawk Series 2 Hour at Watkins Glen, ESPN

1991 Liquid Tide Trans-Am Series at Watkins Glen, ESPN

1991 Budweiser at the Glen, ESPN ("Wild" Satellite Feed)

1991 Champion Spark Plug 400 at Michigan, ESPN

Champions of Speed: Tom Kendall, year unknown.

Inside Winston Cup Racing: 1991 TranSouth 500 at Darlington, TNN

Inside Winston Cup Racing: 1991 Budweiser at the Glen, TNN

Inside Winston Cup Racing: 1991 Champion Spark Plug 400 at Michigan, TNN

Inside Winston Cup Racing: 1991 Peak AntiFreeze 500 at Dover, TNN

Kodak Racing 1991 Highlights, Kodak VHS, 1991.

NASCAR RaceHub, "Riding to work with Joey Gase," August 5, 2015.

Stockcar!, 1977.

The History of the Trans-Am Series, Speedvision Network, LLC, 1997

Tom Usry Interview, Argenta Images, year unknown.

OTHER SOURCES
Alka-Seltzer Racing Press Pack, 1991

Bailey Excavating (https://bailey-excavating.com/about-us/)

Budweiser at the Glen Official Program, August 8-11, 1991. Watkins Glen International, 1991

Carl Long Motorsports (http://www.carllongmotorsports.com/)

eBay (www.ebay.com)

Don Feeley's Photobucket page
  (http://s46.photobucket.com/user/felixdk/library/)
Downtown Sanford: Brick Capital, USA
  (http://www.downtownsanford.com:80/brickcapital_usa.htm)
The Duster and Tex Show #23
  (https://archive.org/details/TheDusterAndTexShow23)
Google Maps (https://www.google.com/maps)
Google News Archives (https://news.google.com/newspapers)
Historical Newspaper Archives (www.newspaperarchive.com)
The Historical Stock Car Racing Forum
  (http://simracin40.proboards.com/)
Ima Jean McDuffie v. Watkins Glen International, Inc., 833
  F.Supp. 197 (W.D.N.Y. 1993), decision published September
  3, 1993.
Jayski's Silly Season Site (www.jayski.com)
Newspapers.com (www.go.newspapers.com/Archive)
RaceNY.com Forums (www.raceny.com)
Racing-Reference.info (www.racing-reference.info)
Racing Sports Cars (http://www.racingsportscars.com/)
The Revs Institute for Automotive Research, photos by Geoffrey
  Hewitt (https://revslib.stanford.edu/)
Rubbin's Racin' Forums (http://www.rubbins-racin.com/forums/)
Rumple Furniture (http://rumplefurniture.com/)
Stock Car Racers Reunion (http://stockcar.racersreunion.com/)
Ultimate Racing History (http://www.ultimateracinghistory.com/)
Watkins Glen Official Website (www.theglen.com)
YouTube (www.youtube.com)

About the Author

 In 2001, college freshman Brock Beard arrived at the University of California at Irvine as a walk-on athlete for the Men's Rowing Team. Despite a complete lack of athletic experience, three years later, he had earned the "twoseat" in the Junior Varsity Eight, a boat which won four races at four different venues. Having graduated as a four-year scholar-athlete with honors in UCI's prestigious Humanities Honors Program, Beard went on to earn his Juris Doctor from John F. Kennedy University with a Witkin Award in Constitutional Law.

As he continues to write his own underdog story, Beard has set to work writing those of others, particularly in his favorite arena of professional stock car racing. Since 2009, Beard's website LASTCAR.info has told the story of NASCAR's last-place finishers and lesser-known competitors.

Beard's unique work, featuring statistics he researched from thousands of race results, has been featured on NASCAR.com, SPEED Channel, RaceTalkRadio.com, Manifold Destiny with Mojo Nixon, and the PETM Podcast. He's also reported trackside for LASTCAR.info during NASCAR events, and in 2013 worked with the Sonoma Raceway's marketing department. He resides in California.

Printed in Great Britain
by Amazon

16624659R00197